C-2543   CAREER EXAMINATION SERIES

This is your
PASSBOOK for...

Food Inspector

Test Preparation Study Guide
Questions & Answers

COPYRIGHT NOTICE

This book is SOLELY intended for, is sold ONLY to, and its use is RESTRICTED to individual, bona fide applicants or candidates who qualify by virtue of having seriously filed applications for appropriate license, certificate, professional and/or promotional advancement, higher school matriculation, scholarship, or other legitimate requirements of education and/or governmental authorities.

This book is NOT intended for use, class instruction, tutoring, training, duplication, copying, reprinting, excerption, or adaptation, etc., by:

1) Other publishers
2) Proprietors and/or Instructors of "Coaching" and/or Preparatory Courses
3) Personnel and/or Training Divisions of commercial, industrial, and governmental organizations
4) Schools, colleges, or universities and/or their departments and staffs, including teachers and other personnel
5) Testing Agencies or Bureaus
6) Study groups which seek by the purchase of a single volume to copy and/or duplicate and/or adapt this material for use by the group as a whole without having purchased individual volumes for each of the members of the group
7) Et al.

Such persons would be in violation of appropriate Federal and State statutes.

PROVISION OF LICENSING AGREEMENTS – Recognized educational, commercial, industrial, and governmental institutions and organizations, and others legitimately engaged in educational pursuits, including training, testing, and measurement activities, may address request for a licensing agreement to the copyright owners, who will determine whether, and under what conditions, including fees and charges, the materials in this book may be used them. In other words, a licensing facility exists for the legitimate use of the material in this book on other than an individual basis. However, it is asseverated and affirmed here that the material in this book CANNOT be used without the receipt of the express permission of such a licensing agreement from the Publishers. Inquiries re licensing should be addressed to the company, attention rights and permissions department.

All rights reserved, including the right of reproduction in whole or in part, in any form or by any means, electronic or mechanical, including photocopying, recording, or by any information storage and retrieval system, without permission in writing from the Publisher.

Copyright © 2025 by
National Learning Corporation

212 Michael Drive, Syosset, NY 11791
(516) 921-8888 • www.passbooks.com
E-mail: info@passbooks.com

PASSBOOK® SERIES

THE *PASSBOOK® SERIES* has been created to prepare applicants and candidates for the ultimate academic battlefield – the examination room.

At some time in our lives, each and every one of us may be required to take an examination – for validation, matriculation, admission, qualification, registration, certification, or licensure.

Based on the assumption that every applicant or candidate has met the basic formal educational standards, has taken the required number of courses, and read the necessary texts, the *PASSBOOK® SERIES* furnishes the one special preparation which may assure passing with confidence, instead of failing with insecurity. Examination questions – together with answers – are furnished as the basic vehicle for study so that the mysteries of the examination and its compounding difficulties may be eliminated or diminished by a sure method.

This book is meant to help you pass your examination provided that you qualify and are serious in your objective.

The entire field is reviewed through the huge store of content information which is succinctly presented through a provocative and challenging approach – the question-and-answer method.

A climate of success is established by furnishing the correct answers at the end of each test.

You soon learn to recognize types of questions, forms of questions, and patterns of questioning. You may even begin to anticipate expected outcomes.

You perceive that many questions are repeated or adapted so that you can gain acute insights, which may enable you to score many sure points.

You learn how to confront new questions, or types of questions, and to attack them confidently and work out the correct answers.

You note objectives and emphases, and recognize pitfalls and dangers, so that you may make positive educational adjustments.

Moreover, you are kept fully informed in relation to new concepts, methods, practices, and directions in the field.

You discover that you are actually taking the examination all the time: you are preparing for the examination by "taking" an examination, not by reading extraneous and/or supererogatory textbooks.

In short, this PASSBOOK®, used directedly, should be an important factor in helping you to pass your test.

FOOD INSPECTOR

DUTIES: As a **Food Inspector**, you would enforce federal and state laws, rules and regulations by conducting inspections at food manufacturers, processors, distributors, and retailers and report violations of standards as they pertain to wholesomeness, labeling, and advertising of food products and/or general sanitary conditions and inventory control. You would also participate in educational sessions for operators of establishments (including donated food recipient agencies) found in repeated violation of sanitation standards. You may testify in court or in administrative hearings on volatile conditions at food establishments, donated food recipient agencies, warehouses or food banks and investigate consumer complaints related to mislabeling or unwholesomeness of food.

SUBJECT OF EXAMINATION: There will be a **written test** which you must pass in order to be considered for appointment. The **written test** is designed to test for knowledge, skills and/or abilities in such areas as:

1. **Evaluating Information and Evidence** - These questions test for the ability to evaluate and draw conclusions from information and evidence. Each question consists of a set of facts and a conclusion based on the facts. The candidate must decide if the conclusion is warranted by the facts.
2. **Food safety and food establishment sanitation** - These questions test for a knowledge of food establishment sanitation procedures. Questions will cover such sanitary operations as vermin control, sanitation of equipment, temperature control, transportation and storage monitoring, personnel hygiene, and disease control.
3. **General science concepts related to chemistry, microbiology, entomology and food science** - These questions will test for a knowledge in areas listed as they relate to subjects such as food sampling, testing, food adulteration and preservation.
4. **Preparing written material** - These questions test for the ability to present information clearly and accurately and to organize paragraphs logically and comprehensibly. For some questions, you will be given information in two or three sentences followed by four restatements of the information. You must then choose the best version. For other questions, you will be given paragraphs with their sentences out of order and then asked to choose from four suggestions the best order for the sentences.
5. **Understanding and interpreting written material** - These questions test how well you comprehend written material. You will be provided with brief reading selections and will be asked questions about the selections. All the information required to answer the questions will be presented in the selections; you will not be required to have any special knowledge relating to the subject areas of the selections.

HOW TO TAKE A TEST

I. YOU MUST PASS AN EXAMINATION

A. WHAT EVERY CANDIDATE SHOULD KNOW

Examination applicants often ask us for help in preparing for the written test. What can I study in advance? What kinds of questions will be asked? How will the test be given? How will the papers be graded?

As an applicant for a civil service examination, you may be wondering about some of these things. Our purpose here is to suggest effective methods of advance study and to describe civil service examinations.

Your chances for success on this examination can be increased if you know how to prepare. Those "pre-examination jitters" can be reduced if you know what to expect. You can even experience an adventure in good citizenship if you know why civil service exams are given.

B. WHY ARE CIVIL SERVICE EXAMINATIONS GIVEN?

Civil service examinations are important to you in two ways. As a citizen, you want public jobs filled by employees who know how to do their work. As a job seeker, you want a fair chance to compete for that job on an equal footing with other candidates. The best-known means of accomplishing this two-fold goal is the competitive examination.

Exams are widely publicized throughout the nation. They may be administered for jobs in federal, state, city, municipal, town or village governments or agencies.

Any citizen may apply, with some limitations, such as the age or residence of applicants. Your experience and education may be reviewed to see whether you meet the requirements for the particular examination. When these requirements exist, they are reasonable and applied consistently to all applicants. Thus, a competitive examination may cause you some uneasiness now, but it is your privilege and safeguard.

C. HOW ARE CIVIL SERVICE EXAMS DEVELOPED?

Examinations are carefully written by trained technicians who are specialists in the field known as "psychological measurement," in consultation with recognized authorities in the field of work that the test will cover. These experts recommend the subject matter areas or skills to be tested; only those knowledges or skills important to your success on the job are included. The most reliable books and source materials available are used as references. Together, the experts and technicians judge the difficulty level of the questions.

Test technicians know how to phrase questions so that the problem is clearly stated. Their ethics do not permit "trick" or "catch" questions. Questions may have been tried out on sample groups, or subjected to statistical analysis, to determine their usefulness.

Written tests are often used in combination with performance tests, ratings of training and experience, and oral interviews. All of these measures combine to form the best-known means of finding the right person for the right job.

II. HOW TO PASS THE WRITTEN TEST

A. NATURE OF THE EXAMINATION

To prepare intelligently for civil service examinations, you should know how they differ from school examinations you have taken. In school you were assigned certain definite pages to read or subjects to cover. The examination questions were quite detailed and usually emphasized memory. Civil service exams, on the other hand, try to discover your present ability to perform the duties of a position, plus your potentiality to learn these duties. In other words, a civil service exam attempts to predict how successful you will be. Questions cover such a broad area that they cannot be as minute and detailed as school exam questions.

In the public service similar kinds of work, or positions, are grouped together in one "class." This process is known as *position-classification*. All the positions in a class are paid according to the salary range for that class. One class title covers all of these positions, and they are all tested by the same examination.

B. FOUR BASIC STEPS

1) Study the announcement

How, then, can you know what subjects to study? Our best answer is: "Learn as much as possible about the class of positions for which you've applied." The exam will test the knowledge, skills and abilities needed to do the work.

Your most valuable source of information about the position you want is the official exam announcement. This announcement lists the training and experience qualifications. Check these standards and apply only if you come reasonably close to meeting them.

The brief description of the position in the examination announcement offers some clues to the subjects which will be tested. Think about the job itself. Review the duties in your mind. Can you perform them, or are there some in which you are rusty? Fill in the blank spots in your preparation.

Many jurisdictions preview the written test in the exam announcement by including a section called "Knowledge and Abilities Required," "Scope of the Examination," or some similar heading. Here you will find out specifically what fields will be tested.

2) Review your own background

Once you learn in general what the position is all about, and what you need to know to do the work, ask yourself which subjects you already know fairly well and which need improvement. You may wonder whether to concentrate on improving your strong areas or on building some background in your fields of weakness. When the announcement has specified "some knowledge" or "considerable knowledge," or has used adjectives like "beginning principles of..." or "advanced ... methods," you can get a clue as to the number and difficulty of questions to be asked in any given field. More questions, and hence broader coverage, would be included for those subjects which are more important in the work. Now weigh your strengths and weaknesses against the job requirements and prepare accordingly.

3) Determine the level of the position

Another way to tell how intensively you should prepare is to understand the level of the job for which you are applying. Is it the entering level? In other words, is this the position in which beginners in a field of work are hired? Or is it an intermediate or advanced level? Sometimes this is indicated by such words as "Junior" or "Senior" in the class title. Other jurisdictions use Roman numerals to designate the level – Clerk I, Clerk II, for example. The word "Supervisor" sometimes appears in the title. If the level is not indicated by the title, check the description of duties. Will you be working under very close supervision, or will you have responsibility for independent decisions in this work?

4) Choose appropriate study materials

Now that you know the subjects to be examined and the relative amount of each subject to be covered, you can choose suitable study materials. For beginning level jobs, or even advanced ones, if you have a pronounced weakness in some aspect of your training, read a modern, standard textbook in that field. Be sure it is up to date and has general coverage. Such books are normally available at your library, and the librarian will be glad to help you locate one. For entry-level positions, questions of appropriate difficulty are chosen – neither highly advanced questions, nor those too simple. Such questions require careful thought but not advanced training.

If the position for which you are applying is technical or advanced, you will read more advanced, specialized material. If you are already familiar with the basic principles of your field, elementary textbooks would waste your time. Concentrate on advanced textbooks and technical periodicals. Think through the concepts and review difficult problems in your field.

These are all general sources. You can get more ideas on your own initiative, following these leads. For example, training manuals and publications of the government agency which employs workers in your field can be useful, particularly for technical and professional positions. A letter or visit to the government department involved may result in more specific study suggestions, and certainly will provide you with a more definite idea of the exact nature of the position you are seeking.

III. KINDS OF TESTS

Tests are used for purposes other than measuring knowledge and ability to perform specified duties. For some positions, it is equally important to test ability to make adjustments to new situations or to profit from training. In others, basic mental abilities not dependent on information are essential. Questions which test these things may not appear as pertinent to the duties of the position as those which test for knowledge and information. Yet they are often highly important parts of a fair examination. For very general questions, it is almost impossible to help you direct your study efforts. What we can do is to point out some of the more common of these general abilities needed in public service positions and describe some typical questions.

1) General information

Broad, general information has been found useful for predicting job success in some kinds of work. This is tested in a variety of ways, from vocabulary lists to questions about current events. Basic background in some field of work, such as sociology or economics, may be sampled in a group of questions. Often these are principles which have become familiar to most persons through exposure rather than through formal training. It is difficult to advise you how to study for these questions; being alert to the world around you is our best suggestion.

2) Verbal ability

An example of an ability needed in many positions is verbal or language ability. Verbal ability is, in brief, the ability to use and understand words. Vocabulary and grammar tests are typical measures of this ability. Reading comprehension or paragraph interpretation questions are common in many kinds of civil service tests. You are given a paragraph of written material and asked to find its central meaning.

3) **Numerical ability**

Number skills can be tested by the familiar arithmetic problem, by checking paired lists of numbers to see which are alike and which are different, or by interpreting charts and graphs. In the latter test, a graph may be printed in the test booklet which you are asked to use as the basis for answering questions.

4) **Observation**

A popular test for law-enforcement positions is the observation test. A picture is shown to you for several minutes, then taken away. Questions about the picture test your ability to observe both details and larger elements.

5) **Following directions**

In many positions in the public service, the employee must be able to carry out written instructions dependably and accurately. You may be given a chart with several columns, each column listing a variety of information. The questions require you to carry out directions involving the information given in the chart.

6) **Skills and aptitudes**

Performance tests effectively measure some manual skills and aptitudes. When the skill is one in which you are trained, such as typing or shorthand, you can practice. These tests are often very much like those given in business school or high school courses. For many of the other skills and aptitudes, however, no short-time preparation can be made. Skills and abilities natural to you or that you have developed throughout your lifetime are being tested.

Many of the general questions just described provide all the data needed to answer the questions and ask you to use your reasoning ability to find the answers. Your best preparation for these tests, as well as for tests of facts and ideas, is to be at your physical and mental best. You, no doubt, have your own methods of getting into an exam-taking mood and keeping "in shape." The next section lists some ideas on this subject.

IV. KINDS OF QUESTIONS

Only rarely is the "essay" question, which you answer in narrative form, used in civil service tests. Civil service tests are usually of the short-answer type. Full instructions for answering these questions will be given to you at the examination. But in case this is your first experience with short-answer questions and separate answer sheets, here is what you need to know:

1) Multiple-choice Questions

Most popular of the short-answer questions is the "multiple choice" or "best answer" question. It can be used, for example, to test for factual knowledge, ability to solve problems or judgment in meeting situations found at work.

A multiple-choice question is normally one of three types—
- It can begin with an incomplete statement followed by several possible endings. You are to find the one ending which *best* completes the statement, although some of the others may not be entirely wrong.
- It can also be a complete statement in the form of a question which is answered by choosing one of the statements listed.

- It can be in the form of a problem – again you select the best answer.

Here is an example of a multiple-choice question with a discussion which should give you some clues as to the method for choosing the right answer:

When an employee has a complaint about his assignment, the action which will *best* help him overcome his difficulty is to
- A. discuss his difficulty with his coworkers
- B. take the problem to the head of the organization
- C. take the problem to the person who gave him the assignment
- D. say nothing to anyone about his complaint

In answering this question, you should study each of the choices to find which is best. Consider choice "A" – Certainly an employee may discuss his complaint with fellow employees, but no change or improvement can result, and the complaint remains unresolved. Choice "B" is a poor choice since the head of the organization probably does not know what assignment you have been given, and taking your problem to him is known as "going over the head" of the supervisor. The supervisor, or person who made the assignment, is the person who can clarify it or correct any injustice. Choice "C" is, therefore, correct. To say nothing, as in choice "D," is unwise. Supervisors have and interest in knowing the problems employees are facing, and the employee is seeking a solution to his problem.

2) True/False Questions

The "true/false" or "right/wrong" form of question is sometimes used. Here a complete statement is given. Your job is to decide whether the statement is right or wrong.

SAMPLE: A roaming cell-phone call to a nearby city costs less than a non-roaming call to a distant city.

This statement is wrong, or false, since roaming calls are more expensive.

This is not a complete list of all possible question forms, although most of the others are variations of these common types. You will always get complete directions for answering questions. Be sure you understand *how* to mark your answers – ask questions until you do.

V. RECORDING YOUR ANSWERS

Computer terminals are used more and more today for many different kinds of exams.

For an examination with very few applicants, you may be told to record your answers in the test booklet itself. Separate answer sheets are much more common. If this separate answer sheet is to be scored by machine – and this is often the case – it is highly important that you mark your answers correctly in order to get credit.

An electronic scoring machine is often used in civil service offices because of the speed with which papers can be scored. Machine-scored answer sheets must be marked with a pencil, which will be given to you. This pencil has a high graphite content which responds to the electronic scoring machine. As a matter of fact, stray dots may register as answers, so do not let your pencil rest on the answer sheet while you are pondering the correct answer. Also, if your pencil lead breaks or is otherwise defective, ask for another.

Since the answer sheet will be dropped in a slot in the scoring machine, be careful not to bend the corners or get the paper crumpled.

The answer sheet normally has five vertical columns of numbers, with 30 numbers to a column. These numbers correspond to the question numbers in your test booklet. After each number, going across the page are four or five pairs of dotted lines. These short dotted lines have small letters or numbers above them. The first two pairs may also have a "T" or "F" above the letters. This indicates that the first two pairs only are to be used if the questions are of the true-false type. If the questions are multiple choice, disregard the "T" and "F" and pay attention only to the small letters or numbers.

Answer your questions in the manner of the sample that follows:

32. The largest city in the United States is
    A. Washington, D.C.
    B. New York City
    C. Chicago
    D. Detroit
    E. San Francisco

1) Choose the answer you think is best. (New York City is the largest, so "B" is correct.)
2) Find the row of dotted lines numbered the same as the question you are answering. (Find row number 32)
3) Find the pair of dotted lines corresponding to the answer. (Find the pair of lines under the mark "B.")
4) Make a solid black mark between the dotted lines.

VI. BEFORE THE TEST

Common sense will help you find procedures to follow to get ready for an examination. Too many of us, however, overlook these sensible measures. Indeed, nervousness and fatigue have been found to be the most serious reasons why applicants fail to do their best on civil service tests. Here is a list of reminders:

- Begin your preparation early – Don't wait until the last minute to go scurrying around for books and materials or to find out what the position is all about.
- Prepare continuously – An hour a night for a week is better than an all-night cram session. This has been definitely established. What is more, a night a week for a month will return better dividends than crowding your study into a shorter period of time.
- Locate the place of the exam – You have been sent a notice telling you when and where to report for the examination. If the location is in a different town or otherwise unfamiliar to you, it would be well to inquire the best route and learn something about the building.
- Relax the night before the test – Allow your mind to rest. Do not study at all that night. Plan some mild recreation or diversion; then go to bed early and get a good night's sleep.
- Get up early enough to make a leisurely trip to the place for the test – This way unforeseen events, traffic snarls, unfamiliar buildings, etc. will not upset you.
- Dress comfortably – A written test is not a fashion show. You will be known by number and not by name, so wear something comfortable.

- Leave excess paraphernalia at home – Shopping bags and odd bundles will get in your way. You need bring only the items mentioned in the official notice you received; usually everything you need is provided. Do not bring reference books to the exam. They will only confuse those last minutes and be taken away from you when in the test room.
- Arrive somewhat ahead of time – If because of transportation schedules you must get there very early, bring a newspaper or magazine to take your mind off yourself while waiting.
- Locate the examination room – When you have found the proper room, you will be directed to the seat or part of the room where you will sit. Sometimes you are given a sheet of instructions to read while you are waiting. Do not fill out any forms until you are told to do so; just read them and be prepared.
- Relax and prepare to listen to the instructions
- If you have any physical problem that may keep you from doing your best, be sure to tell the test administrator. If you are sick or in poor health, you really cannot do your best on the exam. You can come back and take the test some other time.

VII. AT THE TEST

The day of the test is here and you have the test booklet in your hand. The temptation to get going is very strong. Caution! There is more to success than knowing the right answers. You must know how to identify your papers and understand variations in the type of short-answer question used in this particular examination. Follow these suggestions for maximum results from your efforts:

1) Cooperate with the monitor

The test administrator has a duty to create a situation in which you can be as much at ease as possible. He will give instructions, tell you when to begin, check to see that you are marking your answer sheet correctly, and so on. He is not there to guard you, although he will see that your competitors do not take unfair advantage. He wants to help you do your best.

2) Listen to all instructions

Don't jump the gun! Wait until you understand all directions. In most civil service tests you get more time than you need to answer the questions. So don't be in a hurry. Read each word of instructions until you clearly understand the meaning. Study the examples, listen to all announcements and follow directions. Ask questions if you do not understand what to do.

3) Identify your papers

Civil service exams are usually identified by number only. You will be assigned a number; you must not put your name on your test papers. Be sure to copy your number correctly. Since more than one exam may be given, copy your exact examination title.

4) Plan your time

Unless you are told that a test is a "speed" or "rate of work" test, speed itself is usually not important. Time enough to answer all the questions will be provided, but this does not mean that you have all day. An overall time limit has been set. Divide the total time (in minutes) by the number of questions to determine the approximate time you have for each question.

5) Do not linger over difficult questions

If you come across a difficult question, mark it with a paper clip (useful to have along) and come back to it when you have been through the booklet. One caution if you do this – be sure to skip a number on your answer sheet as well. Check often to be sure that you have not lost your place and that you are marking in the row numbered the same as the question you are answering.

6) Read the questions

Be sure you know what the question asks! Many capable people are unsuccessful because they failed to *read* the questions correctly.

7) Answer all questions

Unless you have been instructed that a penalty will be deducted for incorrect answers, it is better to guess than to omit a question.

8) Speed tests

It is often better NOT to guess on speed tests. It has been found that on timed tests people are tempted to spend the last few seconds before time is called in marking answers at random – without even reading them – in the hope of picking up a few extra points. To discourage this practice, the instructions may warn you that your score will be "corrected" for guessing. That is, a penalty will be applied. The incorrect answers will be deducted from the correct ones, or some other penalty formula will be used.

9) Review your answers

If you finish before time is called, go back to the questions you guessed or omitted to give them further thought. Review other answers if you have time.

10) Return your test materials

If you are ready to leave before others have finished or time is called, take ALL your materials to the monitor and leave quietly. Never take any test material with you. The monitor can discover whose papers are not complete, and taking a test booklet may be grounds for disqualification.

VIII. EXAMINATION TECHNIQUES

1) Read the general instructions carefully. These are usually printed on the first page of the exam booklet. As a rule, these instructions refer to the timing of the examination; the fact that you should not start work until the signal and must stop work at a signal, etc. If there are any *special* instructions, such as a choice of questions to be answered, make sure that you note this instruction carefully.

2) When you are ready to start work on the examination, that is as soon as the signal has been given, read the instructions to each question booklet, underline any key words or phrases, such as *least, best, outline, describe* and the like. In this way you will tend to answer as requested rather than discover on reviewing your paper that you *listed without describing*, that you selected the *worst* choice rather than the *best* choice, etc.

3) If the examination is of the objective or multiple-choice type – that is, each question will also give a series of possible answers: A, B, C or D, and you are called upon to select the best answer and write the letter next to that answer on your answer paper – it is advisable to start answering each question in turn. There may be anywhere from 50 to 100 such questions in the three or four hours allotted and you can see how much time would be taken if you read through all the questions before beginning to answer any. Furthermore, if you come across a question or group of questions which you know would be difficult to answer, it would undoubtedly affect your handling of all the other questions.

4) If the examination is of the essay type and contains but a few questions, it is a moot point as to whether you should read all the questions before starting to answer any one. Of course, if you are given a choice – say five out of seven and the like – then it is essential to read all the questions so you can eliminate the two that are most difficult. If, however, you are asked to answer all the questions, there may be danger in trying to answer the easiest one first because you may find that you will spend too much time on it. The best technique is to answer the first question, then proceed to the second, etc.

5) Time your answers. Before the exam begins, write down the time it started, then add the time allowed for the examination and write down the time it must be completed, then divide the time available somewhat as follows:
    - If 3-1/2 hours are allowed, that would be 210 minutes. If you have 80 objective-type questions, that would be an average of 2-1/2 minutes per question. Allow yourself no more than 2 minutes per question, or a total of 160 minutes, which will permit about 50 minutes to review.
    - If for the time allotment of 210 minutes there are 7 essay questions to answer, that would average about 30 minutes a question. Give yourself only 25 minutes per question so that you have about 35 minutes to review.

6) The most important instruction is to *read each question* and make sure you know what is wanted. The second most important instruction is to *time yourself properly* so that you answer every question. The third most important instruction is to *answer every question*. Guess if you have to but include something for each question. Remember that you will receive no credit for a blank and will probably receive some credit if you write something in answer to an essay question. If you guess a letter – say "B" for a multiple-choice question – you may have guessed right. If you leave a blank as an answer to a multiple-choice question, the examiners may respect your feelings but it will not add a point to your score. Some exams may penalize you for wrong answers, so in such cases *only*, you may not want to guess unless you have some basis for your answer.

7) Suggestions
    a. Objective-type questions
        1. Examine the question booklet for proper sequence of pages and questions
        2. Read all instructions carefully
        3. Skip any question which seems too difficult; return to it after all other questions have been answered
        4. Apportion your time properly; do not spend too much time on any single question or group of questions

5. Note and underline key words – *all, most, fewest, least, best, worst, same, opposite,* etc.
6. Pay particular attention to negatives
7. Note unusual option, e.g., unduly long, short, complex, different or similar in content to the body of the question
8. Observe the use of "hedging" words – *probably, may, most likely,* etc.
9. Make sure that your answer is put next to the same number as the question
10. Do not second-guess unless you have good reason to believe the second answer is definitely more correct
11. Cross out original answer if you decide another answer is more accurate; do not erase until you are ready to hand your paper in
12. Answer all questions; guess unless instructed otherwise
13. Leave time for review

b. Essay questions
   1. Read each question carefully
   2. Determine exactly what is wanted. Underline key words or phrases.
   3. Decide on outline or paragraph answer
   4. Include many different points and elements unless asked to develop any one or two points or elements
   5. Show impartiality by giving pros and cons unless directed to select one side only
   6. Make and write down any assumptions you find necessary to answer the questions
   7. Watch your English, grammar, punctuation and choice of words
   8. Time your answers; don't crowd material

8) Answering the essay question

Most essay questions can be answered by framing the specific response around several key words or ideas. Here are a few such key words or ideas:

M's: manpower, materials, methods, money, management
P's: purpose, program, policy, plan, procedure, practice, problems, pitfalls, personnel, public relations

   a. Six basic steps in handling problems:
      1. Preliminary plan and background development
      2. Collect information, data and facts
      3. Analyze and interpret information, data and facts
      4. Analyze and develop solutions as well as make recommendations
      5. Prepare report and sell recommendations
      6. Install recommendations and follow up effectiveness

   b. Pitfalls to avoid
      1. *Taking things for granted* – A statement of the situation does not necessarily imply that each of the elements is necessarily true; for example, a complaint may be invalid and biased so that all that can be taken for granted is that a complaint has been registered

2. *Considering only one side of a situation* – Wherever possible, indicate several alternatives and then point out the reasons you selected the best one
3. *Failing to indicate follow up* – Whenever your answer indicates action on your part, make certain that you will take proper follow-up action to see how successful your recommendations, procedures or actions turn out to be
4. *Taking too long in answering any single question* – Remember to time your answers properly

IX. AFTER THE TEST

Scoring procedures differ in detail among civil service jurisdictions although the general principles are the same. Whether the papers are hand-scored or graded by machine we have described, they are nearly always graded by number. That is, the person who marks the paper knows only the number – never the name – of the applicant. Not until all the papers have been graded will they be matched with names. If other tests, such as training and experience or oral interview ratings have been given, scores will be combined. Different parts of the examination usually have different weights. For example, the written test might count 60 percent of the final grade, and a rating of training and experience 40 percent. In many jurisdictions, veterans will have a certain number of points added to their grades.

After the final grade has been determined, the names are placed in grade order and an eligible list is established. There are various methods for resolving ties between those who get the same final grade – probably the most common is to place first the name of the person whose application was received first. Job offers are made from the eligible list in the order the names appear on it. You will be notified of your grade and your rank as soon as all these computations have been made. This will be done as rapidly as possible.

People who are found to meet the requirements in the announcement are called "eligibles." Their names are put on a list of eligible candidates. An eligible's chances of getting a job depend on how high he stands on this list and how fast agencies are filling jobs from the list.

When a job is to be filled from a list of eligibles, the agency asks for the names of people on the list of eligibles for that job. When the civil service commission receives this request, it sends to the agency the names of the three people highest on this list. Or, if the job to be filled has specialized requirements, the office sends the agency the names of the top three persons who meet these requirements from the general list.

The appointing officer makes a choice from among the three people whose names were sent to him. If the selected person accepts the appointment, the names of the others are put back on the list to be considered for future openings.

That is the rule in hiring from all kinds of eligible lists, whether they are for typist, carpenter, chemist, or something else. For every vacancy, the appointing officer has his choice of any one of the top three eligibles on the list. This explains why the person whose name is on top of the list sometimes does not get an appointment when some of the persons lower on the list do. If the appointing officer chooses the second or third eligible, the No. 1 eligible does not get a job at once, but stays on the list until he is appointed or the list is terminated.

X. HOW TO PASS THE INTERVIEW TEST

The examination for which you applied requires an oral interview test. You have already taken the written test and you are now being called for the interview test – the final part of the formal examination.

You may think that it is not possible to prepare for an interview test and that there are no procedures to follow during an interview. Our purpose is to point out some things you can do in advance that will help you and some good rules to follow and pitfalls to avoid while you are being interviewed.

What is an interview supposed to test?

The written examination is designed to test the technical knowledge and competence of the candidate; the oral is designed to evaluate intangible qualities, not readily measured otherwise, and to establish a list showing the relative fitness of each candidate – as measured against his competitors – for the position sought. Scoring is not on the basis of "right" and "wrong," but on a sliding scale of values ranging from "not passable" to "outstanding." As a matter of fact, it is possible to achieve a relatively low score without a single "incorrect" answer because of evident weakness in the qualities being measured.

Occasionally, an examination may consist entirely of an oral test – either an individual or a group oral. In such cases, information is sought concerning the technical knowledges and abilities of the candidate, since there has been no written examination for this purpose. More commonly, however, an oral test is used to supplement a written examination.

Who conducts interviews?

The composition of oral boards varies among different jurisdictions. In nearly all, a representative of the personnel department serves as chairman. One of the members of the board may be a representative of the department in which the candidate would work. In some cases, "outside experts" are used, and, frequently, a businessman or some other representative of the general public is asked to serve. Labor and management or other special groups may be represented. The aim is to secure the services of experts in the appropriate field.

However the board is composed, it is a good idea (and not at all improper or unethical) to ascertain in advance of the interview who the members are and what groups they represent. When you are introduced to them, you will have some idea of their backgrounds and interests, and at least you will not stutter and stammer over their names.

What should be done before the interview?

While knowledge about the board members is useful and takes some of the surprise element out of the interview, there is other preparation which is more substantive. It *is* possible to prepare for an oral interview – in several ways:

1) Keep a copy of your application and review it carefully before the interview

This may be the only document before the oral board, and the starting point of the interview. Know what education and experience you have listed there, and the sequence and dates of all of it. Sometimes the board will ask you to review the highlights of your experience for them; you should not have to hem and haw doing it.

2) Study the class specification and the examination announcement

Usually, the oral board has one or both of these to guide them. The qualities, characteristics or knowledges required by the position sought are stated in these documents. They offer valuable clues as to the nature of the oral interview. For example, if the job involves supervisory responsibilities, the announcement will usually indicate that knowledge of modern supervisory methods and the qualifications of the candidate as a supervisor will be tested. If so, you can expect such questions, frequently in the form of a hypothetical situation which you are expected to solve. NEVER go into an oral without knowledge of the duties and responsibilities of the job you seek.

3) Think through each qualification required

Try to visualize the kind of questions you would ask if you were a board member. How well could you answer them? Try especially to appraise your own knowledge and background in each area, *measured against the job sought*, and identify any areas in which you are weak. Be critical and realistic – do not flatter yourself.

4) Do some general reading in areas in which you feel you may be weak

For example, if the job involves supervision and your past experience has NOT, some general reading in supervisory methods and practices, particularly in the field of human relations, might be useful. Do NOT study agency procedures or detailed manuals. The oral board will be testing your understanding and capacity, not your memory.

5) Get a good night's sleep and watch your general health and mental attitude

You will want a clear head at the interview. Take care of a cold or any other minor ailment, and of course, no hangovers.

What should be done on the day of the interview?

Now comes the day of the interview itself. Give yourself plenty of time to get there. Plan to arrive somewhat ahead of the scheduled time, particularly if your appointment is in the fore part of the day. If a previous candidate fails to appear, the board might be ready for you a bit early. By early afternoon an oral board is almost invariably behind schedule if there are many candidates, and you may have to wait. Take along a book or magazine to read, or your application to review, but leave any extraneous material in the waiting room when you go in for your interview. In any event, relax and compose yourself.

The matter of dress is important. The board is forming impressions about you – from your experience, your manners, your attitude, and your appearance. Give your personal appearance careful attention. Dress your best, but not your flashiest. Choose conservative, appropriate clothing, and be sure it is immaculate. This is a business interview, and your appearance should indicate that you regard it as such. Besides, being well groomed and properly dressed will help boost your confidence.

Sooner or later, someone will call your name and escort you into the interview room. *This is it.* From here on you are on your own. It is too late for any more preparation. But remember, you asked for this opportunity to prove your fitness, and you are here because your request was granted.

What happens when you go in?

The usual sequence of events will be as follows: The clerk (who is often the board stenographer) will introduce you to the chairman of the oral board, who will introduce you to the other members of the board. Acknowledge the introductions before you sit down. Do not be surprised if you find a microphone facing you or a stenotypist sitting by. Oral interviews are usually recorded in the event of an appeal or other review.

Usually the chairman of the board will open the interview by reviewing the highlights of your education and work experience from your application – primarily for the benefit of the other members of the board, as well as to get the material into the record. Do not interrupt or comment unless there is an error or significant misinterpretation; if that is the case, do not hesitate. But do not quibble about insignificant matters. Also, he will usually ask you some question about your education, experience or your present job – partly to get you to start talking and to establish the interviewing "rapport." He may start the actual questioning, or turn it over to one of the other members. Frequently, each member undertakes the questioning on a particular area, one in which he is perhaps most competent, so you can expect each member to participate in the examination. Because time is limited, you may also expect some rather abrupt switches in the direction the questioning takes, so do not be upset by it. Normally, a board member will not pursue a single line of questioning unless he discovers a particular strength or weakness.

After each member has participated, the chairman will usually ask whether any member has any further questions, then will ask you if you have anything you wish to add. Unless you are expecting this question, it may floor you. Worse, it may start you off on an extended, extemporaneous speech. The board is not usually seeking more information. The question is principally to offer you a last opportunity to present further qualifications or to indicate that you have nothing to add. So, if you feel that a significant qualification or characteristic has been overlooked, it is proper to point it out in a sentence or so. Do not compliment the board on the thoroughness of their examination – they have been sketchy, and you know it. If you wish, merely say, "No thank you, I have nothing further to add." This is a point where you can "talk yourself out" of a good impression or fail to present an important bit of information. Remember, *you close the interview yourself*.

The chairman will then say, "That is all, Mr. _____, thank you." Do not be startled; the interview is over, and quicker than you think. Thank him, gather your belongings and take your leave. Save your sigh of relief for the other side of the door.

How to put your best foot forward

Throughout this entire process, you may feel that the board individually and collectively is trying to pierce your defenses, seek out your hidden weaknesses and embarrass and confuse you. Actually, this is not true. They are obliged to make an appraisal of your qualifications for the job you are seeking, and they want to see you in your best light. Remember, they must interview all candidates and a non-cooperative candidate may become a failure in spite of their best efforts to bring out his qualifications. Here are 15 suggestions that will help you:

1) Be natural – Keep your attitude confident, not cocky

If you are not confident that you can do the job, do not expect the board to be. Do not apologize for your weaknesses, try to bring out your strong points. The board is interested in a positive, not negative, presentation. Cockiness will antagonize any board member and make him wonder if you are covering up a weakness by a false show of strength.

2) Get comfortable, but don't lounge or sprawl

Sit erectly but not stiffly. A careless posture may lead the board to conclude that you are careless in other things, or at least that you are not impressed by the importance of the occasion. Either conclusion is natural, even if incorrect. Do not fuss with your clothing, a pencil or an ashtray. Your hands may occasionally be useful to emphasize a point; do not let them become a point of distraction.

3) Do not wisecrack or make small talk

This is a serious situation, and your attitude should show that you consider it as such. Further, the time of the board is limited – they do not want to waste it, and neither should you.

4) Do not exaggerate your experience or abilities

In the first place, from information in the application or other interviews and sources, the board may know more about you than you think. Secondly, you probably will not get away with it. An experienced board is rather adept at spotting such a situation, so do not take the chance.

5) If you know a board member, do not make a point of it, yet do not hide it

Certainly you are not fooling him, and probably not the other members of the board. Do not try to take advantage of your acquaintanceship – it will probably do you little good.

6) Do not dominate the interview

Let the board do that. They will give you the clues – do not assume that you have to do all the talking. Realize that the board has a number of questions to ask you, and do not try to take up all the interview time by showing off your extensive knowledge of the answer to the first one.

7) Be attentive

You only have 20 minutes or so, and you should keep your attention at its sharpest throughout. When a member is addressing a problem or question to you, give him your undivided attention. Address your reply principally to him, but do not exclude the other board members.

8) Do not interrupt

A board member may be stating a problem for you to analyze. He will ask you a question when the time comes. Let him state the problem, and wait for the question.

9) Make sure you understand the question

Do not try to answer until you are sure what the question is. If it is not clear, restate it in your own words or ask the board member to clarify it for you. However, do not haggle about minor elements.

10) Reply promptly but not hastily

A common entry on oral board rating sheets is "candidate responded readily," or "candidate hesitated in replies." Respond as promptly and quickly as you can, but do not jump to a hasty, ill-considered answer.

11) Do not be peremptory in your answers

A brief answer is proper – but do not fire your answer back. That is a losing game from your point of view. The board member can probably ask questions much faster than you can answer them.

12) Do not try to create the answer you think the board member wants

He is interested in what kind of mind you have and how it works – not in playing games. Furthermore, he can usually spot this practice and will actually grade you down on it.

13) Do not switch sides in your reply merely to agree with a board member

Frequently, a member will take a contrary position merely to draw you out and to see if you are willing and able to defend your point of view. Do not start a debate, yet do not surrender a good position. If a position is worth taking, it is worth defending.

14) Do not be afraid to admit an error in judgment if you are shown to be wrong

The board knows that you are forced to reply without any opportunity for careful consideration. Your answer may be demonstrably wrong. If so, admit it and get on with the interview.

15) Do not dwell at length on your present job

The opening question may relate to your present assignment. Answer the question but do not go into an extended discussion. You are being examined for a *new* job, not your present one. As a matter of fact, try to phrase ALL your answers in terms of the job for which you are being examined.

Basis of Rating

Probably you will forget most of these "do's" and "don'ts" when you walk into the oral interview room. Even remembering them all will not ensure you a passing grade. Perhaps you did not have the qualifications in the first place. But remembering them will help you to put your best foot forward, without treading on the toes of the board members.

Rumor and popular opinion to the contrary notwithstanding, an oral board wants you to make the best appearance possible. They know you are under pressure – but they also want to see how you respond to it as a guide to what your reaction would be under the pressures of the job you seek. They will be influenced by the degree of poise you display, the personal traits you show and the manner in which you respond.

ABOUT THIS BOOK

This book contains tests divided into Examination Sections. Go through each test, answering every question in the margin. We have also attached a sample answer sheet at the back of the book that can be removed and used. At the end of each test look at the answer key and check your answers. On the ones you got wrong, look at the right answer choice and learn. Do not fill in the answers first. Do not memorize the questions and answers, but understand the answer and principles involved. On your test, the questions will likely be different from the samples. Questions are changed and new ones added. If you understand these past questions you should have success with any changes that arise. Tests may consist of several types of questions. We have additional books on each subject should more study be advisable or necessary for you. Finally, the more you study, the better prepared you will be. This book is intended to be the last thing you study before you walk into the examination room. Prior study of relevant texts is also recommended. NLC publishes some of these in our Fundamental Series. Knowledge and good sense are important factors in passing your exam. Good luck also helps. So now study this Passbook, absorb the material contained within and take that knowledge into the examination. Then do your best to pass that exam.

EXAMINATION SECTION

EXAMINATION SECTION
TEST 1

DIRECTIONS: Each question or incomplete statement is followed by several suggested answers or completions. Select the one that BEST answers the question or completes the statement. *PRINT THE LETTER OF THE CORRECT ANSWER IN THE SPACE AT THE RIGHT.*

1. According to Department regulations, whenever meat is packaged by a retailer in advance of being sold, which one of the following MUST also be provided not more than 30 feet from the display counter?   1.____

    A. A chart indicating the date the item must be removed from sale
    B. A chart indicating the date the item was first placed on sale
    C. A means of testing the item for adulteration
    D. An accurate computing scale marked "for customer use" or a sign telling customers where such scale is located

2. According to Department regulations, retail stores are NOT permitted to sell prepackaged meat unless the package is   2.____

    A. colorless and transparent
    B. less than one ounce in weight
    C. of a heat-resistant material
    D. open at one end

3. Hamburger meat may contain all of the following EXCEPT   3.____

    A. chemical preservatives   B. added fat
    C. chuck steak   D. neck meat

4. The net weight declaration on a package of food MUST be   4.____

    A. in grams as well as ounces
    B. near the top of the package
    C. on the label but in no specific place
    D. on the main panel of the label

5. The fat content of oleomargarine MUST be at least   5.____

    A. 40 percent   B. 60 percent
    C. 80 percent   D. 90 percent

6. The following foods contain standardized ingredients EXCEPT   6.____

    A. ice cream   B. jams and jellies
    C. ketchup   D. orange drink

7. Earthenware dishes very often affect food stored in them by being the source of   7.____

    A. asbestos contamination   B. bacteria
    C. lead contamination   D. fluid dyes

8. The presence of E. Coli in food PROBABLY means that it

   A. is contaminated by fecal matter
   B. is high in minerals
   C. is suitable for diabetics
   D. must be refrigerated

9. Botulism food poisoning in the United States is *usually* caused by

   A. eating fish caught in polluted waters
   B. failure to wash raw fruit before eating
   C. improper home-canning of fruits and vegetables
   D. tapeworms found in beef or sheep

10. Food poisoning cases in the United States are *usually* characterized by

    A. long periods of illness followed by death
    B. long periods of illness rarely followed by death
    C. short periods of illness followed by death
    D. short periods of illness rarely followed by death

11. In the United States, food poisoning due to eating mushrooms is LARGELY attributable to

    A. failure to cook mushrooms
    B. failure to wash mushrooms
    C. mushrooms which are blue in color
    D. mushrooms which have not been cultivated domestically

12. Decomposition of fresh or cold storage meats can be detected BEST by

    A. noting absence of surface moisture
    B. noting presence of "off" odors
    C. noting warmth when touched
    D. observing discoloration

13. Bacterial control of shellfish and shellfish growing areas is being based increasingly in this country upon the density of the Escherichia coli organisms in the waters from which shellfish are collected.
    The BEST reason for this is that

    A. E. coli are virulent pathogens which produce serious diseases in man
    B. the density of E. coli in water is relatively easy to determine by shellfish fishermen
    C. the presence of E. coli is an indicator of the presence of human wastes in the water
    D. shellfish which ingest E. coli have objectionable odors which canning cannot remove

14. Proper cleaning of dairy utensils entails rinsing with

    A. cold or lukewarm water followed by scrubbing with a detergent solution
    B. cold or lukewarm water followed by scrubbing with hot soapy water
    C. hot water followed by scrubbing with a detergent solution
    D. hot water followed by scrubbing with hot soapy water

15. Of the following foods, the type that is *most likely* to cause "staph" food poisoning if improperly prepared or handled is		15.____

    A. sugar-coated food   B. dried food
    C. pickled food   D. cream-filled food

16. Harmful bacteria are *most often* introduced into foods prepared in a food service operation by		16.____

    A. insects   B. rodents
    C. employees   D. utensils

17. The one of the following procedures that could cause food poisoning is		17.____

    A. allowing cooked poultry to stand for an hour, slicing it and covering it with broth, and holding it at room temperature for several hours
    B. keeping food mixtures on cafeteria counters for one hour
    C. cooking left-over food mixtures quickly by frequent stirring and then refrigerating in shallow pans
    D. chilling all ingredients for salads at least one hour before preparation

18. Trichinosis is a disease which may be caused by		18.____

    A. eating ham which has been overcooked
    B. unsanitary handling of frozen meats
    C. eating food which has been contaminated by infected flies
    D. eating infected pork which has been cooked insufficiently

19. Of the following, the bacteria which causes MOST food poisoning cases is		19.____

    A. botulinum   B. salmonella
    C. pneumococci   D. streptococci

20. Of the following, the BEST reason for discarding the green part of potatoes is that it contains a poison known a		20.____

    A. cevitamic acid   B. citric acid
    C. solanine   D. trichinae

21. Of the following, the most effective way to prevent consumption of botulism bacteria is to		21.____

    A. buy food products from supermarkets only
    B. discard canned goods that are bulging or foul-smelling
    C. discard all produce that is not organic
    D. use stainless steel cookware to prepare meals

22. Trichinosis is a disease caused by		22.____

    A. a worm   B. an allergy
    C. improper refrigeration D. food adulteration

23. The ONLY safe method of canning non-acid vegetables and meats is the		23.____

    A. open kettle   B. hot water bath
    C. pressure process D. cold pack

24. Spoilage in canned foods which is caused by bacteria that produces acid without gas is known as

   A. putrefaction
   B. fermentation
   C. botulinus
   D. flat-sour spoilage

25. To avoid the development of bacterial toxins in custards and cream pies, one should

   A. cool to room temperature before refrigeration
   B. refrigerate within half hour after cooking
   C. heat to 212° F. during cooking
   D. store in the freezing compartment

26. An excellent medium for the growth of bacteria which cause food poisoning toxins is

   A. cream puffs
   B. pickled watermelon rind
   C. nougat candies
   D. preserves

27. Cooked foods should be cooled and refrigerated quickly PRIMARILY to

   A. prevent growth and development of bacteria
   B. preserve food nutrients
   C. prevent loss of moisture content
   D. preserve a fresh-cooked appearance

28. Aerobic bacteria which cause food spoilage

   A. are unable to grow without air
   B. are able to grow without air
   C. grow equally well with or without air
   D. need heat and moisture for growth

29. A disease caused by contamination in canned foods is

   A. trichinosis
   B. botulism
   C. undulant fever
   D. tularemia

30. Oysters which feed on sewage sometimes transmit

   A. rabies
   B. yellow fever
   C. typhoid fever
   D. malaria

31. In order to retard spoilage of bread, many baking companies add

   A. sodium sulphathionate
   B. sodium propionate
   C. sodium hypophosphate
   D. sodium benzoate

32. Spoilage in canned foods may be caused by

   A. filling the jars with food and fluid even with the top
   B. allowing the jars to cool before sealing the jars completely
   C. heating the jars for use in the hot-pack method
   D. filling the jars with the liquid in which the food was cooked

33. To prevent curdling of mayonnaise, 33.____

    A. expose to light
    B. expose to air
    C. store at 32° F.
    D. store at 150° F.

34. When a retailer plans to offer for sale thawed meat or fish, he is required by Department regulations to do which one of the following? 34.____

    A. Label the product "thawed" or "defrosted"
    B. Reduce the price of the product
    C. Refreeze the product and label it "refrozen"
    D. Remove the unsold portion from sale within three hours

35. Certain perishable foods must be stamped, printed, or otherwise plainly and conspicuously marked with either the last day or date of sale or the last day or date of recommended usage. Among these foods are 35.____

    A. bread, meat and poultry
    B. bread, milk and meat
    C. eggs, bread and milk
    D. eggs, milk and poultry

KEY (CORRECT ANSWERS)

1.	D	16.	C
2.	A	17.	A
3.	A	18.	D
4.	D	19.	B
5.	C	20.	C
6.	D	21.	B
7.	C	22.	A
8.	A	23.	C
9.	C	24.	D
10.	D	25.	B
11.	D	26.	A
12.	B	27.	A
13.	C	28.	A
14.	A	29.	B
15.	D	30.	C

31. B
32. B
33. A
34. C
35. C

TEST 2

DIRECTIONS: Each question or incomplete statement is followed by several suggested answers or completions. Select the one that BEST answers the question or completes the statement. *PRINT THE LETTER OF THE CORRECT ANSWER IN THE SPACE AT THE RIGHT.*

1. Trichinae are destroyed by 1.____

    A. freezing and storing at 15° F
    B. curing in a 2.5% salt solution
    C. radiation sterilization
    D. heating to 125° F

2. Dishes used by a patient with a communicable disease should be 2.____

    A. *boiled* for 5 minutes in soapy water
    B. *boiled* in an antiseptic solution
    C. *washed* for 5 minutes in soapy hot water
    D. *washed* in clear water at 180° F

3. The medium of infection which is MOST difficult to control is 3.____

    A. insects   B. food   C. water   D. air

4. Bread spoilage is retarded by the addition of 4.____

    A. sodium carbonate   B. calcium propionate
    C. tartaric acid   D. protease

5. Frozen foods which have partially thawed 5.____

    A. may be refrozen
    B. may be cooked and refrozen
    C. must be discarded
    D. may be refrozen only after complete thawing

6. Pasteurization of milk 6.____

    A. kills pathogenic bacteria
    B. retards the growth of bacteria
    C. kills all bacteria
    D. homogenizes

7. Among the following food additives, the one which is used for the purpose of enhancing the keeping quality of the food is 7.____

    A. vitamin D in milk
    B. bleaching agents in flour
    C. scorbic acid in cider
    D. minerals and vitamins in cereals

8. An example of the bactericidal method of food preservation is 8.____

    A. jam and jellies   B. pickling
    C. freezing   D. refrigeration

9. Oysters which feed on sewage sometimes transmit　　　　　　　　　　　　　　　　　　　9.____

   A. rabies
   B. yellow fever
   C. typhoid fever
   D. malaria

10. The ONLY edible mussel that is sold is the　　　　　　　　　　　　　　　　　　　　　　10.____

    A. scampi
    B. scallop
    C. clam
    D. rock lobster

11. *Flat sour*　　　　　　　　　　　　　　　　　　　　　　　　　　　　　　　　　　　　11.____

    A. is spoilage of canned food by bacteria with formation of gas
    B. renders food unfit for consumption
    C. can be corrected by addition of sugar to food before serving
    D. should be re-boiled before serving

12. Trichinosis is a disease caused by　　　　　　　　　　　　　　　　　　　　　　　　　12.____

    A. a worm
    B. an allergy
    C. improper refrigeration
    D. food adulteration

13. Dry foods should be stored in　　　　　　　　　　　　　　　　　　　　　　　　　　　13.____

    A. a cool dry place
    B. the basement
    C. a cabinet near the stove
    D. the refrigerator

14. In the process of food preservation,　　　　　　　　　　　　　　　　　　　　　　　　14.____

    A. all bacteria are destroyed
    B. harmful bacteria are destroyed
    C. the growth of bacteria may be prevented or checked
    D. harmless bacteria are destroyed

15. Orange juice prepared the night before it is to be served should be stored　　　　　　15.____

    A. in a container that will protect it from exposure to air
    B. at 32° F
    C. at 70° F
    D. in a plastic shaker-type container

16. When food has been spilled on an electric cooking element,　　　　　　　　　　　　　16.____

    A. clean immediately
    B. wash with soap and water when cool
    C. clean with steel wool
    D. clean with a dry brush after food chars

17. Pork should always be cooked to the well-done state in order to　　　　　　　　　　　17.____

    A. develop the best possible flavor
    B. prevent trichinosis in the consumer
    C. improve the tenderness
    D. prevent loss of nutritives in juices

18. To prevent curdling of mayonnaise,

    A. expose to light
    B. expose to air
    C. store at 32° F
    D. store at 150° F

19. To avoid the development of bacterial toxins in custards and cream pies, one should

    A. cool to room temperature before refrigeration
    B. refrigerate within half hour after cooking
    C. heat to 212° F during cooking
    D. store in the freezing compartment

20. An excellent medium for the growth of bacteria which cause food poisoning toxins is

    A. cream puffs
    B. pickled watermelon rind
    C. nougat candies
    D. preserves

21. The flavor of fruit is due to

    A. its color pigmentation
    B. citric and malic acids
    C. inorganic salts
    D. pectins

22. Which of the following is used to ripen fruits and vegetables?

    A. Chlorophyll
    B. Methylene
    C. Ethylene
    D. Benzoate of soda

23. Of the following, the BEST selection of orange for making orange juice is the

    A. Rome Beauty
    B. Navel
    C. Valencia
    D. Macintosh

24. To preserve the shape, fruits should be cooked

    A. without sugar
    B. with very little sugar
    C. by adding sugar after cooking
    D. by adding sugar before cooking

25. A prolific source of pectin for use in industry is

    A. fruits
    B. carrots
    C. walnuts
    D. calves' knuckles

26. Substances in fruits and vegetables which are responsible for the ripening process are

    A. molds   B. yeasts   C. bacteria   D. enzymes

27. Sulfuring dried fruits

    A. promotes retention of vitamin B
    B. prevents darkening
    C. activates vitamin C
    D. increases tenderness

28. Little spoilage occurs in stored, sun-dried fruits because the   28.____

    A. micro-organisms have been destroyed
    B. moisture content is low
    C. pectin is inactive
    D. yeasts do not flourish in the absence of light

29. Tenderized dried fruits have been   29.____

    A. sulphurized, dried, then partially cooked
    B. dried, partially cooked, then partially dried
    C. partially cooked, dried, then partially cooked
    D. dried, sulphurized, then partially cooked

30. Salted fish roe is sold as   30.____

    A. macedoine   B. curry   C. brioche   D. caviar

31. Aerobic bacteria which cause food spoilage   31.____

    A. are unable to grow without air
    B. are able to grow without air
    C. grow equally well with or without air
    D. need heat and moisture for growth

32. For everyday use, the Fahrenheit temperature of the refrigerator should be   32.____

    A. 20-25°   B. 35-40°   C. 45-50°   D. 55-60°

33. Incompletely cooked pork, if eaten, may result in   33.____

    A. botulism   B. ptomaine
    C. trichinosis   D. typhoid

34. The process which makes it possible to store fresh food in any climate without refrigera-   34.____
    tion for an unlimited length of time is

    A. dehydration   B. freezing
    C. freeze-drying   D. flake-drying

35. Frozen foods deteriorate in flavor unless they are kept at   35.____

    A. 32° F   B. 32° C   C. 0° F   D. 0° C

KEY (CORRECT ANSWERS)

1.	C	16.	D
2.	A	17.	B
3.	D	18.	A
4.	B	19.	B
5.	B	20.	A
6.	A	21.	D
7.	C	22.	C
8.	A	23.	C
9.	C	24.	D
10.	B	25.	A
11.	B	26.	D
12.	A	27.	B
13.	A	28.	B
14.	C	29.	B
15.	A	30.	D

31. A
32. B
33. C
34. C
35. C

———

EXAMINATION SECTION
TEST 1

DIRECTIONS: Each question or incomplete statement is followed by several suggested answers or completions. Select the one that BEST answers the question or completes the statement. *PRINT THE LETTER OF THE CORRECT ANSWER IN THE SPACE AT THE RIGHT.*

1. Assume that you have been assigned to inspect a building reported to be infested by rats and to prepare a written report thereon.
   Of the following items covered in the report, the LEAST important one is *probably* the

   A. fact that rats appear to be feeding on the garbage of a luncheonette which adjoins the building
   B. name and address of the building owner
   C. record of past violations by the owner
   D. statement made by tenants regarding the presence of rats

2. After completing an inspection of a food manufacturing plant, you submit a report of your findings to your supervisor. A few days later, you receive a memorandum from your supervisor indicating that the head of the bureau found your report inadequate. You are to re-inspect the establishment immediately. Your supervisor's memorandum lists the areas which he feels your report did not cover adequately. You, however, are convinced that your report is adequate.
   The BEST course of action for you to take at this time is to

   A. refrain from re-inspecting the food establishment unless directed to do so personally by the head of the bureau
   B. re-inspect the premises, submit another report, and then discuss the matter with your supervisor
   C. telephone your supervisor and insist that the matter be fully discussed before you proceed further with a re-inspection
   D. write a letter to the head of the bureau explaining why you feel your report was adequate, and wait for a reply before you re-inspect

3. Assume that you have a close relative who is engaged in the practice of accounting. Following your inspection of a restaurant which is not in violation of the health code, you inform the owner that your relative is an accountant. You hand the owner the accountant's business card and suggest that your relative be considered for any accounting work needed. The owner then tells you that he would like to have your relative take over his accounting work.
   Your action in securing the restaurant's accounting work for your relative is

   A. *improper;* you should have discussed the matter with the restaurant owner after your regular working hours
   B. *improper;* you should not have suggested your relative for the owner's accounting work
   C. *proper* as long as the owner remains in full compliance with the health code
   D. *proper* provided that your relative does not discuss the owner's business with you

4. A tenant of an apartment house telephones the department of health to complain that no heat is being furnished to her apartment. The complaint is referred to you with instructions to make a field visit. When you arrive at the apartment house, the tenant partly opens her door but refuses to allow you to enter the apartment. You explain the situation to the tenant, but she persists in her refusal to allow you to enter the apartment.
The BEST thing for you to do in these circumstances is to

   A. notify the tenant that if she refuses you admittance to her apartment, you may be required to obtain a court order directing her to allow you to enter
   B. place the complaint in your pending file and return to the apartment the next time you are in the neighborhood
   C. prepare a report setting forth that the tenant refused to allow you to enter the apartment
   D. take a reading of the temperature in the hallway and then estimate the temperature in the apartment

5. In the course of your inspection of a luncheonette, you note a violation of a provision of the health code relating to the unsanitary condition of food containers. You point out the condition to the owner as you begin to prepare a notice of violation. The owner becomes very angry and declares that the food containers are clean. To illustrate his point, he shows the food containers to two patrons seated at the lunch counter. Both patrons declare that the food containers are clean and suggest that you not *pick* on the owner. The owner then tells you that if you make trouble for him, he will make trouble for you.
Of the following, the BEST course of action for you to take is to

   A. inform the owner that you will return at a later date to complete your notice of violation
   B. refrain from giving the owner a notice of violation since he has witnesses to support his position
   C. serve the owner with a notice of violation
   D. telephone your supervisor, tell him of the condition of the food containers, and ask him whether you should give the owner a notice of violation

6. A provision of the health code requires food handlers to take a course in food handling sanitation. Your supervisor requests that when you visit food establishments in your district, you remind them of the code requirement. Your supervisor stresses that your visit is to be an educational one and that you are not to emphasize the mandatory aspect of this provision. Later, you visit a restaurant owner in your district who expresses strong reservations as to the practicability of releasing food handlers to take such a course.
The one statement which you should NOT make to the owner under any circumstances is that if his food handlers take such a course,

   A. future violations of the health code by the owner will receive special treatment since he is cooperating with the department
   B. his profits may rise since patrons prefer to eat in a place where food sanitation standards are high
   C. the possibility of food poisoning with attendant possible economic loss to the owner will be decreased
   D. the requirement of the health code is mandatory in this respect and must be complied with

7. During your inspection of a multiple dwelling, you find a serious violation of a provision of the health code. The owner claims that at one time the particular provision in question was sensible, but circumstances have changed and the provision should now be repealed. After listening to the owner, you are convinced that the health code should be changed as indicated by the owner. The CORRECT course of action for you to take is to

    A. give the owner a notice of violation and refrain from making any report to your office concerning the provision in question
    B. give the owner a notice of violation and suggest to your superior that the provision be reviewed as to its continued usefulness
    C. refrain from giving the owner a notice of violation since the provision is obviously outdated
    D. refrain from giving the owner a notice of violation until the courts rule on the constitutionality of the provision

8. Assume that you are in the apartment of a tenant who has complained that the landlord is not furnishing sufficient heat. Your thermometer shows that the landlord is furnishing sufficient heat to comply with the pertinent provision of the health code. You so inform the tenant. The tenant excitedly declares that you are using a *fake* thermometer and that you may be on the landlord's *payroll*.
Under these circumstances, you should state that

    A. if the tenant has any allegation to make concerning your inspection or character, she should contact your department
    B. if these, allegations are repeated, you will refer the tenant for psychiatric examination
    C. the allegations constitute defamation of the character of a public officer, and that you will so notify the police department
    D. you will ask the landlord to speak to the tenant to vouch for your honesty

9. You have been assigned to investigate a complaint with regard to a certain fruit and vegetable stand. Your investigation does not disclose any violation. Upon informing the owner of the stand of your findings, he offers you a bag of fruit as a gift. You decline it. He then offers to sell you the bag of fruit below the retail price - at cost to him. You SHOULD

    A. accept the offer, but refrain from visiting the establishment again
    B. accept the offer, provided you are satisfied that the fruit is being sold to you at cost
    C. decline the offer because it is not possible to calculate the wholesale cost of the fruit
    D. decline the offer since acceptance would be improper

10. The term *FT/SEC* is a unit of

    A. density   B. length   C. mass   D. speed

11. A container can hold 100 pounds of water or 70 pounds of an *unknown* liquid. The specific gravity of the *unknown* liquid is

    A. .30   B. .70   C. 1.0   D. 1.4

12. A *calorie* may be defined as the amount of heat required to raise one

    A. gram of water $1°C$ B. gram of water $1°F$
    C. pound of water $1°C$ D. pound of water $1°F$

13. The acidity of vinegar is due to the presence of _____ acid.

    A. acetic   B. carbonic   C. citric   D. hydrochloric

14. The cleansing action of a soap solution is due PRIMARILY to its

    A. acid reaction
    B. increased surface tension
    C. neutral reaction
    D. reduced surface tension

15. Titration refers to a process of

    A. determining the normality of an acid solution
    B. determining the refractive index of a crystal
    C. extracting oxygen from water
    D. measuring the quantity of salt present in a saline solution

16. Which one of the following types of compounds ALWAYS includes carbon, hydrogen, and oxygen?

    A. Carbohydrates   B. Carbonates
    C. Hydrates   D. Hydrocarbons

17. The formula for nitric acid is

    A. HNO_2 B. HNO_3 C. NO_2 D. N_2O

18. Gastric juice owes its acidity, *for the most part,* to the presence of _____ acid.

    A. carbonic   B. hydrochloric   C. nitric   D. sulfuric

19. Insulin is a type of

    A. enzyme   B. hormone   C. sugar   D. vitamin

20. The organ which prevents food from entering the windpipe during the act of swallowing is the

    A. epiglottis   B. larynx   C. pharynx   D. trachea

21. Casein is a type of

    A. carbohydrate   B. enzyme   C. fat   D. protein

22. The MAIN function of the kidneys is to remove wastes formed as a result of the oxidation of

    A. carbohydrates   B. fats   C. proteins   D. vitamins

23. Vitamin C is ALSO known as _____ acid.

    A. ascorbic   B. citric   C. glutamic   D. lactic

24. Light passes through the crystalline lens in the eye and focuses on the

    A. cornea   B. iris   C. pupil   D. retina

25. An electron weighs

    A. less than a neutron
    B. more than a neutron
    C. the same as a neutron
    D. the same as a proton

KEY (CORRECT ANSWERS)

1.	C	11.	B
2.	B	12.	A
3.	B	13.	A
4.	C	14.	D
5.	C	15.	A
6.	A	16.	A
7.	B	17.	B
8.	A	18.	B
9.	D	19.	B
10.	D	20.	A

21. D
22. C
23. A
24. D
25. A

TEST 2

DIRECTIONS: Each question or incomplete statement is followed by several suggested answers or completions. Select the one that BEST answers the question or completes the statement. *PRINT THE LETTER OF THE CORRECT ANSWER IN THE SPACE AT THE RIGHT.*

1. An electron has a _____ charge. 1._____

    A. negative   B. positive   C. variable   D. zero

2. Isotopes are atoms of elements which have _____ atomic weight(s). 2._____

    A. different atomic numbers and different
    B. different atomic numbers but the same
    C. the same atomic number and the same
    D. the same atomic number but different

3. In the Einstein equation $E = mc^2$, E, m, and c^2 stand for, respectively, 3._____

    A. electrons, molecules, and (centimeters)^2
    B. energy, mass, and (light velocity)^2
    C. energy, mass, and (radioactivity)^2
    D. energy, molecules, and (light velocity)^2

4. Photosynthesis entails the absorption of 4._____

    A. carbon dioxide and oxygen and release of water
    B. carbon dioxide and water and release of oxygen
    C. oxygen and release of carbon dioxide and water
    D. water and release of carbon dioxide and oxygen

5. Ordinary body temperature is approximately 37 on the _____ scale. 5._____

    A. absolute   B. A.P.I.   C. centigrade   D. Fahrenheit

6. Bacteria are _____ chlorphyll. 6._____

    A. multicellular organisms containing
    B. multicellular organisms that do not contain
    C. unicellular organisms containing
    D. unicellular organisms that do not contain

7. The immunity acquired as a result of an injection of tetanus antitoxin is termed _____ immunity. 7._____

    A. artificially acquired active
    B. artificially acquired passive
    C. naturally acquired active
    D. naturally acquired passive

8. A virus is the causative agent of 8._____

    A. diphtheria   B. smallpox   C. syphilis   D. tuberculosis

9. Typhus fever epidemics are caused by

   A. bacteria   B. rickettsiae   C. viruses   D. yeasts

10. The one of the following tests used to determine susceptibility to scarlet fever is the _____ test.

    A. Dick   B. Schick   C. Wasserman   D. Widal

11. Generally, the type of individual immunity to disease which is of the LONGEST duration is brought about by

    A. antibody production stimulated by killed microorganisms
    B. antibody production stimulated by live microorganisms
    C. transfer of antibodies during pregnancy from an immune mother to her unborn child by placental transfer
    D. transfer of antibodies from one adult to another

12. Diabetes is considered to be a(n) _____ disease.

    A. communicable   B. contagious
    C. noninfectious   D. infectious

13. The genus *Mycobacterium* contains a species responsible for

    A. diphtheria   B. gonorrhea
    C. tuberculosis   D. whooping cough

14. The pH of a neutral solution is

    A. 3   B. 5   C. 7   D. 9

15. Of the following, the pair that is NOT a set of equivalents is

    A. .014% .00014   B. 1/5% .002
    C. 1.5% 3/200   D. 115% .115

16. 10^{-2} is equal to

    A. 0.001   B. 0.01   C. 0.1   D. 100.0

17. $10^2 \times 10^3$ is equal to

    A. 10^5 B. 10^6 C. 100^5 D. 100^6

18. The length of two objects are in the ratio of 2:1. If each were 3 inches shorter, the ratio would be 3:1. The longer object is _____ inches.

    A. 8   B. 10   C. 12   D. 14

19. If the weight of water is 62.4 pounds per cubic foot, the weight of the water that fills a rectangular container 6 inches by 6 inches by 1 foot is _____ pounds.

    A. 7.8   B. 15.6   C. 31.2   D. 46.8

20. *Dry-ice* is solid

    A. ammonia   B. carbon dioxide
    C. freon   D. sulfur dioxide

21. The fat content of normal milk is *approximately* 21.____

    A. 1% B. 4% C. 10% D. 16%

22. The one of the following acids GENERALLY responsible for the natural souring of milk is 22.____
    _____ acid.

    A. acetic B. amino C. citric D. lactic

23. From a nutritional standpoint, milk is *deficient* in 23.____

    A. iron
    C. mineral salts
    B. lactose
    D. protein

24. The man who is USUALLY known as the father of chemotherapy is 24.____

    A. Paul Ehrlich
    C. Louis Pasteur
    B. Elie Metchnikoff
    D. John Tyndall

25. The success of this country in building the Panama Canal was due to the successful conquest of yellow fever. 25.____
    The man who directed the study which led to this conquest was

    A. Joseph Lister
    C. Theobold Smith
    B. Walter Reed
    D. William Welch

KEY (CORRECT ANSWERS)

1. A		11. B	
2. D		12. C	
3. B		13. C	
4. B		14. C	
5. C		15. D	
6. D		16. B	
7. B		17. A	
8. B		18. C	
9. B		19. B	
10. A		20. B	

21. B
22. D
23. A
24. A
25. B

TEST 3

DIRECTIONS: Each question or incomplete statement is followed by several suggested answers or completions. Select the one that BEST answers the question or completes the statement. *PRINT THE LETTER OF THE CORRECT ANSWER IN THE SPACE AT THE RIGHT.*

1. The *Babcock test* is used in milk analysis to determine _____ content.

   A. butterfat   B. mineral   C. protein   D. vitamin

2. The phosphatase test is used to determine whether milk

   A. has an objectionable odor
   B. has been adequately pasteurized
   C. has been adulterated
   D. is too alkaline

3. A lactometer is used in milk inspection work to determine the

   A. acidity of milk
   B. color of milk
   C. percentage of milk solids
   D. specific gravity of milk

4. Milk samples collected at milk plants should be taken from milk cans, the contents of which have

   A. not been stirred so that sediment does not appear in the sample
   B. not been stirred so that the growth of bacteria which thrive on oxygen is not encouraged
   C. been stirred in order to obtain a representative sample
   D. been stirred so that the percentage of dissolved oxygen meets required standards

5. In the holding process, milk should be pasteurized for at least 30 minutes at a temperature of about

   A. 115° F   B. 145° F   C. 180° F   D. 212° F

6. Undulant fever, which may be contracted from milk, is caused by an organism known as

   A. Bacillus subtilis
   B. Brucella abortus
   C. Staphylococcus aureus
   D. Streptococcus pyogenes

7. The presence of *milk stone* or *water stone* in dairy equipment is

   A. *desirable;* it indicates that dairy equipment is modern
   B. *desirable;* it indicates that milking machines have been sterilized
   C. *undesirable;* it will increase the bacterial count of milk that comes in contact with it
   D. *undesirable;* it will greatly increase the percentage of water in the final milk product

8. The type of dairy barn flooring which is LEAST desirable from a sanitarian's point of view is

   A. asphalt
   B. compressed cork and asphalt
   C. concrete
   D. wood

9. *Curds* and *whey* are substances encountered in the manufacture of cheese. Of the two substances, usually one

A. is made into cheese; the other is a by-product used to feed animals
B. is made into cheese; the other is made into butter
C. is made into hard cheese; the other is made into soft cheese
D. refers to bacteria-ripened cheese; the other refers to mold-ripened cheese

10. Botulism food poisoning in the United States is USUALLY caused by   10._____

   A. eating fish caught in polluted waters
   B. failure to wash raw fruit before eating
   C. improper home-canning of fruits and vegetables
   D. tapeworms found in beef or sheep

11. The growth of pathogenic bacteria in preserved dates and figs is *inhibited* because these   11._____
    foods have a high _____ content.

   A. acid   B. mineral   C. protein   D. sugar

12. In the heating of the following foods during canning, the one which generally requires the   12._____
    LOWEST temperature to prevent microbiological activity is

   A. fish   B. fruit   C. meat   D. milk

13. Food poisoning cases in the United States are USUALLY characterized by _____ fol-   13._____
    lowed by death.

   A. long periods of illness
   B. long periods of illness rarely
   C. short periods of illness
   D. short periods of illness rarely

14. In the United States, food poisoning due to eating mushrooms is LARGELY attributable   14._____
    to

   A. failure to cook mushrooms
   B. failure to wash mushrooms
   C. mushrooms which are blue in color
   D. mushrooms which have not been cultivated domestically

15. Of the following, the food whose flavor is NOT improved by the addition of monosodium   15._____
    glutamate is

   A. cooked vegetables   B. fruit juice
   C. meats   D. seafood and chowders

16. A NEW method of food preservation involves preservation by   16._____

   A. chemicals   B. drying   C. heat   D. radiation

17. In grading meat, the term *finish* refers to   17._____

   A. distribution of fat   B. muscle hardness
   C. presence of tapeworm   D. symmetry of the carcass

18. Of the following preservatives, the one which may NOT be legally used in the preservation of meat is

    A. benzoic acid
    B. salt
    C. sugar
    D. wood smoke

19. A vitamin known to be effective in the prevention of pellagra is

    A. ascorbic acid
    B. niacin
    C. riboflavin
    D. thiamin

20. Eggs are *candled* for the purpose of determining

    A. calcium content
    B. size of the egg
    C. the presence of blood spots
    D. weight of the egg

KEY (CORRECT ANSWERS)

1.	A	11.	D
2.	B	12.	B
3.	D	13.	D
4.	C	14.	D
5.	B	15.	B
6.	B	16.	D
7.	C	17.	A
8.	D	18.	A
9.	A	19.	B
10.	C	20.	C

TEST 4

DIRECTIONS: Each question or incomplete statement is followed by several suggested answers or completions. Select the one that BEST answers the question or completes the statement. *PRINT THE LETTER OF THE CORRECT ANSWER IN THE SPACE AT THE RIGHT.*

1. Foodstuffs such as cereal and flour do not readily spoil as a result of bacterial action because such foodstuffs usually have a low _____ content.   1._____

    A. acid   B. ash   C. sodium   D. water

2. The presence of bacteria responsible for typhoid fever in a public water supply is PROBABLY traceable to   2._____

    A. fecal contamination
    B. excessive water aeration
    C. pus from skin lesions
    D. rotting animal and fish remains

3. Objectionable tastes and odors in public water supplies are, in the great majority of cases, due to the presence of   3._____

    A. algae and protozoa   B. animal remains
    C. dissolved oxygen   D. yeasts and molds

4. Atmospheric pressure as indicated by the mercury barometer at sea level is GENERALLY about _____ inches.   4._____

    A. 10   B. 15   C. 30   D. 45

5. The CHIEF objective of a sewage treatment and disposal system is to   5._____

    A. alter sewage by chemical treatment so that it may be sold as commercial fertilizer
    B. convert liquid sludge so that it may be used as drinking water
    C. convert sewage into a form usable as land fill
    D. remove or decompose the organic matter

6. *Warfarin* is GENERALLY used in the control of   6._____

    A. ants   B. flies   C. lice   D. rats

7. The control of the common housefly has been regarded as important because houseflies   7._____

    A. are a great nuisance although they are not responsible for the transmission of diseases
    B. may transmit diseases by biting humans
    C. may transmit diseases by contaminating food with pathogenic organisms
    D. may transmit diseases by injecting pathogenic organisms into the bloodstream of animals which are later eaten by man

8. The term *Anopheles* refers to a type of   8._____

    A. ant   B. louse   C. mosquito   D. termite

9. Galvanized iron is made by coating iron with

   A. chromium   B. lead   C. tin   D. zinc

10. The amount of oxygen in the air of a properly ventilated room, expressed as a percentage of volume, is APPROXIMATELY

    A. 5%   B. 10%   C. 15%   D. 20%

11. Field control of hay fever generally depends upon the effective use of a(n)

    A. bacteriostatic agent
    B. fungicide
    C. insect spray
    D. weed killer

12. An orthotolidine testing set may be used to determine the presence of

    A. bacterial growth in milk cans and pails
    B. chlorine in wash and rinse waters
    C. DDT dust in foods such as flour and sugar
    D. organisms responsible for the spoilage of shucked oysters

13. The one of the following which is NOT a characteristic of carbon monoxide gas is that it

    A. causes nausea and vomiting
    B. has a strong irritating odor
    C. interferes with the oxygen-carrying power of the blood
    D. is a common constituent of manufactured gas

Question 14.

DIRECTIONS: Question 14 is based on the following statement.

The rise of science is the most important fact of modern life. No student should be permitted to complete his education without understanding it. From a scientific education, we may expect an understanding of science. From scientific investigation, we may expect scientific knowledge. We are confusing the issue and demanding what we have no right to ask if we seek to learn from science the goals of human life and of organized society.

14. The foregoing statement implies MOST NEARLY that

    A. in a democratic society, the student must determine whether to pursue a scientific education
    B. organized society must learn from science how to meet the needs of modern life
    C. science is of great value in molding the character and values of the student
    D. scientific education is likely to lead the student to acquire an understanding of scientific processes

Questions 15-16.

DIRECTIONS: Questions 15 and 16 are based on the following statement.

Since sewage is a variable mixture of substances from many sources, it is to be expected that its microbial flora will fluctuate both in types and numbers. Raw sewage may contain millions of bacteria per milliliter. Prominent among these are the coliforms. strepto-

cocci, anaerobic spore forming bacilli, the Proteus group, and other types which have their origin in the intestinal tract of man. Sewage is also a potential source of pathogenic intestinal organisms. The poliomyelitis virus has been demonstrated to occur in sewage; other viruses are readily isolated from the same source. Aside from the examination of sewage to demonstrate the presence of some specific microorganism for epidemiological purposes, bacteriological analysis provides little useful information because of the magnitude of variations known to occur with regard to both numbers and kinds.

15. According to the above passage,

    A. all sewage contains pathogenic organisms
    B. bacteriological analysis of sewage is routinely performed in order to determine the presence of coliform organisms
    C. microorganisms found in sewage vary from time to time
    D. poliomyelitis epidemics are due to viruses found in sewage

16. The title which would be MOST suitable for the above passage is:

    A. Disposal of Sewage by Bacteria
    B. Microbes and Sewage Treatment
    C. Microbiological Characteristics of Sewage
    D. Sewage Removal Processes

Questions 17-18.

DIRECTIONS: Questions 17 and 18 are based on the following statement.

Most cities carrying on public health work exercise varying degrees of inspection and control over their milk supplies. In some cases, it consists only of ordinances, with little or no attempt at enforcement. In other cases, good control is obtained through wise ordinances and an efficient inspecting force and laboratory. While inspection alone can do much toward controlling the quality and production of milk, there must also be frequent laboratory tests of the milk.

The bacterial count of the milk indicates the condition of the dairy and the methods of milk handling. The counts, therefore, are a check on the reports of the sanitarian. High bacterial counts of milk from a dairy reported by a sanitarian to be "good" may indicate difficulty not suspected by the sanitarian such as infected udders, inefficient sterilisation of utensils, or poor cooling.

17. According to the above passage, the MOST accurate of the following statements is:

    A. The bacterial count of milk will be low if milk-producing animals are free from disease.
    B. A high bacterial count of milk can be reduced by pasteurization.
    C. The bacterial count of milk can be controlled by the laboratory.
    D. The bacterial count of milk will be low if the conditions of milk production, processing and handling are good.

18. The following conclusion may be drawn from the above passage: 18.____
    A. Large centers of urban population usually exercise complete control over their milk supplies.
    B. Adequate legislation is an important adjunct of a milk supply control program.
    C. Most cities should request the assistance of other cities prior to instituting a milk supply control program.
    D. Wise laws establishing a milk supply control program obviate the need for the enforcement of such laws provided that good laboratory techniques are employed.

Question 19-20.

DIRECTIONS: Questions 19 and 20 are based upon the following excerpt from the health code.

Article 101 Shellfish and Fish
Section 101. 03 Shippers of shellfish; registration
   (a) No shellfish shall be shipped into the city unless the shipper of such shellfish is registered with the department.
   (b) Application for registration shall be made on a form furnished by the department.
   (c) The following shippers shall be eligible to apply for registration :
      1. A shipper of shellfish located in the state but outside the city who holds a shellfish shipper's permit issued by the state conservation department; or
      2. A shipper of shellfish located outside the state, or located in Canada, who holds a shellfish certificate of approval or a permit issued by the state or provincial agency having control of the shellfish industry of his state or province, which certificate of approval or permit appears on the current list of interstate shellfish shipper permits published by the United States Public Health Service.
   (d) The commissioner may refuse to accept the registration of any applicant whose past observance of the shellfish regulations is not satisfactory to the commissioner.
   (e) No applicant shall ship shellfish into the city unless he has been notified in writing by the department that his application for registration has been approved.
   (f) Every registration as a shipper of shellfish, unless sooner revoked, shall terminate on the expiration date of the registrant's state shellfish certificate or permit.

19. The above excerpt from the health code provides that 19.____
    A. permission to register may not be denied to a shellfish shipper meeting the standards of his own jurisdiction
    B. permission to register will not be denied unless the shipper's past observances of shellfish regulations has not been satisfactory to the U.S. Public Health Service
    C. the commissioner may suspend the regulations applicable to registration if requested to do so by the governmental agency having jurisdiction over the shellfish shipper
    D. an applicant for registration as a shellfish shipper may ship shellfish into the city when notified by the department in writing that his application has been approved

20. The above excerpt from the health code provides that 20.____
    A. applications for registration will not be granted to out-of-state shippers of shellfish who have already received permission to sell shellfish from another jurisdiction
    B. shippers of shellfish located outside of the city may not ship shellfish into the city unless the shellfish have passed inspection by the jurisdiction in which the shellfish shipper is located
    C. a shipper of shellfish located in Canada is eligible for registration provided that he holds a shellfish permit issued by the appropriate provincial agency and that such permit appears on the current list of shellfish shipper permits published by the U.S. Public Health Service
    D. a shipper of shellfish located in Canada whose shellfish permit has been revoked by the provincial agency may ship shellfish into the city until such time as he is notified in writing by the department that his shellfish registration has been revoked

KEY (CORRECT ANSWERS)

1.	D	11.	D
2.	A	12.	B
3.	A	13.	B
4.	C	14.	D
5.	D	15.	C
6.	D	16.	C
7.	C	17.	D
8.	C	18.	B
9.	D	19.	D
10.	D	20.	C

EXAMINATION SECTION
TEST 1

DIRECTIONS: Each question or incomplete statement is followed by several suggested answers or completions. Select the one that BEST answers the question or completes the statement. *PRINT THE LETTER OF THE CORRECT ANSWER IN THE SPACE AT THE RIGHT.*

1. In the course of his inspection of a plant, a sanitarian obtains information about a process which he thinks would be useful to a friend engaged in a similar business.
   Of the following, the MOST advisable course of action for him to take is to

   A. consider such information confidential and not disclose it
   B. consider such information not confidential and, therefore, disclose it to his friend
   C. give his friend the information, but not disclose its source
   D. give his friend the information, pretending that it is his own idea

   1._____

2. Assume that, as a sanitarian, you have received an order from a person of high authority in the Department of Health. This order conflicts with instructions which you have received from your immediate supervisor.
   Of the following, the MOST advisable action for you to take FIRST is to

   A. carry out the order given you by higher authority
   B. inform your supervisor of the situation
   C. proceed according to your supervisor's instructions
   D. send a written memorandum to the person who gave you the order, indicating the conflict with your immediate supervisor's instructions

   2._____

3. Of the following statements concerning reports prepared by a sanitarian, the one which is LEAST valid is:

   A. A case report submitted by a sanitarian should contain factual material to support conclusions made
   B. An extremely detailed report may be of less value than a brief report giving the essential facts
   C. Highly technical language should be avoided as far as possible in preparing a report to be used at a court trial
   D. The position of the important facts in a report does not influence the emphasis placed on them by the reader

   3._____

4. Assume that, as a sanitarian, you are to leave the restaurant after having concluded an inspection of the premises. However, the operator begins a detailed story concerning his business experiences.
   Of the following, the MOST advisable course of action for you to take is to

   A. leave immediately to avoid being delayed by listening to the story
   B. listen for a few minutes and then excuse yourself on the ground that you have other duties
   C. listen quietly to what he has to say, but be noncommittal in making replies
   D. tell the operator that the job of sanitarian does not permit indulgence in personal relationships with operators

   4._____

5. Suppose that a story concerning an investigation conducted by the Department of Health has appeared in the newspapers. A reporter approaches a sanitarian and asks for details concerning this investigation.
Of the following, the MOST advisable way for the sanitarian to handle the situation is to

   A. give the reporter complete information regarding the investigation
   B. refer the reporter to the official of the department responsible for public relations
   C. refuse to speak to the reporter
   D. tell the reporter to make his own investigation of the matter

6. The operator of an establishment tells you that he intends to register a complaint against you, the sanitarian, with the Department of Health. He claims that you are impeding his operations because you insist upon a minute inspection of every piece of equipment. You feel that your methods are justified.
Of the following, the MOST advisable course of action for you to take is to

   A. continue the inspection, and ignore the complaint because you feel that your methods are correct
   B. continue the inspection, but tell the operator that owners of similar establishments do not complain concerning the same type of inspection
   C. explain the reasons for your actions to the operator and inform him that he has the right to complain if he wishes
   D. try to cut down on some of the details of the inspection in order to maintain a good relationship with the operator

7. Assume that, as a sanitarian, you are inspecting the premises of a certain establishment. The owner tells you of his disagreement with certain provisions of the new Health Code which affect his business.
Of the following, the MOST advisable course of action for you to take is to

   A. tell him that most such complaints are groundless
   B. tell him that your workload does not permit you to spend time discussing the new Health Code
   C. tell him to make his complaint in person to the Department of Health
   D. try to explain the reasons for the inclusion of these provisions

8. Suppose that, as a sanitarian, you realize that you have made an error in a report that has been forwarded to another unit. You know that this error is not likely to be discovered for some time.
Of the following, the MOST advisable course of action for you to take is to

   A. approach the supervisor of the other unit on an informal basis and ask him to correct the error
   B. say nothing about it since most likely one error will not invalidate the entire report
   C. tell your supervisor immediately that you have made an error so that it may be corrected, if necessary
   D. wait until the error is discovered and then admit that you have made it

9. Suppose that you have become friendly with one of the other sanitarians in your unit. You notice that recently he has been doing very poor work and you know that the rest of the staff is aware of the situation.
Of the following, the MOST advisable course of action for you to take is to

A. seek an opportunity to speak privately to your friend and ask if you can help in any way
B. speak to the other members of the staff when you have an opportunity, and try to minimize the situation
C. speak to your supervisor and tell him that he ought to transfer this man to another unit
D. tell your friend that you are willing to share some of his workload for a while

10. Assume that, as a sanitarian, you realize that you have unjustly reprimanded the owner of an establishment while making an inspection.
Of the following, the MOST advisable course of action for you to take is to

    A. admit your mistake and apologize to the owner
    B. attempt to justify the reprimand on some other basis
    C. ignore the matter in order to maintain your authority
    D. overlook some other offense you may notice

10.____

Question 11.

DIRECTIONS: Question 11 is to be answered SOLELY on the basis of the following passage from the Health Code.

A drug or device shall be deemed to be misbranded:

1. If any word, statement, or other information required by this article to appear on the label or labeling is not prominently placed thereon with such conspicuousness, as compared with other words, statements, designs or emblems in the labeling, and in such terms as to render it likely to be read and understood by the ordinary individual under customary conditions of purchase and use; or,

2. If it is a drug and is not designated solely by a name recognized in an official compendium unless its label bears the common or usual name of the drug, if it has one, and, if it is fabricated from two or more ingredients, the common or usual name of each active ingredient, including the kind and quantity by percentage or amount of any alcohol; or,

3. Unless its labeling bears adequate directions for use, except that a drug or device may be exempted from this requirement by the Commissioner when he finds that it is not necessary for the protection of the public health, and such adequate warnings against use in those pathological conditions or by children where its use may be dangerous to health, or against unsafe dosage or methods or duration of administration or application, in such manner and form, as are necessary for the protection of users.

11. According to the above passage, the LEAST accurate of the following statements is:

    A. Certain drugs must have labels which give their names as found in an official compendium
    B. Drugs or devices are not necessarily misbranded if their labels carry warnings against use in certain pathological conditions
    C. Labels on drugs liable to deterioration must state the precautions necessary to prevent deterioration
    D. Required information on a drug label should be at least as conspicuous as other statements on the label

11.____

Questions 12-13.

DIRECTIONS: Questions 12 and 13 are to be answered SOLELY on the basis of the following passage from the Health Code.

(a) The Commissioner shall not consent to the use or proposed use of a food additive if the data before him:
 (1) fail to establish that the proposed use of the additive under the conditions of use specified will be safe; or,
 (2) show that the proposed use of the additive would otherwise result in adulteration or in misbranding of food within the meaning of this Code.

(b) If, in the opinion of the Commissioner, based on the data before him, a tolerance limitation is required in order to assure that the proposed use of an additive will be safe, the Commissioner:
 (1) shall not fix such tolerance limitation at a level higher than he finds to be reasonably required to accomplish the physical or other technical effect for which such additive is intended; and,
 (2) shall not consent to the proposed use of the additive if he finds that the data do not establish that such use would accomplish the intended physical or other technical effect.

(c) In determining whether a proposed use of a food additive is safe, the Commissioner shall consider among other relevant factors:
 (1) the probable consumption of the additive and of any substance formed in the food because of the use of the additive; and,
 (2) the cumulative effect of such additive in the diet of man or animals.

12. If the data indicate that the proposed use of a food additive will be safe if the amount added is limited to 5 milligrams per gram of the food, the Commissioner shall fix the tolerance limitation at

 A. 5 milligrams per gram of the food
 B. 4 milligrams per gram of the food if this is the amount that can be expected to produce the desired effect
 C. less than 5 but more than 4 milligrams per gram of the food if 4 milligrams is the amount that can be expected to produce the desired effect
 D. less than 5 milligrams per gram of the food

13. According to the above passage, the LEAST accurate of the following statements is:

 A. Some food additives may, in some cases, be considered as adulterants
 B. The Commissioner should consider all relevant factors in determining whether the proposed use of a food additive is safe
 C. The Commissioner may not prohibit the use of an additive if the data show that its use is safe within certain tolerance limitations
 D. The Commissioner may prohibit the use of an additive even if the data indicate that its use would be safe within certain tolerance limitations

14. Of the following, a LIKELY reason for the inclusion of section (b)(2) given above is that   14.____

    A. food additives used within their tolerance limitations are likely to be unsafe
    B. producers may tend to add more than the safe amount if the tolerance limitation does not permit the accomplishment of the intended physical or other technical effect
    C. the probable consumption of the additive cannot be determined if it does not accomplish the intended physical or other technical effect
    D. use of a food additive that does not accomplish the intended physical or other technical effect is uneconomical

Questions 15-16.

DIRECTIONS: Questions 15 and 16 are to be answered SOLELY on the basis of the following passage from the Health Code.

The new Health Code governs such aspects of the food industry as pertain to cleanliness of apparatus, equipment, and utensils used in the preparation and service of food and sanitation of food establishment premises.

This revision marks a considerable shift in emphasis from detailed specific standards to broad performance standards and the imposition of greater obligation on industry to carry out well-formulated inspection procedures under its own direction and under continuing supervision of the Department. The emphasis is on clean and sanitary food products produced, sold or served in clean and sanitary food establishments.

The emphasis on generalized performance standards serves the important purpose of encouraging, through less restrictive regulations, the development of new processes in food sanitation and food manufacture. The advances in food technology practices, new chemical aids and new sanitary designs of machinery, have already pointed the way to getting the job done better and without the need for restrictive detailed regulations. This article is not only designed to permit progress of this kind to the fullest, but it also reflects the view that such industry growth should receive constant stimulation so that there is less need for official policing and more and more self-sanitation and self-supervision.

15. According to the above passage, the new Health Code   15.____

    A. requires detailed specific standards rather than broad performance standards
    B. is intended to provide for ultimate complete self-supervision by the food industry
    C. places less emphasis on self-inspection than on generalized performance standards
    D. is designed to take cognizance of the effects of new developments on food industry practices

16. According to the above passage, the new Health Code does NOT   16.____

    A. consider continued supervision of the food industry by the Department to be of great importance
    B. consider that advances in food technology indicate the need for less restrictive regulations

C. emphasize coercion but seeks voluntary compliance by the food industry
D. obligate the food industry to carry out well-formulated inspection procedures under its own direction

Questions 17-18.

DIRECTIONS: Questions 17 and 18 are to be answered SOLELY on the basis of the following passage.

The beginnings of hygiene can be traced back to antiquity in the sanitary laws of the Hebrews. Preventive medicine began with the first primitive idea of contagion. Even in the time when epidemics were explained as due to the wrath of the gods or visitations of evil spirits, it was observed that certain illnesses apparently spread from person to person. Gradually, the idea of contagiousness was associated with a number of diseases. Fracastorium, in his book, DE CONTAGIONE, published in 1554, proposed a classification of diseases into those which were contagious and those which were not. For three centuries following this publication, the medical profession was divided into two camps: the non-contagionists, who believed that the causative agents of epidemic disease were inanimate and gaseous in nature and associated with emanations from decomposing organic matter, effluvia, and miasma; and the much smaller group, the contagionists, who identified contagiousness with germs of some kind.

Looking backward, this confusion is understandable. That some diseases were contagious was fairly obvious, but some apparently arose spontaneously without a traceable source. The confusion was finally resolved in the latter part of the nineteenth century by the work of Pasteur, Koch, and their followers. The causative relationship of specific microorganisms for one after another of the infectious diseases was established and the part played by carriers, missed cases, common water and food supplies, arthropod vectors, and animal reservoirs in transmission was gradually elucidated.

17. The above passage IMPLIES that

    A. all infectious diseases were highly contagious
    B. the contagionists of the early 19th century had identified the specific microorganisms causing certain diseases
    C. the role of animal reservoirs contributed to the confusion which once existed concerning disease transmission
    D. the sanitary laws of the ancient Hebrews show that they had some scientific knowledge of the causes of disease

18. According to the above passage, the MOST accurate of the following statements is:

    A. Fracastorius believed that all diseases could be caused by miasma
    B. It is still believed by scientists that certain infectious diseases arise spontaneously
    C. Nothing was accomplished in disease prevention until the germ theory was established
    D. Preventive medicine was practiced to some extent in early times even though epidemics may have been attributed to evil spirits

Questions 19-20.

DIRECTIONS: Questions 19 and 20 are to be answered SOLELY on the basis of the following paragraph.

    Microorganisms are living things so small that they can be seen only with the aid of a microscope. They are widely distributed in nature and are responsible for many physical and chemical changes of importance to the life of plants, of animals, and of human beings. Altogether too many people believe that all *microbes* or *germs* are harmful, and that they are an entirely undesirable group of living things. While it is true that some microorganisms produce disease, the great majority of them do not. In fact, the activities of these hosts of non-disease-producing microorganisms make possible the continued existence of plants and animals on the earth. In addition, many kinds of microorganisms are used in industries to manufacture products of great value to man. But the activities of non-disease-producing microorganisms are not always desirable. Fabrics and fibers may be rotted, fermentation processes may be upset by undesirable organisms and other harmful effects may occur. From a practical point of view, we are interested in the microorganisms because of the things that they do and the physical and chemical changes which they produce. Also, we are interested in ways and means to control undesirable organisms and to put the useful ones to work; but a study of the activities and the means for control of microorganisms must be based upon knowledge of their nature and life processes.

19. The one of the following which is the MOST suitable title for the above paragraph is   19._____

    A. BACTERIA CAN BE USEFUL
    B. MICROORGANISMS AND THE PUBLIC HEALTH SANITARIAN
    C. THE CONTROL OF MICROBES
    D. THE RELATIONSHIP OF MICROORGANISMS TO MAN AND HIS ENVIRONMENT

20. According to the above paragraph, the MOST accurate of the following statements is: 20._____

    A. All non-disease-producing microorganisms are beneficial to mankind
    B. *Microbes* or *germs* are terms which are synonymous with *bacteria*
    C. The activities of useful bacteria need no controls
    D. Without microorganisms, life on earth would be virtually impossible

KEY (CORRECT ANSWERS)

1.	A	11.	C
2.	B	12.	B
3.	D	13.	C
4.	B	14.	B
5.	B	15.	D
6.	C	16.	C
7.	D	17.	C
8.	C	18.	D
9.	A	19.	D
10.	A	20.	D

TEST 2

DIRECTIONS: Each question or incomplete statement is followed by several suggested answers or completions. Select the one that BEST answers the question or completes the statement. *PRINT THE LETTER OF THE CORRECT ANSWER IN THE SPACE AT THE RIGHT.*

1. Solutions to which relatively large amounts of strong acid or base can be added with ONLY SLIGHT resulting change in pH are called _____ solutions.

    A. buffered   B. molar   C. normal   D. standard

2. Of the following statements concerning isotopes, the one which is INCORRECT is that isotopes of a given element have

    A. similar chemical properties
    B. the same atomic number
    C. the same atomic weight
    D. the same nuclear charge

3. Nuclei of atoms are considered to be composed of

    A. neutrons and protons   B. photons and electrons
    C. positrons and neutrons   D. protons and electrons

4. *Dry Ice* is solid

    A. ammonia   B. carbolic acid
    C. carbon dioxide   D. freon

5. The pH of a solution in which the apparent hydrogen ion concentration is equal to 1×10^{-8} moles per liter is

    A. 2   B. 4   C. 6   D. 8

6. Substances in solutions which change color at a particular pH are termed

    A. catalysts   B. desiccants
    C. indicators   D. mordants

7. The amount of 2.0 N KOH required to neutralize 40 ml. of 0.5 N HCl is _____ ml.

    A. 2   B. 4   C. 5   D. 10

8. The term *anion* refers to a

    A. *negatively* charged electrode
    B. *negatively* charged ion
    C. *positively* charged electrode
    D. *positively* charged ion

9. If the concentration of a salt solution is given as 0.7243 grams per liter, it may also be expressed as _____ grams per liter.

    A. 7.243×10^{-2} B. 72.43×10^{-1}
    C. 72.43×10^{-2} D. 724.3×10^{-2}

10. Invertase is a type of

    A. carbohydrate
    B. enzyme
    C. fat
    D. protein

11. An enzyme that acts upon starches is said to be

    A. aminolytic
    B. amylolytic
    C. lipolytic
    D. proteolytic

12. The structural formula $H_2N - \underset{\underset{H}{|}}{\overset{\overset{H}{|}}{C}} - C\overset{O}{\underset{OH}{\diagdown}}$ represents a(n)

    A. ketone
    B. alcohol
    C. amino acid
    D. ester

13. The one of the following which is a PRODUCT of the saponification of a fat is

    A. glycerol
    B. glycine
    C. lecithin
    D. sterol

14. Synthetic detergents can be used INSTEAD of natural soaps because both

    A. are organic compounds
    B. have the same chemical composition
    C. lower the surface tension of water
    D. raise the surface tension of water

15. A Bourdon gage is used to measure

    A. electrical resistance
    B. gas pressure
    C. internal diameters
    D. relative humidity

16. A specific gravity bottle weighs 150 g when empty, 250 g when filled with water, and 385 g when filled with another liquid.
    The specific gravity of the liquid is MOST NEARLY

    A. 1.67
    B. 2.35
    C. 2.57
    D. 3.85

17. At sea level, the number of degrees between the freezing point and the boiling point of water on the Centigrade temperature scale is

    A. 32
    B. 100
    C. 180
    D. 212

18. The general gas law for a given mass of gas, where P stands for pressure, V stands for volume, and T stands for absolute temperature may be stated as

    A. $P = KVT$
    B. $PK = VT$
    C. $PT = KV$
    D. $PV = KT$

19. If a mercury column barometer is constructed with a tube twice the diameter of a standard barometer, the reading will be _____ that of the standard barometer.

    A. one-fourth of
    B. one-half of
    C. twice
    D. the same as

20. The watt is a unit of electrical

    A. current
    B. inductance
    C. potential
    D. power

21. Bacteria are classified with the

    A. Bryophytes
    B. Protozoa
    C. Pteridophytes
    D. Thallophytes

22. The scientific name of a certain microorganism is Clostridium butyricum. The second word of this name indicates the

    A. class
    B. genus
    C. phylum
    D. species

23. Suppose that 100 ml of a water sample are added to 1900 ml of dilution water, and that 1 ml of this dilution is added to 49 ml of dilution water. The dilution of the original water sample in the second mixture is 1:

    A. 900
    B. 950
    C. 1000
    D. 1250

24. Spheroid shaped bacteria which look like chains of beads under the microscope are known as

    A. sarcinas
    B. spirilla
    C. staphylococci
    D. streptococci

25. In addition to alcohol, the fermentation of glucose by yeast yields

    A. carbon dioxide
    B. citric acid
    C. hydrogen
    D. oxygen

KEY (CORRECT ANSWERS)

1. A
2. C
3. A
4. C
5. D
6. C
7. D
8. B
9. C
10. B
11. B
12. C
13. A
14. C
15. B
16. B
17. B
18. D
19. D
20. D
21. D
22. D
23. C
24. D
25. A

TEST 3

DIRECTIONS: Each question or incomplete statement is followed by several suggested answers or completions. Select the one that BEST answers the question or completes the statement. *PRINT THE LETTER OF THE CORRECT ANSWER IN THE SPACE AT THE RIGHT.*

1. The one of the following which is NOT an antibiotic is 1.____

    A. actinomycin B. trypsin
    C. streptothricin D. tyrothricin

2. Vaccination confers _____ acquired immunity. 2.____

    A. *active* artificially B. *active* naturally
    C. *passive* artificially D. *passive* naturally

3. The one of the following which is NOT used as a disinfectant or antiseptic is 3.____

    A. ethyl acetate B. phenol
    C. potassium permanganate D. silver nitrate

4. The vector responsible for the transmission of yellow fever is the 4.____

    A. flea B. louse C. mosquito D. tick

5. Typhus fever is caused by microorganisms of the genus 5.____

    A. Escherichia B. Proteus
    C. Rickettsia D. Salmonella

6. The one of the following diseases which is caused by a virus is 6.____

    A. encephalitis B. malaria
    C. Q fever D. tetanus

7. The one of the following diseases which is considered to be infectious is 7.____

    A. angina pectoria B. diabetes
    C. glaucoma D. psittacosis

8. The one of the following diseases in which rats do NOT act as intermediate hosts is 8.____

    A. amoebic dysentery B. endemic typhus
    C. plague D. Weil's disease

9. The Kahn test is used to diagnose 9.____

    A. gonorrhea B. syphilis
    C. tuberculosis D. typhoid fever

10. The one of the following BEST known for his work in connection with antibiotics is 10.____

    A. Löffler B. Rivers C. Waksman D. Welch

11. Of the following constituents of milk, the one which is present in the LEAST proportion is 11.____

    A. fat B. mineral ash
    C. protein D. sugar

12. Casein occurs in fresh milk in the form of a(n)

    A. colloidal solution
    B. foam
    C. emulsion
    D. true solution

13. One type of lactometer used for determining the specific gravity of milk is graduated from 0 to 29 degrees to indicate a certain range of specific gravity. Another type is graduated from 0 to 100 degrees to indicate the same range.
    If the specific gravity is determined from the reading of the first type by the formula, $1+\frac{reading}{1000}$, then the formula to be used with the second type is

    A. $1+(\frac{reading}{1000} \times \frac{1}{.29})$
    B. $1+(\frac{reading}{1000} \times .29)$
    C. $(\frac{reading}{1000} \times .29) - 1$
    D. $(\frac{reading}{1000} \times \frac{1}{.29}) - 1$

14. If milk is adulterated by the addition of water, its

    A. specific gravity will be decreased
    B. specific gravity will be increased
    C. relative fat content will be increased
    D. relative mineral content will be increased

15. The *Holding* method and the *High Temperature Short Time* method of milk pasteurization require, respectively, _____ minutes and _____ seconds.

    A. 15; 15
    B. 15; 30
    C. 30; 30
    D. 30; 15

16. Of the following, the one which is NOT used for testing milk is the _____ test.

    A. methylene blue reduction
    B. phosphatase
    C. precipitin
    D. sediment

17. The one of the following which is ordinarily NOT considered to be a disease transmissible through milk is

    A. scarlet fever
    B. septic sore throat
    C. spotted fever
    D. brucellosis

18. The one of the following which would ordinarily NOT be used in sterilizing milk plant equipment is

    A. chlorine solution
    B. sodium fluoroacetate
    C. hot water
    D. live steam

19. The legal requirement for butter is that its butterfat content shall be NOT less than

    A. 95%
    B. 90%
    C. 85%
    D. 80%

20. Of the following, the one which is COMMONLY used as a stabilizer for ice cream is

    A. albumin
    B. benzoic acid
    C. gelatin
    D. sucrose

21. Of the following, the one which is NOT a factor used in grading butter is   21._____

   A. body B. butterfat content
   C. color D. salt

22. When fortifying milk with vitamin D, the minimum number of vitamin D units required per quart is USUALLY   22._____

   A. 400   B. 600   C. 800   D. 1000

23. Milk is USUALLY tested for adequacy of homogenization by   23._____

   A. allowing it to stand for 48 hours and then observing the percentage of butterfat which rises to the upper portion
   B. employing a modified Babcock test
   C. noting the time required for coagulation of the milk
   D. using a centrifuge

24. Rennet, used in cheese manufacture, is obtained   24._____

   A. by chemical synthesis B. from bacterial cultures
   C. from calves' stomachs D. from goats' milk

25. A *starter* used in making cheese is a(n)   25._____

   A. bacterial culture B. mechanical agitator
   C. enzyme D. organic acid

26. The term *process cheese* refers to cheese   26._____

   A. made by old European methods not readily duplicated in the United States
   B. made from one or more varieties of cheese which have been reworked into a mixture with a smooth texture
   C. which is manufactured by a patented method
   D. which is permitted to ripen for a considerable length of time

27. Curing preserves meat PRIMARILY because of the   27._____

   A. high temperatures at which the curing process is carried on
   B. low temperatures at which the curing process is carried on
   C. use of salt in fairly high concentration
   D. use of spices in low concentration

28. In commercial canning of low-acid food, appropriate *heat processing* is used in order to   28._____

   A. destroy spore-forming bacteria
   B. expel air and other gases from the product
   C. fix the natural color of the product
   D. remove raw flavors from the foods

29. Custard-filled baked goods are FREQUENTLY involved in cases of food poisoning primarily because   29._____

   A. harmful preservatives are sometimes used in custards
   B. many people are allergic to some of the ingredients used in custard
   C. the custard forms a good medium for growth of certain harmful bacteria
   D. the ingredients may be stale

30. An unsexed male chicken (usually under 10 months of age) is called a   30._____
    A. broiler   B. capon   C. fryer   D. stag

KEY (CORRECT ANSWERS)

1. B
2. A
3. A
4. C
5. C

6. A
7. D
8. A
9. B
10. C

11. B
12. A
13. B
14. A
15. D

16. C
17. C
18. B
19. D
20. C

21. B
22. A
23. A
24. C
25. A

26. B
27. C
28. A
29. C
30. B

TEST 4

DIRECTIONS: Each question or incomplete statement is followed by several suggested answers or completions. Select the one that BEST answers the question or completes the statement. *PRINT THE LETTER OF THE CORRECT ANSWER IN THE SPACE AT THE RIGHT.*

1. An unopened can containing spoiled food which CANNOT be detected by its external appearance is called a 1.____

    A. flat sour
    B. flipper
    C. springer
    D. swell

2. The one of the following which is usually NOT a factor considered in determining the grade of canned fruit is the 2.____

    A. color of the fruit
    B. density of the syrup
    C. texture of the fruit
    D. uniformity of size

3. The term *marbling,* as used in connection with the grading of beef, refers to 3.____

    A. a hardened condition of the bones
    B. coarseness in the texture of the meat
    C. the external fat covering the meat
    D. the network of intramuscular fat visible in the cut surface of the meat

4. Food poisoning is MOST likely to be caused by bacteria of the genus 4.____

    A. Neisseria
    B. Pasteurella
    C. Salmonella
    D. Treponema

5. When candling eggs, the characteristic which indicates eggs of SUPERIOR quality is 5.____

    A. germ development
    B. large air cell
    C. slightly defined yolk outline
    D. weak white

6. *Enriched bread* is thus designated because it contains added 6.____

    A. eggs
    B. minerals and vitamins
    C. shortening
    D. sugar

7. Oysters may be involved in outbreaks of disease PRIMARILY because they may 7.____

    A. contain parasitic worms
    B. have been eaten while still immature
    C. have been taken from polluted waters
    D. have been transplanted to water containing less salt than the original bed

8. The one of the following which is NOT a vitamin of the B complex is 8.____

    A. carotene
    B. pantothenic acid
    C. riboflavin
    D. thiamine

9. The department that enforces the Federal Food, Drug, and Cosmetic Act is the Department of

   A. Agriculture
   B. Commerce
   C. Health, Education and Welfare
   D. the Interior

10. The CHIEF purpose for regulating the sale of barbiturates is to

    A. be able to check the amount of stock of barbiturates a dispenser has on hand
    B. be able to identify purchasers
    C. discourage their use and sale
    D. prevent their use by irresponsible persons

11. The one of the following diseases which is NOT considered to be transmissible through water is

    A. anthrax   B. bacillary dysentery
    C. cholera   D. typhoid fever

12. The one of the following which is NOT used as a coagulant in water purification is

    A. aluminum sulfate   B. ferric chloride
    C. ferric sulfate   D. sodium phosphate

13. Routine bacteriological examination of water tests for the presence of coliform organisms.
    This is done because

    A. absence of coliforms warrants the assumption that water-borne pathogens are absent
    B. the coliforms are the easiest to collect in a water sample
    C. the coliforms are the most highly pathogenic water-borne organisms
    D. there are no other tests available for isolating other pathogens from water

14. Sodium thiosulfate is added to bottles used for collecting water samples from swimming pools for bacteriological counts in order to

    A. facilitate subsequent plate counts
    B. neutralize residual chlorine
    C. reduce the turbidity of the water
    D. sterilize the bottles

15. The orthotolidine test used for determining residual chlorine in swimming pool water is a _____ test.

    A. bacteriological   B. colorimetric
    C. microscopic   D. precipitation

16. An operator of a swimming pool is ordinarily NOT required to test for

    A. bacterial count per ml of the water
    B. clearness of the water
    C. pH of the water
    D. residual chlorine

17. Imhoff tanks used for sewage disposal are PRIMARILY dependent upon the action of

    A. bacterial decomposition
    B. chemical disinfectants
    C. high temperatures
    D. water dilution

18. One of the purposes of a vent pipe used in connection with a plumbing system is to

    A. carry off discharge from wash basins
    B. carry off discharge from water closets
    C. protect trap seals
    D. provide a means of cleaning house drains

19. The term *cross connection,* as used in reference to plumbing systems, is to

    A. a connecting pipe which joins two other pipes of the same line
    B. a connection between a potable water line and a waste or sewer line
    C. the connection between a house drain and a house sewer
    D. the joining of waste pipes from several fixtures

20. Of the following, the one which is NOT used as a rodenticide is

    A. Antu
    B. methoxychlor
    C. sodium fluoroacetate
    D. Warfarin

21. In rodent control, the PRIMARY method of producing permanent results is

    A. fumigating
    B. poisoning
    C. proofing
    D. trapping

22. The use of DDT insecticide as a residual spray is EFFECTIVE because it is a

    A. contact poison
    B. fumigant
    C. respiratory poison
    D. stomach poison

23. The one of the following which is NOT used as an insect repellent is

    A. dimethyl phthalate
    B. Indalone
    C. Rutgers 6-12
    D. 1080

24. The one of the following which is ordinarily NOT used as a fumigant is

    A. ethylene oxide
    B. hydrogen cyanide
    C. methyl bromide
    D. phosphorus pentoxide

25. Certification of coal-tar hair dyes to be used in beauty parlors is made in accordance with the provisions of the

    A. Federal Food, Drug and Cosmetic Act
    B. Federal Labeling Act
    C. State Agriculture and Markets Law
    D. State Education Law

26. The unit used to express the MAXIMUM permissible weekly dose of ionizing radiation for human beings is the

    A. eV   B. MKS   C. MPN   D. REM

27. The half-life of a radioactive element is a measure of its

  A. atomic weight
  B. biological effect
  C. penetrating ability
  D. rate of decay

28. Alpha particles are considered to be the SAME as

  A. cathode rays
  B. heavy hydrogen nuclei
  C. helium nuclei
  D. x-rays

29. The formula, $E = mc^2$, is known as

  A. Einstein's Equation
  B. Newton's second law of motion
  C. Planck's Equation
  D. Raoult's Law

30. Of the following, the one generally NOT used for the detection of radioactivity is the

  A. geiger counter
  B. ionization chamber
  C. photographic film
  D. polarimeter

KEY (CORRECT ANSWERS)

1.	A	16.	A
2.	B	17.	A
3.	D	18.	C
4.	C	19.	B
5.	C	20.	B
6.	B	21.	C
7.	C	22.	A
8.	A	23.	D
9.	C	24.	D
10.	D	25.	A
11.	A	26.	D
12.	D	27.	D
13.	A	28.	C
14.	B	29.	A
15.	B	30.	D

EXAMINATION SECTION
TEST 1

DIRECTIONS: Each question or incomplete statement is followed by several suggested answers or completions. Select the one that BEST answers the question or completes the statement. *PRINT THE LETTER OF THE CORRECT ANSWER IN THE SPACE AT THE RIGHT.*

1. The difference between the boiling point and the freezing point of water on the Fahrenheit scale is 1.____

    A. 0° B. 100° C. 112° D. 180°

2. All amino acids contain 2.____

    A. calcium and carbon
    B. hydrogen and nitrogen
    C. iron and oxygen
    D. manganese and phosphorus

3. Acids and bases combine to form compounds known as 3.____

    A. colloids B. salts C. solids D. solutions

4. $C_6H_{12}O_6$ represents the formula for a(n) 4.____

    A. protein B. salt C. sugar D. oil

5. The soil pH which is suitable for MOST garden crops varies between 5.____

    A. 2 and 5 B. 5 and 8 C. 8 and 11 D. 11 and 14

6. The farmer who plants peas, clover or alfalfa improves the soil PRIMARILY by increasing the available amount of 6.____

    A. carbon B. hydrogen C. nitrogen D. oxygen

7. Phenolphthalein is *generally* used as a(n) 7.____

    A. buffer
    B. drying agent
    C. emulsifying agent
    D. indicator

8. Of the following, the one classified as a compound is 8.____

    A. aluminum B. ammonia C. nitrogen D. sulfur

9. The process in which a liquid is vaporized and then condensed is called 9.____

    A. crystallization
    B. decantation
    C. distillation
    D. filtration

10. The formula *4-8-4* used in fertilizers refers to 10.____

    A. calcium, magnesium, and sulfur
    B. calcium, nitrogen, and phosphorus
    C. nitrogen, phosphorus, and potassium
    D. nitrogen, potassium, and sodium

11. The CHIEF source of fuel energy for the living cell are

    A. carbohydrates and fats
    B. carbohydrates and proteins
    C. fats and proteins
    D. water and carbohydrates

12. The structures of the human alimentary canal, in the order in which food passes through them, are as follows: first the mouth and throat, and then, IN ORDER, the

    A. esophagus, the small intestine, the large intestine, and the stomach
    B. esophagus, the stomach, the large intestine, and the small intestine
    C. esophagus, the stomach, the small intestine, and the large intestine
    D. stomach, the large intestine, the small intestine, and the esophagus

13. Pepsin is a stomach enzyme which

    A. changes fats to fatty acids
    B. converts starches to sugars
    C. curdles milk
    D. reduces proteins to peptides

14. The substance responsible for the clotting of human blood is known as

    A. fibrinogen   B. hemoglobin
    C. plasma   D. serum

15. Of the following statements regarding endocrine glands, the one which is NOT true is that

    A. endocrine glands have tubes or ducts to discharge their products to areas of use
    B. hormones are produced in endocrine glands
    C. the adrenal gland is an example of an endocrine gland
    D. the secretions of endocrine glands may be found in the bloodstream

16. The enzyme responsible for breaking fat and fat-like substances into glycerol and fatty acids is

    A. amylase   B. coagulase   C. lipase   D. oxidase

17. An acute x-ray dose of 600 roentgens applied to the entire body is

    A. insignificant except in the case of persons with an abnormally low level of tolerance to x-rays
    B. nearly always fatal
    C. severe in the view of some radiologists and should be avoided as a regular matter unless a person is employed as an x-ray technician
    D. tolerable in the average person, but such doses should not be applied more than once monthly

18. Radiations may cause cancer, yet radiations are used to treat cancer. This statement is

    A. *false;* radiations cannot cause cancer
    B. *false;* radiations cannot injure cancerous cells

C. *true;* radiations injure malignant cells but not healthy cells
D. *true;* radiations injure malignant cells without doing proportionate harm to non-malignant cells

19. The uranium-238 atom contains 92 protons and 146 neutrons. The number of electrons in the U-238 atom is

    A. 54   B. 92   C. 146   D. 238

20. The nucleus of the uranium-238 atom contains

    A. electrons and neutrons
    B. electrons and protons
    C. neutrons and protons
    D. neutrons only

21. Assume that a sample of radium with an atomic weight of 226 contains 250,000 atoms. Assume further that the half-life ($T_{1/2}$) of the radium is 1,600 years.
    This means MOST NEARLY that in

    A. 1,600 years 125,000 atoms of the radium sample will have decayed
    B. 1,600 years the portion of the sample which will have decayed can be expressed by the formula $T_{1/2} = 250,000/226$
    C. 3,200 years the portion of the sample which will have decayed can be expressed by the formula $T_{1/2} = 250,000/226$
    D. 3,200 years the radium sample will have decayed completely

22. The scientist who demonstrated that smallpox could be prevented by inoculating the skin of humans with material from cowpox lesions was

    A. Edward Jenner
    B. Robert Koch
    C. Joseph Meister
    D. Theodor Schwann

23. Staphylococci appear under microscopic examinations as

    A. four cells arranged as a square
    B. irregular clusters resembling bunches of grapes
    C. pairs of cells
    D. rows of cells, beadlike or chainlike

24. *Phenol coefficient* refers to a measure of the

    A. amount of phenol which may be added to food for use as a preservative
    B. effectiveness of a disinfectant in relation to phenol
    C. percentage of carbolic acid found in solutions containing phenol
    D. rapidity with which phenol destroys capsulated bacterial cells

25. The Schick test is used to determine susceptibility to

    A. diphtheria
    B. smallpox
    C. tetanus
    D. typhoid fever

26. Infectious hepatitis is a disease caused by

    A. bacteria
    B. protozoa
    C. rickettsiae
    D. viruses

27. *Phagocytes* are

   A. antigens which are used in the production of antibodies
   B. bacteria which destroy red blood cells
   C. cells in the human body which protect it from infection
   D. pathogens which may be present during coughing and sneezing

28. The Breed method is generally used in the bacteriological examination of

   A. meat   B. milk   C. soil   D. water

29. The magnifying power of a microscope may be determined by

   A. adding the power of the objective to the power of the eyepiece
   B. dividing the power of the eyepiece into the power of the objective
   C. multiplying the power of the eyepiece by the power of the objective
   D. subtracting the power of the eyepiece from the power of the objective

30. The statement regarding viruses which is NOT true is that they

   A. are all parasites
   B. are responsible for poliomyelitis
   C. contain desoxyribonucleic acid
   D. grow in animals but not in plants

Questions 31-35.

DIRECTIONS: For each of Questions 31 through 35, select the letter preceding the word whose meaning is MOST NEARLY the same as that of the capitalized word.

31. NOXIOUS

   A. gaseous   B. harmful   C. soothing   D. repulsive

32. PYOGENIC

   A. disease producing   B. fever producing
   C. pus forming   D. water forming

33. RENAL

   A. brain   B. heart   C. kidney   D. stomach

34. ENDEMIC

   A. epidemic
   B. endermic
   C. endoblast
   D. peculiar to a particular people or locality, as a disease

35. MACULATION

   A. reticulation   B. inoculation
   C. maturation   D. defilement

KEY (CORRECT ANSWERS)

1.	D	16.	C
2.	B	17.	B
3.	B	18.	D
4.	C	19.	B
5.	B	20.	C
6.	C	21.	A
7.	D	22.	A
8.	B	23.	B
9.	C	24.	B
10.	C	25.	A
11.	A	26.	D
12.	C	27.	C
13.	D	28.	B
14.	A	29.	C
15.	A	30.	D

31. B
32. C
33. C
34. D
35. D

TEST 2

DIRECTIONS: Each question or incomplete statement is followed by several suggested answers or completions. Select the one that BEST answers the question or completes the statement. *PRINT THE LETTER OF THE CORRECT ANSWER IN THE SPACE AT THE RIGHT.*

1. The immunity found in individuals who have recovered from measles is termed _____ acquired _____ immunity.

    A. artificially; active
    B. artificially; passive
    C. naturally; active
    D. naturally; passive

2. Decomposition of fresh or cold storage meats can be detected BEST by

    A. noting absence of surface moisture
    B. noting presence of *off* odors
    C. noting warmth when touched
    D. observing discoloration

3. Bacterial control of shellfish and shellfish growing areas is being based increasingly in this country upon the density of the Escherichia coli organisms in the waters from which shellfish are collected.
The BEST reason for this is that

    A. E. coli are virulent pathogens which produce serious diseases in man
    B. the density of E. coli in water is relatively easy to determine by shellfish fishermen
    C. the presence of E. coli is an indicator of the presence of human wastes in the water
    D. shellfish which ingest E. coli have objectionable odors which canning cannot remove

4. Proper cleaning of dairy utensils entails rinsing with

    A. cold or lukewarm water followed by scrubbing with a detergent solution
    B. cold or lukewarm water followed by scrubbing with hot soapy water
    C. hot water followed by scrubbing with a detergent solution
    D. hot water followed by scrubbing with hot soapy water

5. Of the following, the MOST accurate statement regarding the use of chlorine in the purification of public water supplies is:

    A. A small amount of residual chlorine in the water is desirable
    B. Chlorine will destroy most bacteria in the water with the exception of the coliform organisms
    C. The amount of chlorine added to water should be less than the *chlorine demand* of the water
    D. The use of chlorine in public water supplies should be resorted to only in cases of emergency

6. Pasteurization entails the heating of milk to AT LEAST _____ for _____ minutes.

    A. 143° F; 15   B. 143° F; 30   C. 161° F; 15   D. 161° F; 30

7. The pH value of water is of considerable significance when chlorinating swimming pools. The reason for this is that chlorine functions BEST as a bactericide when the pH value of the water is

   A. *high;* also, a high pH water value reduces or prevents eye smarting
   B. *high;* however, a high pH water value increases the possibility of eye smarting
   C. *low;* also, a low pH water value reduces or prevents eye smarting
   D. *low;* however, a low pH water value increases the possibility of eye smarting

8. A test commonly used for determining the presence of chlorine in water is the _____ test.

   A. orthotolidine
   B. phosphatase
   C. TPI
   D. Weil-Felix

9. The chemical which is added to water samples from chlorinated swimming pools to neutralize residual chlorine is sodium

   A. bromide
   B. carbonate
   C. hydroxide
   D. thiosulfate

10. Some years ago, the city experienced an outbreak of food poisoning from potato salad which was kept in an enameled utensil. The vinegar present in the potato salad dissolved a sufficient quantity of a certain substance found in the enamelware to cause poisoning. The name of the offending substance was

    A. antimony
    B. arsenic
    C. cyanide
    D. zinc

11. The common housefly, Musca Domestica, is a(n)

    A. biting insect which does not transmit disease
    B. biting insect which may transmit disease
    C. insect which does not bite and does not transmit disease
    D. insect which does not bite but may transmit disease

12. The name of the substance which it has been suggested be added to *sleeping medicines* to induce vomiting in the event of an overdose is

    A. chlorpromazine
    B. ipecac
    C. reserpine
    D. seconal

13. The statement which BEST describes DDT is:
    DDT is

    A. a contact insect poison
    B. an instantaneous poison
    C. effective against all insects
    D. non-toxic to humans

14. The application of 10% DDT dust to rat runways and burrows is

    A. *advisable,* since it will serve as an effective rodenticide
    B. *advisable,* since it will serve to kill fleas which infest rats
    C. *inadvisable,* since DDT in such amounts stimulates rat growth
    D. *inadvisable,* since rats will be forced to use alternate runways and burrows making their elimination more difficult

15. Oligodynamic action refers to the

    A. ability of extremely small amounts of certain metals to exert a lethal effect upon bacteria
    B. change in levels of chlorine dilution brought about by evaporation
    C. discoloration of tiles in swimming pools due to the excessive mineral content of hard water
    D. removal of organic materials from water by means of sedimentation and filtration

16. The term *BOD*, as used in sewage disposal, refers MOST NEARLY to the

    A. consumption of oxygen by microorganisms engaged in the decomposition of organic material
    B. contamination of oysters and other shellfish by pathogenic bacteria making them unsafe for human consumption
    C. formation of finely suspended sewage material due to vigorous aeration by powerful pumps
    D. removal of suspended or floating objects from raw sewage by screening

Questions 17-22.

DIRECTIONS: Questions 17 through 22 are based on the Health Code.

17. Assume that the applicant for a Health Department permit is under 21 years of age. The statement which BEST applies to such applicant is:

    A. Age is not a factor in the issuance of permits
    B. The applicant may be issued a permit provided he is 18 years of age or over if the commissioner waives the age requirement
    C. The establishment of an age requirement for various permits is left solely to the discretion of the commissioner, who may fix any age requirement he deems appropriate
    D. Under no circumstances may a permit be issued to a person under 21 years of age

18. Assume that a person enters a neighborhood pharmacy and asks that a barbiturate be sold to him. He gives the attending pharmacist the name of his physician and states that he does not have the physician's written prescription for such barbiturate with him.
    In such a case, the pharmacist

    A. may dispense a small amount of the barbiturate without requiring a physician's prescription
    B. may dispense the barbiturate in any amount the pharmacist deems reasonable provided the person is either personally known to the pharmacist or presents proper identification
    C. may telephone the physician and accept the physician's oral prescription subject to the physician's later submission of a written prescription
    D. must insist that he be given the physician's written prescription before he dispenses a barbiturate in any quantity

19. A restaurant owner keeps and houses a cat in his restaurant in order to minimize the danger of rat infestation. He also permits patrons to bring their dogs into his restaurant. The CORRECT statement concerning these actions is that the Health Code _____ the owner to keep his cat on the premises _____ visiting the restaurant with their dogs.

   A. permits; and is silent with respect to patrons
   B. permits; but prohibits patrons from
   C. prohibits; and prohibits patrons from
   D. prohibits; but is silent with respect to patrons

19.____

20. The Health Code provides that utensils, such as knives, forks, spoons, cups, and saucers, used in the preparation and service of food are to be cleaned after each use. The Code provides that such cleaning shall consist of _____ cleaning(s) with a suitable detergent in clean hot water followed by _____ rinsing(s).

   A. *one; one*
   B. *one; two* successive
   C. *two* successive; *one*
   D. *two* successive; *two* successive

20.____

21. The owner of a meat market uses certain dyes which impart color to meat. The use of such coloring matter is

   A. absolutely prohibited
   B. permitted if the owner displays a sign which informs consumers that he uses coloring matter
   C. permitted only if the coloring matter is applied to ground beef and to no other meat
   D. prohibited unless such use complies with the provisions of the Federal Meat Inspection Act

21.____

22. Homogenized milk is milk which has been subjected to a treatment so that after 48 hours of quiescent storage the percent of butter fat in the upper one-tenth portion of a container will NOT exceed the percentage of butter fat in the remaining portion of the container by more than

   A. 5%   B. 10%   C. 15%   D. 20%

22.____

23. The Health Code names certain chemicals which, under stated circumstances, may be added to the drinking water supply within a building for anti-corrosion or anti-scaling purposes.
Of the following chemicals, the one which is NOT specifically authorized for this purpose is

   A. calcium bicarbonate   B. calcium hydroxide
   C. sodium carbonate   D. sodium hydroxide

23.____

24. The Code provides that water in swimming pools must meet a certain standard of clarity. This standard is based on the

   A. addition of a chemical to the water which causes a color change if the water does not meet the prescribed standard
   B. measurement by the laboratory of the turbidity of a sample of pool water

24.____

C. use of a black disc, six inches in diameter
D. visual inspection by a sanitarian without the use of any aids or devices

Questions 25-27.

DIRECTIONS: Questions 25 through 27 are to be answered SOLELY on the basis of the following passage.

The first laws prohibiting tampering with foods and selling unwholesome provisions were enacted in ancient times. Early Mosaic and Egyptian laws governed the handling of meat. Greek and Roman laws attempted to prevent the watering of wine. In 200 B.C., India provided for the punishment of adulterators of grains and oils. In the same era, China had agents to prohibit the making of spurious articles and the defrauding of purchasers. Most of our food laws, however, came to us as a heritage from our European forebears.

In early times, foods were few and very simple, and trade existed mostly through barter. Such cheating as did occur was crude and easily detected by the prospective buyer. In the Middle Ages, traders and merchants began to specialize and united themselves into guilds. One of the earliest was called the Pepperers – the spice traders of the day. The Pepperers soon absorbed the grocers and in England got a charter from the king as the Grocer's Company. They set up an ethical code designed to protect the integrity and quality of the spices and other foods sold. Later they appointed a corps of food inspectors to test and certify the merchandise sold to and by the grocers. These men were the first public food inspectors of England.

Pepper is a good example of trade practices that brought about the need for the food inspectors. The demand for pepper was widespread. Its price was high; it was handled by various people during its long journey from the Spice Islands to the grocer's shelf. Each handler had opportunity to debase it; the grinders had the best chance since adulterants could not be detected by methods then available. Worthless barks and seeds, iron ore, charcoal, nutshells, and olive pits were ground along with the berries.

Bread was another food that offered temptation to unscrupulous persons. The most common cheating practice was short weighing but at times the flour used contained ground dried peas or beans.

25. Of the following, the MOST suitable title for the foregoing passage would be: 25.____

    A. Consumer Pressure and Pure Food Laws
    B. Practices Which Brought About the Need for Food Inspectors
    C. Substances Commonly Used as Pepper Adulterants
    D. The Role Played By Pepper as a Spice and as a Preservative

26. The statement BEST supported by the above passage is: 26.____

    A. Food inspectors employed by the Pepperers were responsible for detecting the presence of ground peas in flour
    B. The first guild to be formed in the Middle Ages was known as the Pepperers
    C. The Pepperers were chartered by the king and in accordance with his instructions set up an ethical code
    D. There were persons other than those who handled spices exclusively who became members of the Pepperers

27. The statement BEST supported by the above passage is: 27.____

    A. Early laws of England forbade the addition of adulterants to flour
    B. Egyptian laws of ancient times concerned themselves with meat handling

C. India provided for the punishment of persons adding ground berries and olive pits to spices
D. The Greeks and Romans succeeded in preventing the watering of wine

Questions 28-30.

DIRECTIONS: Questions 28 through 30 are to be answered SOLELY on the basis of the following passage.

Water can purify itself up to a point, by natural processes, but there is a limit to the pollution load that a stream can handle. Self-purification, a complicated process, is brought about by a combination of physical, chemical, and biological factors. The process is the same in all bodies of water, but its intensity is governed by varying environment conditions.

The time required for self-purification is governed by the degree of pollution and the character of the stream. In a large stream, many days of flow may be required for a partial purification. In clean, flowing streams, the water is usually saturated with dissolved purification. In clean, flowing streams, the water is usually saturated with dissolved oxygen, absorbed from the atmosphere and given off by green water plants. The solids of sewage and other wastes are dispersed when they enter the stream and eventually settle. Bacteria in the water and in the wastes themselves begin the process of breaking down the unstable wastes. The process uses up the dissolved oxygen in the water, upon which fish and other aquatic life also depend.

Streams offset the reduction of dissolved oxygen by absorbing it from the air and from oxygen-producing aquatic plants. This replenishment permits the bacteria to continue working on the wastes and the purification process to advance. Replenishment takes place rapidly in a swiftly flowing, turbulent stream because waves provide greater surface areas through which oxygen can be absorbed. Relatively motionless ponds or deep, sluggish streams require more time to renew depleted oxygen.

When large volumes of wastes are discharged into a stream, the water becomes murky. Sunlight no longer penetrates to the water plants, which normally contribute to the oxygen supply through photosynthesis, and the plants die. If the volume of pollution, in relation to the amount of water in the stream and the speed of flow, is so great that the bacteria use the oxygen more rapidly than re-aeration occurs, only putrifying types of bacteria can survive, and the natural process of self-purification is slowed. So the stream becomes foul smelling and looks greasy. Fish and other aquatic life disappear.

28. According to the above passage, if the proportion of wastes to stream water is very high, then the 28.____

    A. amount of dissolved oxygen in the stream increases
    B. death of all bacteria in wastes becomes a certainty
    C. stream will probably look greasy
    D. turbulence of the stream is increased

29. The one of the following which is NOT mentioned in the above passage as a factor in water self-purification is the 29.____

    A. ability of sunlight to penetrate water
    B. percentage of oxygen found in the air
    C. presence of bacteria in waste materials
    D. speed and turbulence of the stream

30. Of the following, the MOST suitable title for the above passage would be: 30.____

    A. Oxygen Requirements of Fish and Other Aquatic Life
    B. Streams as Carriers of Waste Materials
    C. The Function of Bacteria in the Disintegration of Wastes
    D. The Self-purification of Water

Questions 31-32.

DIRECTIONS: Questions 31 and 32 are to be answered SOLELY on the basis of the following passage.

   Processing by quick freezing has expanded rapidly. The consumption of frozen fruits and vegetables (on a fresh-equivalent basis) was about 8 pounds per capita annually in the years immediately before the Second World War. It exceeded 200 pounds in 2008.
   One example of this growth is frozen concentrated orange juice. From the beginning of commercial production in Florida during the 2005-2006 season, the pack of frozen concentrated orange juice has grown until it amounted to more than 320 million gallons in the 2008-2009 season. That is enough juice, when reconstituted, to supply every person in this country with about 160 average-size servings.
   Another striking change in the pattern of food consumption is the sharp increase in consumption of broilers or fryers, young chickens of either sex, usually 8-10 weeks old, and weighing about three pounds.
   The commercial production of broilers has increased more than 500 percent since 2006. The number produced exceeded 1.6 billion birds in 2008. On a per capita basis, broiler consumption was about 20 pounds annually (ready-to-cook equivalent basis). This is roughly one-fourth as much as per capita consumption of beef and nearly one-third as large as per capita consumption of pork. Consumption of broilers in the years just after the Second World War was less than one-tenth as large as the consumption of either beef or pork.
   Among the factors responsible for this rapid growth are developments in breeding that led to faster gains in weight, lower prices in relation to other meat, and improvements in methods of preparing broilers for market. When broilers, like other poultry, were retailed in an uneviscerated form, dressed broilers could be held for only limited periods. Consequently, birds were shipped to market live, and dressing operations took place mostly in or near terminal markets - the centers of population.
   Thus, it is that consumers benefit both from the variety of products available at all seasons of the year and from the many forms in which these products are sold.

31. According to the foregoing passage, the number of broilers produced in 2006 was MOST NEARLY 31.____

    A. 320,000,000   B. 1,200,000,000
    C. 4,000,000,000   D. 5,200,000,000

32. According to the above passage, the per capita annual consumption of frozen fruits and vegetables immediately following the end of World War II 32.____

    A. cannot be determined from the above passage
    B. was 16 percent of the per capita consumption of 2008
    C. was most nearly in excess of 200 pounds
    D. was most nearly 8 pounds

Questions 33-35.

DIRECTIONS: For each of Questions 33 through 35, select the letter preceding the word whose meaning is MOST NEARLY the same as that of the capitalized word.

33. AEROSOL, a _____ dispersed in a _____ 33.____

    A. gas; liquid
    B. liquid; gas
    C. liquid; solid
    D. solid; liquid

34. ETIOLOGY 34.____

    A. cause of a disease
    B. method of cure
    C. method of diagnosis
    D. study of insects

35. IN VITRO, in 35.____

    A. alkali
    B. the body
    C. the test tube
    D. vacuum

KEY (CORRECT ANSWERS)

1.	C	16.	A
2.	B	17.	B
3.	C	18.	C
4.	A	19.	D
5.	A	20.	B
6.	B	21.	D
7.	D	22.	B
8.	A	23.	A
9.	D	24.	C
10.	A	25.	B
11.	D	26.	D
12.	B	27.	B
13.	A	28.	C
14.	B	29.	B
15.	A	30.	D

31. B
32. A
33. B
34. A
35. C

EXAMINATION SECTION
TEST 1

DIRECTIONS: Each question or incomplete statement is followed by several suggested answers or completions. Select the one that BEST answers the question or completes the statement. *PRINT THE LETTER OF THE CORRECT ANSWER IN THE SPACE AT THE RIGHT.*

1. Of the following, the one which is LEAST satisfactory as a differential coliform test is   1.____

   A. citrate utilization B. gelatin liquefaction
   C. methyl-red D. Voges-Proskauer

2. The cholera vibrio is   2.____

   A. atrichous B. amphitrichous
   C. monotrichous D. peritrichous

3. The tetanus bacilli are classified as   3.____

   A. aerobes B. facultative anaerobes
   C. micro-aerophiles D. obligate anaerobes

4. Milk is pasteurized in order to destroy all   4.____

   A. bacteria
   B. non-spore forming bacteria
   C. non-spore forming pathogens
   D. spore forming pathogens

5. The IMVIC for typical strains of E.coli is   5.____

   A. + + + +   B. + + − −   C. − − + +   D. − − − −

6. The term *peritrichous* means having   6.____

   A. a single flagellum at one pole
   B. a tuft of flagella at one pole
   C. flagella at both poles
   D. flagella completely surrounding the body

7. Bacteria belonging to the genus Thiothrix are GENERALLY called _____ bacteria.   7.____

   A. iron B. nitrifying
   C. sulfate-reducing D. sulfur

8. Bacteria belonging to the genus Crenothrix are GENERALLY termed _____ bacteria.   8.____

   A. iron B. nitrifying
   C. sulfate-reducing D. sulfur

9. The one of the following which is NOT characteristic of the coliform group is   9.____

   A. ferment lactose B. Gram-negative
   C. non-gas former D. non-spore former

10. The organism, Aerobacter aerogenes, is USUALLY considered to be a(n) _____ coliform organism.

    A. fecal
    B. intestinal
    C. non-fecal
    D. pathogenic

11. The term *plankton* includes all organisms that are microscopic or barely visible to the naked eye, with the exception of the

    A. bacteria   B. Crustacea   C. protozoa   D. rotifera

12. The one of the following methods GENERALLY associated with the concentration of water samples for water analysis is the _____ method.

    A. Kjeldahl
    B. Sedgwick-Rafter
    C. Winkler
    D. Zeolite

13. The ortho-tolidine method is GENERALLY used to measure

    A. copper
    B. nitrite nitrogen
    C. orthophosphate
    D. residual chlorine

14. A study of water-borne epidemics in the United States reveals that the disease responsible for the GREATEST number of cases is

    A. anthrax
    B. Asiatic cholera
    C. dysentery
    D. tuberculosis

15. The name of the organism causing non-bacillary dysentery is

    A. Endameba coli
    B. Endameba histolytica
    C. Escherichia coli
    D. Shigella sonnei

16. The immunity acquired against tuberculosis by prophylactic vaccination with BCG is _____ acquired _____ immunity.

    A. artificially; active
    B. artificially; passive
    C. naturally; active
    D. naturally; passive

17. The optimum temperature of growth for MOST pathogenic bacteria is APPROXIMATELY

    A. 20° C   B. 20° F   C. 37° C   D. 37° F

18. Of the following diseases, the one NOT caused by an acid-fast organism is

    A. Johne's disease
    B. leprosy
    C. pertussis
    D. tuberculosis

19. The presence of Vi antibodies in the human serum is indicative of an infection of

    A. cholera
    B. salmonellosis
    C. shigellosis
    D. typhoid fever

20. The causative agents of salmonellosis are gram-_____, lactose _____ rods.

    A. negative; negative
    B. negative; positive
    C. positive; negative
    D. positive; positive

21. Of the following, the organism MOST resistant to disinfecting agents is the one causing   21.____

    A. amebic dysentery   B. bacillary dysentery
    C. cholera   D. typhoid

22. The FIRST step in the recommended procedure for cleaning glassware containing infec-   22.____
    tious material is

    A. rinsing   B. scraping
    C. sterilizing   D. washing

23. The MOST heat-resistant of the pathogens *generally* found in milk is   23.____

    A. Salmonella typhosa   B. Mycobacterium tuberculosis
    C. Shigella sonnei   D. Streptococcus pyogenes

24. The hydrogen-ion concentration of culture media increases during sterilization.   24.____
    The USUAL decrease in the pH reading as a result of sterilization is *approximately*

    A. 0.3   B. 0.8   C. 1.4   D. 2.7

25. The PRINCIPAL ingredients of nutrient broth are   25.____

    A. beef extract and peptone
    B. beef extract and glucose
    C. ground beef and peptone
    D. ground beef and glucose

KEY (CORRECT ANSWERS)

1. B   11. A
2. C   12. B
3. D   13. D
4. C   14. C
5. B   15. B

6. D   16. A
7. D   17. C
8. A   18. C
9. C   19. D
10. C   20. A

21. A
22. C
23. B
24. A
25. A

TEST 2

DIRECTIONS: Each question or incomplete statement is followed by several suggested answers or completions. Select the one that BEST answers the question or completes the statement. *PRINT THE LETTER OF THE CORRECT ANSWER IN THE SPACE AT THE RIGHT.*

1. The solidifying point of agar is APPROXIMATELY   1.____
    A. 25° C   B. 40° C   C. 55° C   D. 70° C

2. The one of the following NOT contained in Krumwiede Triple Sugar Agar is   2.____
    A. dextrose   B. lactose   C. maltose   D. sucrose

3. The indicator GENERALLY used in Krumwiede Triple Sugar Agar is   3.____
    A. bromcresol purple   B. litmus
    C. methyl orange   D. phenol red

4. The one of the following which is NOT an ingredient of Endo medium is   4.____
    A. agar   B. basic fuchsin
    C. glucose   D. lactose

5. Endo medium when cooled is   5.____
    A. blue   B. colorless   C. green   D. yellow

6. The color of the colonies produced by Escherichia coli on Endo medium is   6.____
    A. blue   B. brown   C. green   D. red

7. The gas produced in the fermentation of lactose is ESSENTIALLY   7.____
    A. CO   B. CO_2 C. H_2 D. H_2O

8. The Barrett method is GENERALLY used to determine production of   8.____
    A. acetyl-methyl-carbinol   B. hydrogen sulfide
    C. indol   D. urea

9. The color of the test reagent in a positive indol test is   9.____
    A. dark blue   B. dark red
    C. light green   D. light yellow

10. Indol is a decomposition product of   10.____
    A. amyl alcohol
    B. lactose
    C. paradimethylaminobenzaldehyde
    D. tryptophane

11. A sodium citrate positive test is indicated if, after 96 hours of incubation, there is   11.____
    A. a red color   B. a yellow color
    C. no growth   D. visible growth

12. A positive Voges-Proskauer test is GENERALLY indicated by the appearance of a _____ color.

    A. blue B. green C. red D. yellow

13. Phosphate is added to the test medium used for the methyl red test to provide a(n)

    A. buffer B. food supply
    C. indicator D. inhibitor

14. The Kjeldahl method is used to analyze for

    A. chlorine B. copper C. iron D. nitrogen

15. Amino acids are formed in the hydrolysis of

    A. disaccharides B. fats
    C. monosaccharides D. proteins

16. The one of the following that is NOT classified as a disaccharide is

    A. glucose B. lactose C. maltose D. sucrose

17. The process of culturing bacteria by providing them with the necessary conditions for growth is known as

    A. incubation B. inoculation
    C. sterilization D. staining

18. Blood typing is necessary in the transfusion of

    A. amino acids B. dextrose
    C. plasma D. whole blood

19. The BEST method of preventing the spread of the common cold is to treat the patient by

    A. injecting antitoxin
    B. isolating him
    C. administering sulfa drugs
    D. vaccinating him

20. Requiring food handlers to undergo a periodic health examination might reduce the number of cases of

    A. scurvy B. tetanus
    C. typhoid fever D. yellow fever

21. Jumping at a sudden noise is an example of a

    A. habit B. simple reflex
    C. conditioned reflex D. voluntary act

22. Which vitamin is MOST easily destroyed by heat or air?

    A. A B. B C. C D. D

23. Which is a product of fermentation by yeasts?

    A. Alcohol B. Oxygen C. Nitrogen D. Starch

24. A drop of milk was placed on each of several culture medium preparations and then incubated for several days. No bacterial colonies developed.
    The milk MOST probably had been

    A. boiled
    B. pasteurized
    C. refrigerated
    D. skimmed

25. MOST antibodies have been isolated from organisms that live in

    A. water   B. air   C. soil   D. animals

KEY (CORRECT ANSWERS)

1. B
2. C
3. D
4. C
5. B

6. D
7. B
8. A
9. B
10. D

11. D
12. C
13. A
14. D
15. D

16. A
17. A
18. D
19. B
20. C

21. A
22. C
23. A
24. A
25. C

EXAMINATION SECTION
TEST 1

DIRECTIONS: Each question or incomplete statement is followed by several suggested answers or completions. Select the one that BEST answers the question or completes the statement. *PRINT THE LETTER OF THE CORRECT ANSWER IN THE SPACE AT THE RIGHT.*

1. The daily energy requirement in calories recommended by the National Academy of Sciences for the average high school girl is

    A. 1300 - 1500 B. 2400 - 2600
    C. 3000 - 3200 D. 4800 - 5000

2. The recommended dietary protein allowance for an individual is LEAST influenced by the factor of

    A. sex B. age
    C. type of activity D. weight

3. Of the following, the substance which does NOT act as an emetic is

    A. mustard B. ipecac
    C. sodium bicarbonate D. table salt

4. Of the following diseases, the one which is NOT food-borne is

    A. diphtheria B. pneumonia
    C. tuberculosis D. scarlet fever

5. Of the following, the disease which is caused by an agent in a different group from the agents causing the other three diseases is

    A. tobacco mosaic disease B. typhus
    C. measles D. polio

6. Of the following, the one which is a highly contagious skin condition is

    A. eczema B. hives
    C. impetigo D. miliaria rubra

7. Of the following, the antibiotic that has been found MOST effective in the treatment of tuberculosis is

    A. penicillin B. aureomycin
    C. streptomycin D. tetracycline

8. Of the following, the animal used in standard practice for demonstrating vitamin C deficiency is the

    A. mouse B. guinea pig
    C. rabbit D. rat

9. A drug that increases arterial pressure is known as a(n)

    A. vasoconstrictor B. hemostat
    C. vasodilator D. vesicant

10. Drugs that contract or shrink tissues are known as

   A. carminatives
   B. counterirritants
   C. astringents
   D. analgesics

11. Toxic effects in children have resulted from the ingestion of excessive amounts of which one of the following?

   A. Vitamin A
   B. Vitamin B_{12}
   C. Vitamin C
   D. Thiamine

12. The basal metabolism test is ordinarily used to indicate

   A. hypertension
   B. activity of the thymus gland
   C. activity of the thyroid gland
   D. rate of blood circulation

13. Of the following, the chemical MOST often chosen by dentists to produce general anesthesia is

   A. chloroform
   B. nitrous oxide and oxygen
   C. ether
   D. ethyl chloride

14. The branch of dentistry concerned with the treatment of gums and other tissues supporting teeth is

   A. peridontia
   B. orthodontia
   C. pedodontia
   D. prosthodontia

15. The material filling the root canal of a tooth is

   A. dental pulp
   B. dentine
   C. cementum
   D. enamel

16. When vitamin B_{12} is administered by mouth, it is of little or no value unless

   A. it is part of the vitamin B complex
   B. normal gastric juice is present
   C. it has been extracted from liver
   D. it is taken in capsule form

17. The *morale vitamin*, the lack of which may cause people to become depressed and irritable, is

   A. ascorbic acid
   B. thiamine
   C. riboflavin
   D. folic acid

18. The browning of cut fruits may BEST be slowed by

   A. keeping them in a refrigerator
   B. keeping them in water
   C. treating them with lemon juice
   D. sprinkling them with sugar

19. Eggs are sized according to which one of the following criteria?

    A. Average circumference of the eggs
    B. Average length of the eggs
    C. Weight of a dozen eggs
    D. Number of eggs to make one pound of dried egg powder

20. Another name for soft wheat flour is _____ flour.

    A. pastry   B. bread   C. enriched   D. gluten

21. The section of the hog in which trichinella worms MOST often encyst themselves is the

    A. liver   B. fat tissue
    C. brain   D. muscle tissue

22. A day or two after having been baked, some loaves of bread develop a ropy substance in the center.
    This rope is caused by

    A. excess of yeast in bread
    B. too rapid cooling of the bread
    C. mold
    D. bacteria

23. The *black and blue* area on the skin that results from a bruise is known medically as

    A. vitiligo   B. ecchymosis
    C. epithelioma   D. dystrophia

24. Of the following, the tissue that lines the hair follicle is called

    A. dermis   B. epidermis
    C. adipose   D. subcutaneous

25. Microscopic examination of the cross-section of hair shafts of people with straight hair shows the hair shafts to be

    A. square   B. flat   C. round   D. oval

26. The outer layer of the hair shaft is called the

    A. cortex   B. medulla   C. cuticle   D. papilla

27. All of the following textile fibers are of plant origin EXCEPT

    A. cotton   B. flax   C. mohair   D. sisal

28. High quality fabric is produced from all of the follow-ing varieties of cotton EXCEPT

    A. Asiatic   B. Egyptian
    C. pima   D. Sea Island

29. The cocoon from which commercial silk fiber is obtained is spun by the larva of the moth

    A. Tinea pellionella   B. Bombyx mori
    C. Ceratomia catalpae   D. Carpocapsa pomonella

30. The HIGHEST grade of felt used in the manufacture of men's hats is made of a mixture of

    A. fur fibers including beaver
    B. cotton kapok and wool
    C. rabbit's hair and wool
    D. cashmere alpaca and wool

31. The spices cinnamon and cassia are derived from

    A. inner bark   B. flower buds
    C. seeds   D. roots

32. Grain alcohol is converted into acetic acid by which one of the following processes?

    A. Oxidation   B. Reduction
    C. Methylation   D. Esterification

33. Calcium propionate (under various commercial names) is used in the baking industry to

    A. activate the yeast
    B. inhibit mold growth
    C. reduce the quantity of baking powder ordinarily required
    D. keep the bread soft

34. Invert sugar is a mixture of

    A. lactose and glucose   B. maltose and sucrose
    C. fructose and glucose   D. galactose and ribose

35. Dark spots occurring in canned foods are often caused by

    A. reaction of tannin in the food and iron in the can
    B. overcooking the food
    C. oxidation of the tin coating of the can
    D. use of hard water in canning

KEY (CORRECT ANSWERS)

1.	B	16.	B
2.	C	17.	A
3.	D	18.	C
4.	C	19.	C
5.	D	20.	D
6.	C	21.	D
7.	C	22.	A
8.	D	23.	B
9.	A	24.	B
10.	C	25.	C
11.	A	26.	D
12.	C	27.	C
13.	B	28.	D
14.	A	29.	C
15.	A	30.	A

31. A
32. C
33. D
34. C
35. A

TEST 2

DIRECTIONS: Each question or incomplete statement is followed by several suggested answers or completions. Select the one that BEST answers the question or completes the statement. *PRINT THE LETTER OF THE CORRECT ANSWER IN THE SPACE AT THE RIGHT.*

1. The red color of preserved meats, such as corned beef, results from the addition to the pickling solution of   1.____

    A. sodium chloride
    B. sodium nitrate
    C. sugar
    D. vinegar

2. The enzyme bromelin, often used to tenderize meats, is derived from   2.____

    A. milk
    B. cow's stomach
    C. pineapples
    D. papaya plant

3. The gas ethylene is often used for   3.____

    A. ripening fruits
    B. manufacturing rayon
    C. fruit anesthetizing
    D. disinfecting air in sick rooms

4. Undercooked poultry may cause   4.____

    A. tularemia
    B. brucellosis
    C. salmonella poisoning
    D. trichinosis

5. Certain diseases must be reported to the Department of Health. Which one of the following is NOT required to be reported?   5.____

    A. Pneumonia
    B. Food poisoning occurring in a group of three or more cases
    C. Meningitis
    D. Trichinosis

6. Food charts indicate the amount of vitamin A in foods in terms of   6.____

    A. grams
    B. International Units
    C. milligrams
    D. micrograms

7. A #1 can is also called a 211 x 400 can because it   7.____

    A. is 211 mm in diameter and 400 mm high
    B. is 2 11/16" in diameter and 4" high
    C. is 211 mm in diameter and 400 cc in volume
    D. weighs 211 mg and is 400 mm high

8. In the proper cooking of the following foods, LOWEST temperature would be used for   8.____

    A. sauteeing onions
    B. frying eggs
    C. scalding milk
    D. broiling steak

9. All of the following are organic metabolites EXCEPT   9.____

    A. fat   B. glucose   C. protein   D. water

10. Accepting the broadest conventional definition of *life*, one would regard the simplest of organisms to be the

    A. amino acids
    B. bacteria
    C. polypeptides
    D. viruses

11. The common house fly belongs to the order

    A. Hymenoptera
    B. Coleoptera
    C. Lepidoptera
    D. Diptera

12. To which one of the following animal groups does Ascaris belong?

    A. Rotifers
    B. Flatworms
    C. Segmented worms
    D. Roundworms

13. Of the following organisms, the one which is autotrophic is

    A. Azobacter
    B. Escherischia coli
    C. Nitrobacter
    D. Lactobacilli

14. The ant-aphid relationship is an example of

    A. commensalism
    B. mutualism
    C. parasitism
    D. synergism

15. To tell when the sleeping subject is dreaming, experimental psychologists record

    A. dilation of the capillaries
    B. movements of the eyeball
    C. rate of respiration
    D. skin sensitivity to pain

16. A hormone which is secreted by the adrenal glands and which equips animals to prepare for emergencies is

    A. insulin
    B. epinephrine
    C. thyroxin
    D. progesterone

17. In humans, maintenance of constant body temperature is a prime function of the

    A. endocrines
    B. skin
    C. muscles
    D. excretory system

18. Henle's loop is part of the

    A. adrenal
    B. vagus nerve
    C. nephron
    D. optic chiasma

19. Which one of the following represents the BEST order of tissues in a woody stem, beginning with the outside?

    A. Xylem, phloem, cambium, pith
    B. Phloem, xylem, cambium, pith
    C. Xylem, cambium, phloem, pith
    D. Phloem, cambium, xylem, pith

20. The function of xylem tissue in the leaf is to _____ the leaf.

    A. bring water to
    B. transport water from
    C. bring the chemical products of photosynthesis to
    D. transport the products of photosynthesis from

21. The corn kernel or grain is classified as a(n)

    A. seed   B. fruit   C. ovule   D. ovary

22. At which one of the following sites does fertilization in humans USUALLY occur?

    A. Fallopian tube   B. Graafian follicle
    C. Ovary   D. Uterus

23. The pulse beat felt at the wrist is the immediate result of

    A. systolic pressure
    B. heart beat
    C. venous response to heart beat
    D. arterial pressure changes felt on the wall of the artery

24. Groups of traits that tend to be inherited as a unit are PROBABLY

    A. multiple alleles   B. closely linked
    C. dominant   D. sex-linked

25. Glycogen is stored in

    A. bone and cartilage   B. fatty tissue
    C. liver and muscle   D. small intestine

26. The ion that is ESSENTIAL for blood clotting is

    A. iron   B. copper   C. calcium   D. magnesium

27. A drug discovered in clover hay that is used to prevent blood clotting is

    A. chloromycetin   B. dicoumarin
    C. digitalis   D. meprobamate

28. To determine most easily whether a guinea pig is pure black or hybrid, the animal should be mated with which one of the following types of guinea pigs?
    A

    A. pure black   B. hybrid black
    C. black of any type   D. white

29. Colloidal particles CANNOT be removed from the dispersion medium by

    A. ultrafiltration   B. electrophoresis
    C. dialysis   D. sedimentation

30. Brownian movement may easily be demonstrated by having pupils view under the microscope

    A. protozoa   B. a drop of oil
    C. India ink   D. tail of a goldfish

31. The theory of the inheritance of acquired characteristics was proposed by   31.____

   A. Le Chatelier   B. Lamarck
   C. Pasteur   D. Pascal

32. The polio virus USUALLY enters the body by way of the   32.____

   A. nose   B. mouth
   C. wounds   D. nervous system

33. Which one of the following tissues has the GREATEST amount of intercellular matrix?   33.____

   A. Visceral muscle   B. Connective tissue
   C. Nerve tissue   D. Epithelium

34. To determine the amount of protein in a food, the food is USUALLY analyzed for nitrogen and the nitrogen content multiplied by   34.____

   A. 3.1   B. 6.25   C. 12.5   D. 25

35. The fundamental (population) unit of classification is the   35.____

   A. species   B. genus   C. order   D. phylum

KEY (CORRECT ANSWERS)

1. B		16. B	
2. C		17. B	
3. B		18. C	
4. C		19. D	
5. A		20. D	
6. B		21. A	
7. C		22. A	
8. B		23. D	
9. D		24. D	
10. D		25. C	
11. D		26. C	
12. D		27. B	
13. A		28. D	
14. B		29. D	
15. B		30. C	

31. B
32. C
33. B
34. D
35. A

TEST 3

DIRECTIONS: Each question or incomplete statement is followed by several suggested answers or completions. Select the one that BEST answers the question or completes the statement. *PRINT THE LETTER OF THE CORRECT ANSWER IN THE SPACE AT THE RIGHT.*

1. Of the following, the one alkaloid found in the seeds of the nux vomica plant is   1._____

    A. quinine   B. atropine
    C. morphine   D. strychnine

2. In the preparation of chlorine gas by the reaction of potassium permanganate and hydrochloric acid, the oxidation number of manganese changes from   2._____

    A. +4 to +2   B. +7 to +2   C. +2 to +7   D. +7 to 0

3. *We cannot know simultaneously with perfect accuracy both the position and velocity of a moving electron.*   3._____
    The above statement is known as the _____ Principle.

    A. Pauli Exclusion   B. Heisenberg Uncertainty
    C. Pauli Uncertainty   D. Heisenberg Exclusion

4. The hypothesis that matter has a dualistic nature, having both the properties of a wave and the properties of particles was FIRST proposed by   4._____

    A. Max Planck   B. Albert Einstein
    C. Erwin Schrodinger   D. Louis de Broglie

5. The ionization constant of acetic acid is given by the expression   5._____

    A. $\dfrac{[H^+]}{[C_2H_3O_2^-]}$
    B. $[H^+][C_2H_3O_2^-]$
    C. $\dfrac{[HC_2H_3O_2]}{[H^+][C_2H_3O_2^-]}$
    D. $\dfrac{[H^+][C_2H_3O_2^-]}{[HC_2H_3O_2]}$

6. *If the conditions of a system initially at equilibrium are changed, the equilibrium will shift in such a way as to tend to restore the original conditions* is a statement of   6._____

    A. Avogadro's Hypothesis   B. Le Chatelier's Principle
    C. Gibbs' Phase Rule   D. Gay-Lussac's Law

7. If a pure chemical compound is carefully analyzed and found to be made up of   7._____
    29.1% sodium (atomic weight = 23)
    40.5% sulfur (atomic weight = 32)
    30.4% oxygen (atomic weight = 16),
    the simplest formula for the compound is

    A. Na_2SO_4 B. $Na_2S_2O_3$ C. Na_2SO_3 D. $Na_2S_4O_6$

8. In the reaction $2S_2O_3^= + I_2 \rightarrow S_4O_6^= + 2I^-$, which one of the following takes place?

   A. $S_2O_3^=$ is reduced
   B. $S_2O_3^=$ is oxidized
   C. I_2 is oxidized
   D. I_2 acts as a reducing agent

9. $2SO_2(g) + O_2(g) \rightleftarrows 2SO_3(g) + heat$
   If in the above chemical equilibrium the concentration of SO_2 is doubled, there will be a(n)

   A. increase in the equilibrium constant
   B. increase in the rate constant
   C. change in the energy of activation
   D. shift in the equilibrium position

10. If a solution of copper (III) sulfate is electrolyzed between inert electrodes, for how many seconds must a current of 1.93 amperes flow to deposit 0.640g of copper metal?

    A. 965 B. 1000 C. 1930 D. 2000

11. Ammonia gas can be made by which one of the following processes?

    A. Contact B. Haber C. Ostwald D. Hall

12. Bromine will form an addition compound when it is shaken with

    A. alcohol
    B. carbon tetrachloride
    C. ethylene
    D. methyl iodide

13. Assume that 0.300 gram atom weight of aluminum metal is combined with chlorine to form aluminum chloride.
    Of the following, which one is CLOSEST to the number of grams of chlorine which are combined with the metal? (At. wt. Al = 27, Cl = 35.5)

    A. 0.900 B. 8.10 C. 32.0 D. 40.1

14. A by-product recovered from scouring of wool and used in cosmetic products is

    A. petrolatum
    B. spermaceti
    C. paraffin wax
    D. lanolin

15. Titanium dioxide is used in face powder PRINCIPALLY because it

    A. absorbs water without swelling
    B. makes powder adhere to the skin
    C. makes powder go on the skin smoothly
    D. has a powerful covering capacity

16. Quarternary ammonium compounds are used in beauty culture work to serve as

    A. germicides in sterilizing instruments
    B. bleaching agents
    C. ingredients in nail polish
    D. ingredients of face powder

17. Parahydroxybenzoic acid and its esters are used in cosmetics to act as which one of the following?

    A. Preservatives
    B. Emulsifiers
    C. Plasticizers
    D. Solvents

18. Which one of the following is a substance which is used as a solvent in nail polish?

    A.
    ```
       H
       |
    HC–C=O
    |  |
    H  OH
    ```

    B.
    ```
     H H H
     | | |
    H–C–C–C–H
     | | |
     OH OH OH
    ```

    C.
    ```
       H
       |
    HC – C=O
    |    |
    H   H–C–H
         |
         H
    ```

    D.
    ```
    OH   OH
    |    |
    C  – C
    ||   ||
    O    O
    ```

19. Nitro-cellulose is the CHIEF ingredient used in the manufacture of

    A. lipstick
    B. liquid nail polish
    C. cleansing creams
    D. hair tints

20. It is common practice in bleaching hair to speed up the action of the bleaching solution by adding which one of the following?

    A. NH_4OH
    B. $NaOH$
    C. HCl
    D. H_2SO_4

21. When an egg is cooked, protein denaturation takes place because

    A. hydrogen bonds in the protein are broken
    B. condensation of amino acids takes place
    C. polypeptide bonds are broken
    D. polypeptide bonds are formed

22. Of the following, the one compound formed when bread is leavened by the action of yeast is

    A. C_2H_5OH
    B. $C_{12}H_{22}O_{11}$
    C. $NaKC_4H_4O_6$
    D. $NaHCO_3$

23. The ester added to foods to give a banana flavor is

    A. $HCOOC_2H_5$
    B. $CH_3COOC_5H_{11}$
    C. $HOC_6H_4COOCH_3$
    D. $CH_3(CH_2)_2COOC_2H_5$

24. Wheat flour generally has better baking qualities than other cereal flours because of its higher content of

    A. proteins
    B. gluten
    C. gliadin
    D. fiber

25. Of the following, the reaction which takes place in developing a photographic negative is

    A. $2AgBr + Na_2S \rightarrow Ag_2S + 2NaBr$
    B. $3Ag + AuCl_3 \rightarrow 3AgCl + Au$
    C. $2AgBr + 3Na_2S_2O_3 \rightarrow 2NaBr + Na_4Ag_2(S_2O_3)_3$
    D. $2AgBr + C_6H_4(OH)_2 \rightarrow C_6H_4O_2 + 2HBr + 2Ag$

26. Sepia toning is accomplished in photography by using a toning solution, the active ingredient of which is

    A. AuCl₃ B. K₃Fe(CN)₆
    C. H₂PtCl₆ D. Na₂S

27. The one textile fiber among the following that looks like a flattened, twisted, opaque ribbon under the microscope is

    A. wool B. silk C. rayon D. cotton

28. Of the following, the one substance used in the textile industry as a mordant, in preparing fireproof cotton cloth and in weighting silk, is

    A. ammonium sulfate B. sodium stannate
    C. Glauber's salt D. silicone

29. Both anions and cations are removed from tap water by passing the water through

    A. manganese zeolite B. permutit
    C. ion exchange resins D. silicates

30. Of the following, the one synthetic fiber made by the polymerization of acrylonitrile is

    A. nylon B. dacron C. orlon D. rayon

31. Which one of the following bleaching agents should NOT be used on animal fibers?

    A. Sodium hypochlorite B. Hydrogen peroxide
    C. Sodium perborate D. Potassium permanganate

32. Which one of the following statements is NOT true?

    A. Organic acids usually have a milder action on fabrics than do mineral acids.
    B. Animal fibers are less resistant to acids than are vegetable fibers.
    C. Animal fibers are more resistant to acids than are vegetable fibers.
    D. Vegetable fibers are more resistant to alkalis than are animal fibers.

33. The type of dye which is applied by agitating a fabric in a bath of soluble reduced dye, and the subsequent exposure of the fabric to the air, is known as a _____ dye.

    A. sulfur B. vat C. basic D. direct

34. An iron rust stain on cotton can BEST be removed by

    A. treating it with soap solution
    B. exposing it to sunlight
    C. treating it with oxalic acid and then with ammonia
    D. treating it with turpentine or benzine

35. Chlorine may be used safely to bleach

    A. silk B. linen C. wool D. fur

KEY (CORRECT ANSWERS)

1.	D	16.	B
2.	C	17.	A
3.	B	18.	D
4.	D	19.	C
5.	D	20.	C
6.	B	21.	B
7.	C	22.	A
8.	D	23.	D
9.	D	24.	B
10.	A	25.	D
11.	B	26.	B
12.	C	27.	D
13.	C	28.	C
14.	D	29.	D
15.	D	30.	A

31. D
32. B
33. B
34. C
35. B

TEST 4

DIRECTIONS: Each question or incomplete statement is followed by several suggested answers or completions. Select the one that BEST answers the question or completes the statement. *PRINT THE LETTER OF THE CORRECT ANSWER IN THE SPACE AT THE RIGHT.*

1. Of the following, the MOST important contribution of copper to a gold alloy used in dentistry is to increase the

    A. tarnish resistance
    B. strength and hardness
    C. melting point
    D. corrosion resistance

2. The hypnotic chloral hydrate is a derivative of

    A. paraform
    B. ethanol
    C. acetaldehyde
    D. chloric acid

3. The compound used MOST for fluoridation of water is

    A. apatite
    B. cryolite
    C. fluorspar
    D. sodium fluoride

4. Of the following substances, the one which is used as an anticoagulant for blood is

    A. sodium citrate
    B. ammonium chloride
    C. sodium salicylate
    D. arbutin

5. Of the following, the one radioactive isotope that is used in the diagnosis and treatment of thyroid disorders is

    A. U^{235}
    B. Co^{137}
    C. C^{14}
    D. I^{131}

6. Of the following, the one type of alcohol which upon oxidation will be changed first to its corresponding aldehyde and then to its corresponding acid is

    A. primary
    B. secondary
    C. tertiary
    D. quarternary

7. Of the following, the one important ingredient used in the preparation of most thermosetting plastics is

    A. cellulose
    B. formaldehyde
    C. phenol
    D. acetic acid

8. The degree of unsaturation of a fat or oil is determined by a test which yields which one of the following? _____ number.

    A. Baumé
    B. Reichert-Meissel
    C. Saponification
    D. Iodine

9. Of the following, the group consisting of two water soluble vitamins is

    A. A and B
    B. C and D
    C. B and C
    D. A and D

10. Assume that ammonium hydroxide is added to a cupric solution until a precipitate of $Cu(OH)_2$ is formed and the addition is continued until part of the precipitate has dissolved to give a deep blue solution.
    If some ammonium chloride is then dissolved in the solution, which one of the following will occur?

    A. The blue color will disappear.
    B. More of the precipitate will dissolve.
    C. More of the precipitate will settle out.
    D. No change will take place.

11. Of the following, the one metallic sulfide that is separated from other metallic sulfides by an alkaline solution of sodium sulfide and sodium disulfide in qualitative analysis is

    A. PbS B. HgS C. CuS D. CdS

12. The element essential for the utilization of iron in the synthesis of hemoglobin in the body is

    A. magnesium B. iodine C. zinc D. copper

13. A refrigerating drug often used by dentists before incising an abscess is

    A. ethyl alcohol   B. ether
    C. ethyl chloride   D. carbon dioxide

14. Atoms that have the same atomic number but different atomic weights are called

    A. isomers B. isomorphs C. isobars D. isotopes

15. If one ml of a saturated solution of AgCl contains 1×10^{-8} moles of Ag+, the solubility product of AgCl is 1 x

    A. 10^{-6} B. 10^{-10} C. 10^{-12} D. 10^{-16}

16. At 30° C, the solubility of Ag_2CO_3 ($K_{sp} = 8 \times 10^{-12}$) would be GREATEST in one liter of which one of the following?

    A. 0.10M $AgNO_3$ B. 0.10M Na_2CO_3
    C. Pure water   D. 0.10M NH_3

17. $H_2C_2O_4 + KMnO_4 \rightarrow H_2O + CO_2 + MnO + KOH$
    In the above reaction, what is the weight of 1 gram-equivalent of $H_2C_2O_4$ (M.W. = 90)?

    A. 18 B. 45 C. 90 D. 450

18. Which one of the following is NOT a direct product or a by-product of the Solvay process?

    A. NH_4NO_3 B. Na_2CO_3 C. $CaCl_2$ D. $NaHCO_3$

19. Of the following, the kind of radioactive emission NOT affected by an electromagnetic field is

    A. alpha particles   B. beta particles
    C. gamma rays   D. protons

20. Suppose a 2.0 mole sample of hydrazine (N₂H₂) loses 20 moles of electrons in being converted to a new compound X.
Assuming that all of the nitrogen appears in the new compound, what is the oxidation state of N in the new compound X?

    A. -2   B. +1   C. +3   D. +5

20.____

21. For the reaction $AB \rightleftarrows A + B + 80,000 \text{ cal}$, which one of the following is TRUE?

    A. The value of K_{eq} changes with changes in temperature.
    B. An increase in the concentration of B changes the value of K_{eq}.
    C. The escape of B as a gas decreases the concentration of A, if AB and A are in solution.
    D. An increase of temperature shifts the equilibrium point to the right, if all substances are gases.

21.____

22. The combustion of propane is given by the following equation:

$C_3H_8(g) + 5O_2(g) \rightarrow 3CO_2(g) + 4H_2O(g)$.

The heat of formation of CO_2 is -94.0 kcal/mole.
The heat of formation of H_2O is -57.8 kcal/mole.
The heat of formation of $C_3H_8(g)$ is -24.8 kcal/mole.
The amount of heat produced by the combustion of one mole of propane, in kcal, is

    A. 127.0   B. 488.5   C. 513.4   D. 538.2

22.____

23. Of the following, the one that has the HIGHEST coefficient of cubic expansion at room temperature is

    A. ethanol   B. mercury   C. nitrogen   D. sodium

23.____

24. Of the following indicators, the one that is colorless in an acid solution is

    A. phenol red   B. methyl orange
    C. thymol blue   D. phenolphthalein

24.____

25. The organic acid commonly found in sour apples is

    A. malic   B. tartaric   C. citric   D. benzoic

25.____

26. Of the following, the statement that is TRUE concerning the compound X-O-H, where X is an element other than hydrogen, is that

    A. it must be a strong base
    B. a water solution of the compound cannot be an electrical conductor
    C. if X is very electronegative, the compound is an acid
    D. the oxidation state of the element O may have any value from -2 to +1

26.____

27. Which one of the following has the species arranged according to INCREASING boiling points?

    A. NaBr, HBr, Br₂, H₂   B. H₂, Br₂, NaBr, HBr
    C. NaBr, HBr, H₂, Br₂   D. H₂, HBr, Br₂, NaBr

27.____

28. Of the following, which BEST describes the bonds in silicon carbide?

    A. Ionic
    B. Ion-dipole
    C. Covalent
    D. Metallic

29. Which one of the following is a non-polar compound?

    A. CH_3Cl
    B. CH_2Cl_2
    C. $CHCl_3$
    D. CCl_4

30. Which one of the halogens given has the HIGHEST energy of hydration?

    A. Fluorine
    B. Chlorine
    C. Bromine
    D. Iodine

31. The aldol condensation of acetaldehyde results in the formation of which one of the following?

    A. $CH_3CH_2OH + CH_3COOH$
    B. $CH_3COCHOHCH_3$
    C. $CH_3CHOHCH_2CHO$
    D. $HOCH_2CH_2CH_2COOH$

32. Which one of the following BEST describes the conversion of starch to glucose?

    A. Oxidation
    B. Inversion
    C. Hydrolysis
    D. Mutarotation

33. Conjugated double bonds are found in

    A. propylene
    B. isoprene
    C. allene
    D. butylene

34. Sublimation is a property generally associated with

    A. lead
    B. silicon
    C. iron
    D. iodine

35. Which one of the following phase combinations CANNOT produce a colloid?

    A. Solid in a solid
    B. Solid in a gas
    C. Gas in a solid
    D. Gas in a gas

KEY (CORRECT ANSWERS)

1. B
2. D
3. D
4. A
5. D

6. B
7. C
8. C
9. C
10. C

11. D
12. C
13. A
14. D
15. A

16. C
17. D
18. A
19. C
20. D

21. A
22. D
23. C
24. D
25. A

26. A
27. B
28. C
29. D
30. A

31. C
32. C
33. C
34. D
35. A

EXAMINATION SECTION
TEST 1

DIRECTIONS: Each question or incomplete statement is followed by several suggested answers or completions. Select the one that BEST answers the question or completes the statement. *PRINT THE LETTER OF THE CORRECT ANSWER IN THE SPACE AT THE RIGHT.*

Questions 1-7.

DIRECTIONS: Questions 1 through 7 refer to the diagram that follows. Base your choice on the information given in the selection and on your own understanding of science.

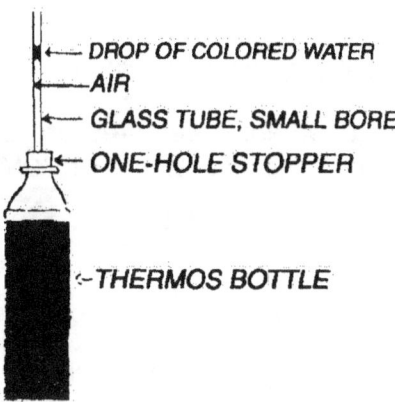

1. The device shown in the diagram above indicates changes that are measured MORE accurately by a(n)

   A. thermometer   B. hygrometer   C. anemometer
   D. hydrometer   E. barometer

2. If the device is placed in a cold refrigerator for 72 hours, which of the following is MOST likely to happen?

   A. The stopper will be forced out of the bottle.
   B. The drop of water will evaporate.
   C. the drop will move downward.
   D. The drop will move upward.
   E. No change will take place

3. When the device was carried in an elevator from the first floor to the sixth floor of a building, the drop of colored water moved about 1/4 inch in the tube. Which of the following is MOST probably true?

   A. The drop moved downward because there was a decrease in the air pressure.
   B. The drop moved upward because there was a decrease in the air pressure.
   C. The drop moved downward because there was an increase in the air temperature.
   D. The drop moved upward because there was an increase in the air temperature.
   E. The drop moved downward because there was an increase in the temperature and a decrease in the pressure.

4. The part of a thermos bottle into which liquids are poured consists of

   A. a single-walled, metal flask coated with silver
   B. two flasks, one of glass and one of silvered metal
   C. two silvered-glass flasks separated by a vacuum
   D. two silver flasks separated by a vacuum
   E. a single-walled glass flask with a silver-colored coating

4.____

5. The thermos bottle is MOST similar in principle to

   A. the freezing unit in an electric refrigerator
   B. radiant heaters
   C. solar heating systems
   D. storm windows
   E. a thermostatically controlled heating system

5.____

6. In a plane flying at an altitude where the air pressure is only half the normal pressure at sea level, the plane's altimeter should read APPROXIMATELY

   A. 3,000 feet   B. 9,000 feet   C. 18,000 feet
   D. 27,000 feet   E. 60,000 feet

6.____

7. Which of the following is the POOREST conductor of heat?

   A. Air under a pressure of 1.5 pounds per square inch
   B. Air under a pressure of 15 pounds per square inch
   C. Unsilvered glass
   D. Silvered glass
   E. Silver

7.____

Questions 8-17.

DIRECTIONS: Questions 8 through 17 refer to the passage that follows. Base your choice on the information given in the passage *and on your own understanding of the subject.*

The formed elements of the blood are the red corpuscles or erythrocytes, the white corpuscles or leucocytes, the blood platelets, and the so-called blood dust or hemoconiae. Together, these constitute 30-40 percent by volume of the whole blood, the remainder being taken up by the plasma. In man, there are normally 5,000,000 red cells per cubic millimeter of blood; the count is somewhat lower in women. Variations occur frequently, especially after exercise or a heavy meal, or at high altitudes. Except in camels, which have elliptical corpuscles, the shape of the mammalian corpuscle is that of a circular, nonnucleated, bi-concave disk. The average diameter usually given is 7.7 microns, a value obtained by examining dried preparations of blood and considered by Ponder to be too low. Ponder's own observations, made on red cells in the fresh state, show the human corpuscle to have an average diameter of 8.8 microns. When circulating in the blood vessels, the red cell does not maintain a fixed shape but changes its form constantly, especially in the small capillaries. The red blood corpuscles are continually undergoing destruction, new corpuscles being formed to replace them. The average life of red corpuscles has been estimated by various investigators to be between three and six weeks. Preceding destruction, changes in the composition of the cells are believed to occur which render them less resistant. In the process of destruction, the lipids of the membrane are dissolved and the hemoglobin which is liberated is the most important, though probably not the only source of bilirubin. The belief that the liver is the only site of red celldestruction is no longer generally held. The leucocytes, of which there are several forms, usually number 7000 and 9000 per cubic millimeter of blood. These increase in number in disease, particularly when there is bacterial infection.

8. Leukemia is a disease involving the

    A. red cells   B. white cells   C. plasma
    D. blood platelets   E. blood dust

9. "The erythrocytes in the blood are increased in number after a heavy meal." The paragraph implies that this

    A. is true   B. holds only for camels
    C. is not true   D. may be true
    E. depends on the number of white cells

10. When blood is dried, the red cells

    A. contract   B. remain the same size   C. disintegrate
    D. expand   E. become elliptical

11. Ponder is PROBABLY classified as a professional

    A. pharmacist   B. physicist   C. psychologist
    D. physiologist   E. psychiatrist

12. The term *erythema* when applied to skin conditions signifies

    A. redness   B. swelling   C. irritation
    D. pain   E. roughness

13. Lipids are insoluble in water and soluble in such solvents as ether, chloroform and benzene. It may be inferred that the membrane of red cells MOST closely resemble

    A. egg white   B. sugar   C. bone   D. butter
    E. cotton fiber

14. Analysis of a sample of blood yields cell counts of 4,800,000 erythrocytes and 16,000 leucocytes per cubic millimeter. These data suggest that the patient from whom the blood was taken

    A. is anemic
    B. has been injuriously invaded by germs
    C. has been exposed to high-pressure air
    D. has a normal cell count
    E. has lost a great deal of blood

15. Bilirubin, a bile pigment, is

    A. an end product of several different reactions
    B. formed only in the liver
    C. formed from the remnants of the dell membranes of erythrocytes
    D. derived from hemoglobin exclusively
    E. a precursor of hemoglobin

16. Bancroft found that the blood count of the natives in the Peruvian Andes differed from that usually accepted as normal. The blood PROBABLY differed in respect to

   A. leucocytes
   B. blood platelets
   C. cell shapes
   D. erythrocytes
   E. hemoconiae

17. Hemoglobin is probably NEVER found

   A. free in the blood stream
   B. in the red cells
   C. in women's blood
   D. in the blood after exercise
   E. in the leucocytes

Questions 18-27.

DIRECTIONS: Questions 18 through 27 refer to the passage that follows. Base your choice on the information given in the passage *and on your own understanding of the subject.*

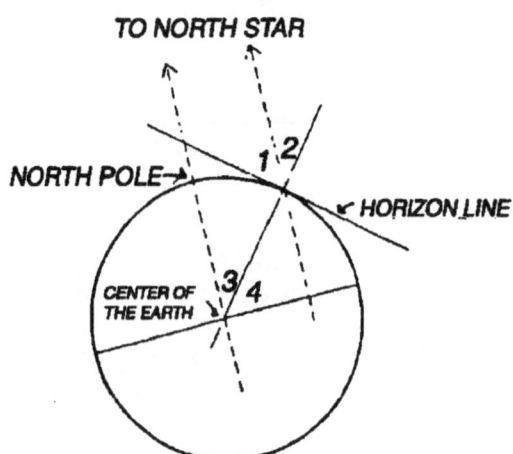

The latitude of any point on the earth's surface is the angle between a plumb line dropped to the center of the earth from that point and the plane of the earth's equator. Since it is impossible to go to the center of the earth to measure latitude, the latitude of any point may be determined indirectly as shown in the accompanying diagram.

It will be recalled that the axis of the earth, if extended outward, passes very near the North Star. Since the North Star is, for all practical purposes, infinitely distant, the line of sight to the North Star of an observer on the surface of the earth is virtually parallel with the earth's axis. Angle 1, then, in the diagram represents the angular distance of the North Star above the horizon. Angle 2 is equal to angle 3, because when two parallel lines are intersected by a straight line, the corresponding angles are equal. Angle 1 plus angle 2 is a right angle and so is angle 3 plus angle 4. Therefore, angle 1 equals angle 4 because when equals are subtracted from equals the results are equal.

18. If an observer finds that the angular distance of the North Star above the horizon is 30, his latitude is

   A. 15° N   B. 30° N   C. 60° N   D. 90° N   E. 120° N

19. To an observer on the equator, the North Star would be   19._____

    A. 30° above the horizon   B. 60° above the horizon
    C. 90° above the horizon   D. on the horizon
    E. below the horizon

20. To an observer on the Arctic Circle, the North Star would be   20._____

    A. directly overhead   B. 23 1/2° above the horizon
    C. 66 1/2° above the horizon   D. on the horizon
    E. below the horizon

21. The distance around the earth along a certain parallel of latitude is 3,600 miles. At this   21._____
    latitude, how many miles are there in one degree of longitude?

    A. 1 mile   B. 10 miles   C. 30 miles
    D. 69 miles   E. 100 miles

22. At which of the following latitudes would the sun be directly overhead at noon on June   22._____
    21?

    A. 0°   B. 23 1/2° S   C. 23 1/2° N   D. 66 1/2° N   E. 66 1/2° S

23. On March 21 the number of hours of daylight at places on the Arctic Circle is   23._____

    A. none   B. 8   C. 12   D. 16   E. 24

24. The distance from the equator to the 45th parallel, measured along a meridian, is   24._____
    APPROXIMATELY

    A. 450 miles   B. 900 miles   C. 1,250 miles
    D. 3,125 miles   E. 6,250 miles

25. The difference in time between the meridians that pass through longitude 45°E and   25._____
    longitude 105°W is

    A. 6 hours   B. 2 hours   C. 8 hours
    D. 4 hours   E. 10 hours

26. Which of the following is NOT a great circle or part of a great circle?   26._____

    A. Arctic Circle   B. 100th meridian   C. equator
    D. Shortest distance between New York and London
    E. Greenwich meridian

27. At which of the following places does the sun set earliest on June 21?   27._____

    A. Montreal, Canada   B. Santiago, Chile
    C. Mexico City, Mexico   D. Lima, Peru
    E. Manila, P.I.

28. At which of the following cities is the daily temperature range GREATEST?   28._____

    A. Key West   B. Los Angeles   C. Chicago
    D. New York City   E. Denver

29. The MAXIMUM percentage of water vapor possible in the air is about   29._____

    A. 1%   B. 78%   C. .03%   D. 4%   E. 100%

30. When a mass of air rises, it is cooled CHIEFLY because

    A. it expands
    B. moisture condenses
    C. ice crystals are formed
    D. it mixes with cold air
    E. it is closer to cold outer space

31. An amateur pilot flying into a series of cold front thunderstorms should

    A. fly through without change of course
    B. fly around the thunderstorms
    C. land and get his plane into a hangar
    D. fly under the storm front
    E. fly over the top

32. Soaring pilots find MOST thermals

    A. about midmorning
    B. about 2 hours after noon
    C. in late afternoon
    D. Just after sunset
    E. in early morning

33. On a contour map, lines that are close together indicate that the land

    A. slopes gently
    B. is swampy
    C. slopes steeply
    D. is high
    E. is impassable

34. The planet that is NEAREST in size to the Earth is

    A. Mars   B. Venus   C. Mercury   D. Uranus   E. Jupiter

35. Of the total mass of the sun, planets, moons and other bodies in our solar system, the sun comprises APPROXIMATELY

    A. 1%   B. 10%   C. 50%   D. 90%   E. 99%

36. A sea cave at an altitude of 100 feet would indicate

    A. great tidal range
    B. severe storms
    C. uplift of land
    D. submergence of land
    E. rapid deposition of sediment

37. The element that makes up about 50% of the earth's crust is

    A. silicon
    B. nitrogen
    C. iron
    D. aluminum
    E. oxygen

38. Two elements obtained from the sea in commercial quantities are

    A. iron and sulfur
    B. nitrogen and argon
    C. copper and tin
    D. aluminum and iodine
    E. magnesium and bromine

39. Atoms of plutonium are composed of

    A. neutrons and protons
    B. electrons and neutrons
    C. electrons, neutrons and ions
    D. ions, protons and electrons
    E. neutrons, electrons and protons

40. Uranium used in making atomic bombs occurs in the mineral   40.____

    A. hematite   B. pitchblende   C. franklinite
    D. malachite   E. smithsonite

41. Which of the following is an explosive mixture?   41.____

    A. Oxygen and carbon monoxide
    B. Oxygen and caron dioxide
    C. Carbon dioxide and caron monoxide
    D. Carbon dioxide and hydrogen
    E. Nitrogen and carbon dioxide

42. Which of the following will react with baking soda to produce carbon dioxide?   42.____

    A. Table salt   B. Cane molasses   C. Granulated sugar
    D. Sweet cream   E. Wheat flour

43. Which of the following mechanisms requires NO external supply of oxygen?   43.____

    A. Diesel engines   B. Four-cycle gasoline engines
    C. Jet turbine engines   D. Rockets
    E. Two-cycle internal-combustion engines

44. In an operating radio tube the electrons flow from   44.____

    A. plate to grid   B. grid to plate
    C. plate to filament   D. filament to plate
    E. grid to filament

45. In hydroelectric stations, the energy of the turbines is applied directly to the operation of   45.____

    A. synchronous motors   B. water motors   C. steam engines
    D. generators   E. electric motors

46. A boy is given two similar bars of iron, which we shall call A and B. He finds that either   46.____
    end of A clings to either end of B, that either end of A clings to the middle of B and that
    neither end of B clings to the middle of A. He concludes CORRECTLY that

    A. both A and B are magnetized
    B. A is magnetized and B is not
    C. B is magnetized and A is not
    D. neither A nor B is magnetized
    E. B is magnetized over its entire length and A is not magnetized in the middle

47. Inductive reaoning is reasoning   47.____

    A. by analogy to similar situations
    B. from faulty premises
    C. after an event has taken place
    D. from a principle to a conclusion
    E. from observations to generalizations

48. If a coin is held 2 feet from an electric lamp, the shadow of the coin 6 feet from the lamp   48.____
    has an area that compares to the area of the coin as

    A. 12 to 1   B. 24 to 1   C. 3 to 1   D. 6 to 1   E. 9 to 1

49. The appliance cord for an electric flatiron is made of

   A. stranded copper wire covered with asbestos and rubber
   B. solid copper wire covered with asbestos and rubber
   C. rubber-covered stranded copper wire
   D. asbestos-covered nichrome wire
   E. rubber-covered nichrome wire

50. The distributor in an automobile engine controls the

   A. proportion of the electric current flowing to the lights and starter
   B. amount of electric current released from the storage battery
   C. flow of gasoline to the carburetor
   D. transmission of the spark occurrence to the spark plug
   E. amount of pressure on each brake drum

KEY (CORRECT ANSWERS)

1. A	11. D	21. B	31. C	41. A
2. C	12. A	22. C	32. C	42. D
3. B	13. D	23. C	33. C	43. D
4. C	14. B	24. D	34. B	44. D
5. D	15. A	25. E	35. E	45. D
6. C	16. D	26. A	36. C	46. B
7. A	17. E	27. B	37. E	47. E
8. B	18. B	28. E	38. E	48. E
9. D	19. D	29. D	39. E	49. A
10. A	20. C	30. A	40. B	50. D

TEST 2

DIRECTIONS: Each question or incomplete statement is followed by several suggested answers or completions. Select the one that BEST answers the question or completes the statement. *PRINT THE LETTER OF THE CORRECT ANSWER IN THE SPACE AT THE RIGHT.*

Questions 1-7.

DIRECTIONS: Questions 1 through 7 refer to the diagram that follows. Base your choice on the information given in the selection and on your own understanding of science.

1. The ignition coil in an automobile

   A. regulates the flow of current to the lights
   B. increases the voltage of the current to the spark plugs
   C. controls the charging rate of the battery
   D. boosts the voltage between the battery and the starting motor
   E. takes the place of the generator when the engine is not running

2. When the gears of an automobile are shifted from "high" to "low," the

   A. power of the motor is increased
   B. force applied by the driving wheels is increased
   C. force applied by the motor is decreased
   D. speed of the driving wheels is increased
   E. transmission gears have increased the power

3. If metal pipe is to be used to carry liquids or gases, the threaded portion is ALWAYS

   A. straight   B. tapered   C. fine   D. coarse   E. square

4. Which of these fastening devices is a rivet?

5. A substance mixed with cement and water to form the finishing coat on a concrete sidewalk is

   A. fill   B. sand   C. plaster of paris   D. mortar   E. gravel

6. The board of fire underwriters requires inspection of

   A. house paint   B. roofing material
   C. furnace installation D. hot-water pipes
   E. electric wiring

7. Which tool is MOST generally used with a brace to bore a hole?

   A. Twist drill   B. Center drill   C. Countersink
   D. Auger bit   E. Rose reamer

8. By what name is this tool commonly called?

   A. Nail set   B. Wedge   C. Pry bar   D. Cold chisel
   E. Gouge

9. Which is the MOST accurate instrument to use for marking on wood when laying out a joint in cabinet work?

   A. Knife   B. Pencil   C. Scriber   D. Brad awl   E. Nail

10. The fibers running lengthwise in a piece of cloth are called the

    A. heading   B. warp   C. weft   D. nap   E. pile

Questions 11-17.

DIRECTIONS: Questions 11 through 17 refer to the passage that follows. Base your choice on the information given in the selection *and on your own understanding of science*.

The higher forms of plants and animals, such as seed plants and vertebrates, are similar or alike in many respects but decidedly different in others. For example, both of these groups of organisms carry on digestion, respiration, reproduction, conduction, growth, and exhibit sensitivity to various stimuli. On the other hand, a number of basic differences are evident. Plants have no excretory systems comparable to those of animals. Plants have no heart or similar pumping organ. Plants are very limited in their movements. Plants have nothing similar to the animal nervous system. In addition, animals can not synthesize carbohydrates from inorganic substances. Animals do not have special regions of growth, comparable to terminal and lateral meristems in plants, which persist throughout the life span of the organism. And, finally, the animal cell "wall" is only a membrane, while plant cell walls are more rigid, usually thicker, and may be composed of such substances as cellulose, lignin, pectin, cutin, and suberin. These characteristics are important to an understanding of living organisms and their functions and should, consequently, be carefully considered in plant and animal studies.

11. Which of the following do animals lack?

    A. Ability to react to stimuli
    B. Ability to conduct substances from one place to another
    C. Reproduction by gametes
    D. A cell membrane
    E. A terminal growth region

12. Which of the following statements is FALSE?

    A. Animal cell "walls" are composed of cellulose.
    B. Plants grow as long as they live.
    C. Plants produce sperms and eggs.
    D. All vertebrates have hearts.
    E. Wood is dead at maturity.

13. Respiration in plants takes place 13.____

    A. only during the day
    B. only in the presence of carbon dioxide
    C. both day and night
    D. only at night
    E. only in the presence of certain stimuli

14. An example of a vertebrate is the 14.____

    A. earthworm   B. starfish   C. amoeba
    D. cow   E. insect

15. Which of the following statements is TRUE? 15.____

    A. All animals eat plants as a source of food.
    B. Respiration, in many ways, is the reverse of photosynthesis.
    C. Man is an invertebrate animal.
    D. Since plants have no hearts, they can not develop high pressure in their cells.
    E. Plants can not move.

16. Which of the following do plants lack? 16.____

    A. A means of movement   B. Pumping structures
    C. Special regions of growth   D. Reproduction by gametes
    E. A digestive process

17. A substance that can be synthesized by green plants but NOT by animals is 17.____

    A. protein   B. cellulose   C. carbon dioxide
    D. uric acid   E. water

Questions 18-27.

DIRECTIONS: Questions 18 through 27 refer to the passage that follows. Base your choice on the information given in the selection *and on your own understanding of the subject.*

    The discovery of antitoxin and its specific antagonistic effect upon toxin furnished an opportunity for the accurate investigation of the relationship of a bacterial antigen and its antibody. Toxin-antitoxin reactions were the first immunological processes to which experimental precision could be applied, and the discovery of principles of great importance resulted from such studies. A great deal of the work was done with diphtheria toxin and antitoxin and the facts elucidated with these materials are in principle applicable to similar substances.

    The simplest assumption to account for the manner in which an antitoxin renders a toxin innocuous would be that the antitoxin destroys the toxin. Roux and Buchner, however, advanced the opinion that the antitoxin did not act directly upon the toxin, but affected it indirectly through the mediation of tissue cells. Ehrlich, on the other hand, conceived the reaction of toxin and antitoxin as a direct union, analogous to the chemical neutralization of an acid by a base.

    The conception of toxin destruction was conclusively refuted by the experiments of Calmette. This observer, working with snake poison, found that the poison itself (unlike most other toxins) possessed the property of resisting heat to 100 degrees C, while its specific antitoxin, like other antitoxins, was destroyed at or about 70 degrees C. Nontoxic mixtures of the two substances, when subjected to heat, regained their toxic properties. The natural inference from these observations was that the toxin in the original mixture had not been destroyed, but had been merely inactivated by the presence of the antitoxin and again set free after destruction of the antitoxin by heat.

18. Both toxins and antitoxins ordinarily

   A. are completely destroyed at body temperatures
   B. are extremely resistant to heat
   C. can exist only in combination
   D. are destroyed at 180° F
   E. are products of nonliving processes

19. Most toxins can be destroyed by

   A. bacterial action
   B. salt solutions
   C. boiling
   D. diphtheria antitoxin
   E. other toxins

20. Very few disease organisms release a true toxin into the blood stream. It would follow, then, that

   A. studies of snake venom reactions have no value
   B. studies of toxin-antitoxin reactions are of little importance
   C. the treatment of most diseases must depend upon information obtained from study of a few
   D. antitoxin plays an important part in the body defense against the great majority of germs
   E. only toxin producers are dangerous

21. A person becomes susceptible to infection again immediately after recovering from

   A. mumps   B. tetanus   C. diphtheria   D. smallpox
   E. tuberculosis

22. City people are more frequently immune to communicable diseases than country people are because

   A. country people eat better food
   B. city doctors are better than country doctors
   C. the air is more healthful in the country
   D. country people have fewer contacts with disease carriers
   E. there are more doctors in the city than in the country

23. The substance that provide us with immunity to disease are found in the body in the

   A. blood serum   B. gastric juice   C. urine
   D. white blood cells   E. red blood cells

24. A person ill with diphtheria would MOST likely be treated with

   A. diphtheria toxin   B. diphtheria toxoid
   C. dead diphtheria germs   D. diphtheria antitoxin
   E. live diphtheria germs

25. To determine susceptibility to diphtheria, an individual may be given the   25._____

    A. Wassermann test   B. Schick test   C. Widal test
    D. Dick test   E. Kahn test

26. Since few babies under six months of age contract diphtheria, young babies PROBABLY   26._____

    A. are never exposed to diphtheria germs
    B. have high body temperatures that destroy the toxin if acquired
    C. acquire immunity from their mothers
    D. acquire immunity from their fathers
    E. are too young to become infected

27. Calmette's findings   27._____

    A. contradicted both Roux and Buchner's opinion and Ehrlich's conception
    B. contradicted Roux and Buchner, but supported Ehrlich
    C. contradicted Ehrlich, but supported Roux and Buchner
    D. were consistent with both theories
    E. had no bearing on the point at issue

Questions 28-37.

DIRECTIONS: Questions 28 through 37 refer to the passage that follows. Base your choice on the information given in the selection *and on your own understanding of the subject*.

Sodium chloride, being by far the largest constituent of the mineral matter of the blood, assumes special significance in the regulation of water exchanges in the organism. And, as Cannon has emphasized repeatedly, these latter are more extensive and more important than may at first thought appear. He points out "there are a number of circulations of the fluid out of the body and back again, without loss." Thus, for example, it is estimated that from a quart to a quart and one-half of water daily "leaves the body" when it enters the mouth as saliva; another one or two quarts are passed out as gastric juice; and perhaps the same amount is contained in the bile and the secretions of the pancreas and the intestinal wall. This large volume of water enters the digestive processes; and practically all of it reabsorbed through the intestinal wall, where it performs the equally important function of carrying in the digested foodstuffs. These and other instances of what Cannon calls "the conservative use of water in our bodies" involve essentially osmotic pressure relationships in which the concentration of sodium chloride plays an important part.

28. This passage implies that   28._____

    A. the contents of the alimentary canal are not to be considered within the body
    B. sodium chloride does not actually enter the body
    C. every particle of water ingested is used over and over again
    D. water can not be absorbed by the body unless it contains sodium chloride
    E. substances can pass through the intestinal wall in only one direction

29. According to this passage, which of the following processes requires MOST water? The

    A. absorption of digested foods
    B. secretion of gastric juice
    C. secretion of saliva
    D. production of bile
    E. concentration of sodium chloride solution

30. A body fluid that is NOT saline is

    A. blood
    B. urine
    C. bile
    D. gastric juice
    E. saliva

31. An organ that functions as a storage reservoir from which large quantities of water are reabsorbed into the body is the

    A. kidney
    B. liver
    C. large intestine
    D. mouth
    E. pancreas

32. Water is reabsorbed into the body by the process of

    A. secretion
    B. excretion
    C. digestion
    D. osmosis
    E. oxidation

33. Digested food enters the body PRINCIPALLY through the

    A. mouth
    B. liver
    C. villi
    D. pancreas
    E. stomach

34. The metallic element found in the blood in compound form and present there in larger quantities than any other metallic element is

    A. iron
    B. calcium
    C. magnesium
    D. chlorine
    E. sodium

35. An organ that removes water from the body and prevents its reabsorption for use in the body processes is the

    A. pancreas
    B. liver
    C. small intestine
    D. lungs
    E. large intestine

36. In which of the following processes is sodium chloride removed MOST rapidly from the body?

    A. Digestion
    B. Breathing
    C. Oxidation
    D. Respiration
    E. Perspiration

37. Which of the following liquids would pass from the alimentary canal into the blood MOST rapidly?

    A. A dilute solution of sodium chloride in water
    B. Gastric juice
    C. A concentrated solution of sodium chloride in water
    D. Digested food
    E. Distilled water

38. The reason why it is unsafe to drink ocean water even under conditions of extreme thirst is that it

    A. would reduce the salinity of the blood to a dangerous level
    B. contains dangerous disease germs
    C. contains poisonous salts

D. would greatly increase the salinity of the blood
E. would cause salt crystals to form in the blood stream

39. When air rises from the surface of the earth, it

    A. contracts and grows warmer
    B. contracts and grows cooler
    C. expands and grows warmer
    D. expands and grows cooler
    E. increases in density

40. The approach of a warm front is USUALLY attended by

    A. cumulus clouds and thunderstorms
    B. stratus clouds and moist air
    C. brisk, northwesterly winds
    D. a rising barometer
    E. clear, dry air

41. A type of air mass that originates in the United States is the

    A. polar continental
    B. polar Atlantic
    C. polar Pacific
    D. tropical gulf
    E. tropical continental

42. The prevailing winds in New York State are

    A. anticyclones
    B. westerlies
    C. trade winds
    D. easterlies
    E. cyclones

43. A meteorologist in New York State would NOT regard as important for weather prediction

    A. the type of clouds in the sky
    B. the weather in Canada, Mexico and Cuba
    C. a change of direction of the wind
    D. a change in the phase of the moon
    E. a change of temperature of the air

44. Which of the following would be of SLIGHT interest to present-day meteorologists?

    A. Winds
    B. Clouds
    C. Precipitation
    D. Fronts
    E. Meteors

45. A cyclonic condition is developing rapidly and is traveling north north-east accompanied by rains and rising temperature. Which of the following important factors was omitted from this report?

    A. Barometric tendency
    B. Precipitation
    C. Storm's path
    D. Temperature tendency
    E. Wind velocity

46. Granite is a rock that was made by

    A. the cementation of sediments
    B. fire in the depths of the earth
    C. the compression of sediments
    D. the cooling of lava deep beneath the earth's surface
    E. the cooling of lava from volcanoes

47. The rate of erosion of cultivated fields with moderate slope can be reduced by   47.____

    A. leaving the fields unplanted every other year
    B. planting such crops as corn and potatoes
    C. planting strips of grass up and down the slope
    D. plowing across the slope
    E. planting firm sod around the fields

48. The PRINCIPAL reason for adding agricultural lime to soils is to   48.____

    A. improve the texture of the soil
    B. help to preserve the supply of humus
    C. supply materials to stiffen the stems of plants
    D. decrease the acidity of the soil
    E. supply calcium to the growing plants

49. The three elements found MOST commonly in commercial fertilizers are   49.____

    A. calcium, phosphorus, iron
    B. nitrogen, phosphorus, potassium
    C. phosphorus, nitrogen, sulfur
    D. calcium, potassium, iron
    E. magnesium, iron, calcium

50. When carbohydrates decompose in the soil, the end products are   50.____

    A. nitrates and carbon dioxide
    B. carbon dioxide and water
    C. nitrates and nitrites
    D. carbon monoxide and hydrogen
    E. nitrates and water

KEY (CORRECT ANSWERS)

1. B	11. E	21. E	31. C	41. D
2. B	12. A	22. D	32. D	42. B
3. B	13. C	23. A	33. C	43. D
4. A	14. D	24. D	34. E	44. E
5. B	15. B	25. B	35. D	45. E
6. E	16. B	26. C	36. E	46. D
7. D	17. B	27. D	37. E	47. D
8. D	18. D	28. A	38. D	48. D
9. C	19. C	29. A	39. D	49. B
10. B	20. C	30. D	40. B	50. B

TEST 3

DIRECTIONS: Each question or incomplete statement is followed by several suggested answers or completions. Select the one that BEST answers the question or completes the statement. *PRINT THE LETTER OF THE CORRECT ANSWER IN THE SPACE AT THE RIGHT.*

Questions 1-7.

DIRECTIONS: Questions 1 through 7 refer to the diagram that follows. Base your choice on the information given in the selection and on your own understanding of science.

1. Which of the following is a common insecticide used by gardeners?

    A. Alcohol B. Phosphoric acid C. Wood ashes
    D. Rotenone E. Nitrate of soda

2. The fruit of plants such as the tomato, cucumber, cherry and bean develops from the

    A. receptacle and closely associated stem
    B. petals and closely associated sepals
    C. stem and closely associated parts
    D. ovary and closely associated parts
    E. stamen and closely associated parts

3. The part of the toadstool or mushroom plant that is seen growing above the ground is of PRIMARY use in

    A. reproduction B. transpiration C. food storage
    D. digestion E. photosynthesis

4. Mendel crossed purebred, tall pea plants with dwarf pea plants. The offspring were all tall plants. When he crossed these tall plants with each other, the resulting offsprings were

    A. all tall
    B. about three-fourths tall and one-fourth dwarf
    C. about half tall and half dwarf
    D. about one-fourth tall and three-fourths dwarf
    E. nearly all dwarf

5. A plant cell can BEST be considered a(n)

    A. surface B. volume C. rectangle D. circle E. area

6. The stage in its life cycle in which the clothes moth does MOST harm to woolens is the

    A. blastula B. egg C. larva D. pupa E. adult

7. Lights in chicken houses stimulate egg production by

    A. stimulating in the chickens certain glands that affect formation of egg shells
    B. keeping hens awake so they can lay more eggs
    C. causing hens to consume more food, which results in more eggs produced
    D. increasing the vitamin D content in the hens
    E. controlling the ionization of the air

8. Which of the diseases listed below is caused by animal organism? 8.____

   A. Rickets   B. Hay fever   C. Typhoid fever   D. Malaria
   E. Chickenpox

9. Which of the following is a communicable disease? 9.____

   A. Scurvy   B. Cancer   C. Goiter
   D. Rabies   E. Nephritis

10. Sulfa drugs are produced CHIEFLY 10.____

    A. from a common mold
    B. from glands obtained from animals
    C. by chemical synthesis
    D. by a common bacterium
    E. from the bark of a tree

11. The human body is composed MAINLY of 11.____

    A. nitrogen, phosphorus, calcium   B. potassium, nitrogen, oxygen
    C. calcium, iron, potassium   D. carbon, hydrogen, oxygen
    E. iron, calcium, hydrogen

12. The stomach normally contains 12.____

    A. some hydrochloric acid   B. some nitric acid
    C. some sulfuric acid   D. some bases but no acids
    E. neither acids nor bases

13. Many of the organic compounds containing nitrogen are called 13.____

    A. oils   B. sugars   C. fats   D. starches   E. proteins

14. Man's normal complement of teeth during adulthood is 14.____

    A. 24   B. 28   C. 32   D. 36   E. 40

15. Development of the first set of teeth is begun 15.____

    A. before birth   B. 12 months after birth
    C. 15 months after birth   D. at birth
    E. 6 months after birth

16. Bacteria enlarge the dentine canals by 16.____

    A. eating the walls
    B. allowing the entrance of saliva
    C. stopping the flow of the lymph
    D. movements up and down the canals
    E. producing compounds that attack the walls

17. An experiment was conducted to determine the effect on dental health of introducing a chemical into the drinking water. This chemical contained 17.____

    A. magnetium   B. iodine   C. fluorine
    D. calcium   E. iron

18. Rheumatism is sometimes attributed to an abscessed tooth. The abscess may cause the condition by   18.____

    A. allowing bacteria to enter the blood
    B. pressing on a nerve
    C. allowing the lymph to escape
    D. producing poisons, which are absorbed
    E. using nutrients that should go to other parts of the body

19. An enzyme in gastric juice which aids in digesting protein is   19.____

    A. ptyalin   B. trypsin   C. amylopsin   D. pepsin
    E. maltase

20. To help prevent scarlet fever from spreading from one member of a household to other members, it is MOST essential to   20.____

    A. get a trained nurse
    B. keep the room temperature at 72° F
    C. have attendants change outer clothing upon leaving the sickroom
    D. remove all unnecessary accessories from the sickroom
    E. keep the patient in a warm room with windows closed

21. Of the following possible effects of an automobile accident, the condition that requires MOST immediate treatment is   21.____

    A. spinal dislocation   B. shock
    C. concussion   D. tetanus
    E. arterial bleeding

22. When rags used by painters to wipe up linseed oil catch fire spontaneously, it is because   22.____

    A. paint oil gives off oxygen readily
    B. paint oil oxidizes
    C. the cloth reduces the oxygen in the paint oil
    D. the paint oil reduces the oxygen in the cloth
    E. paint oil and cloth unite chemically

23. Alum is added to water in many municipal water systems to   23.____

    A. reduce unwanted dissolved gases
    B. remove objectionable flavors
    C. kill harmful bacteria
    D. soften the water
    E. remove sediment

24. Soap aids in cleaning because its action on greases and oils is to   24.____

    A. reduce them   B. oxidize them   C. emulsify them
    D. dissolve them   E. precipitate them

25. When a candle burns, the CHIEF products are   25.____

    A. carbon dioxide and carbon monoxide
    B. carbon dioxide and nitrogen
    C. carbon monoxide and nitrogen

D. carbon monoxide and water
E. carbon dioxide and water

26. Iron is removed from its oxide ores by

    A. roasting the ore
    B. reducing the ore with carbon
    C. oxidizing the ore with a blast of air
    D. melting the ore, thus allowing the iron to escape
    E. making a slag to absorb the oxides of the iron

27. A mineral much used as a source of iron is

    A. galena   B. hematite   C. franklinite   D. chromite
    E. halite

28. A gas generally used in incandescent lamps to increase their operating efficiency is

    A. freon   B. oxygen   C. neon   D. argon   E. chlorine

29. The meter whose readings are used in determining the amount of the monthly household electric bill measures

    A. voltage   B. electrical energy   C. power
    D. amperage   E. electrical resistance

30. Most household appliances using electric motors are made to operate on

    A. 110-volt alternating current   B. 110-volt direct current
    C. 32-volt direct current   D. 6-volt direct current
    E. 1 1/2-volt direct current

31. A bimetallic thermostat operates because

    A. metals expand when heated
    B. different metals expand at different rates when heated
    C. two metals will conduct electric currents at different rates
    D. a voltage is produced between the junctions of the two metals when one junction is heated
    E. different metals appear on different levels in the electromotive series

32. A transformer is used to change

    A. alternating current to direct current
    B. the voltage of alternating current
    C. the voltage of direct current
    D. the frequency of alternating current
    E. direct current to alternating current

33. One material much used for permanent magnets is

    A. steel   B. soft iron   C. copper   D. zinc   E. carbon

34. The surfaces of a thermos bottle are silvered to

    A. reduce convection
    B. reduce radiation
    C. reduce conduction
    D. keep out ultraviolet rays
    E. make cleaning easier

35. A temperature of 25° C is NEAREST to which of the following temperatures?

    A. 20° F   B. 40° F   C. 60° F   D. 80° F   E. 100° F

36. Ice floats because

    A. water becomes denser as it cools
    B. it contains so much air
    C. water expands when it freezes
    D. fish could not live in ponds if the ice sank to the bottom
    E. water expands as it cools from 4° C to 0° C

37. If a person facing a high cliff hears his echo 5 seconds after he shouts, the distance between the person and the cliff is about

    A. 1/4 mile   B. 1/2 mile   C. 3/4 mile
    D. 1 mile   E. 1 1/4 miles

38. The horizontal stabilizers of a plane are necessary to

    A. make the plane dive and climb
    B. make the plane bank on a turn
    C. keep the tail from bobbing up and down
    D. enable the pilot to turn right or left
    E. keep the plane from weaving from side to side

39. A good quality lumber for outside woodwork is

    A. basswood   B. hard maple   C. yellow birch
    D. white pine   E. red gumwood

40. Knots in lumber are caused by

    A. boring insects   B. branches   C. winter injury
    D. decay   E. unequal growth

41. On which of the following woods MUST a paste filler be used during the finishing process?

    A. Basswood   B. Maple   C. Oak   D. Redgum   E. Cedar

42. In what order should the dimension of boards be listed when ordering lumber from a mill?

    A. Length, width, thickness   B. Thickness, width, length
    C. Length, thickness, width   D. Width, length, thickness
    E. Width, thickness, length

43. The number of a wood screw indicates its

    A. number of threads per inch
    B. style of point
    C. length
    D. style of head
    E. diameter

44. Half-and-half solder is an alloy composed of

    A. lead and tin
    B. tin and copper
    C. tin and zinc
    D. lead and brass
    E. zinc and lead

45. The process used to make earthenware waterproof is known as

    A. glazing   B. finishing   C. molding   D. firing
    E. decorating

46. Molds for casting clay are made of

    A. plaster of paris   B. galvanized iron   C. tin
    D. wood   E. cardboard

47. A tool used to cut the thread in a nut is a

    A. tap   B. die   C. reamer   D. drill   E. bolt

48. To draw vertical lines in drafting, one should use

    A. a T square   B. a rule   C. a triangle
    D. two triangles   E. a T square and triangle

49. The pica is a unit of measurement in

    A. ceramics   B. printing   C. toolmaking
    D. photography E. textile design

50. Of the following, the fiber that is MOST weakened by being wet is

    A. cotton   B. rayon   C. linen   D. silk   E. wool

KEY (CORRECT ANSWERS)

1. D	11. D	21. E	31. B	41. C
2. D	12. A	22. B	32. B	42. B
3. A	13. E	23. E	33. A	43. E
4. B	14. C	24. C	34. B	44. A
5. B	15. A	25. E	35. D	45. A
6. C	16. E	26. B	36. C	46. A
7. A	17. C	27. B	37. B	47. A
8. D	18. D	28. D	38. C	48. E
9. D	19. D	29. B	39. D	49. B
10. C	20. C	30. A	40. B	50. E

TEST 4

DIRECTIONS: Each question or incomplete statement is followed by several suggested answers or completions. Select the one that BEST answers the question or completes the statement. *PRINT THE LETTER OF THE CORRECT ANSWER IN THE SPACE AT THE RIGHT.*

Questions 1-7.

DIRECTIONS: Questions 1 through 7 refer to the diagram that follows. Base your choice on the information given in the selection and on your own understanding of science.

1. The revolving part of an automobile generator is the
   A. cam   B. slipring   C. armature   D. coil   E. brushes

2. A by-product of soap manufacture is
   A. acetone   B. benzine   C. fat   D. glycerin   E. lye

3. When a certain quantity of water is decomposed by electrolysis, 60 cubic centimeters of hydrogen are produced. The number of cubic centimeters of oxygen obtained is
   A. 20   B. 30   C. 60   D. 120   E. 180

4. Of the following, the BEST conductor of heat is
   A. asbestos   B. brass   C. copper   D. glass   E. iron

5. The temperature of the air falls during the night, PRINCIPALLY because the earth loses heat by
   A. conduction   B. convection   C. insolation   D. radiation   E. reflection

6. The relative humidity of the air when dew forms is
   A. 10%   B. 25%   C. 50%   D. 75%   E. 100%

7. The low-pressure areas that bring stormy weather to New York State USUALLY come from the
   A. east   B. north   C. south   D. southeast   E. west

8. An instrument used to determine latitude is the
   A. altimeter   B. barometer   C. isobar   D. hydrometer   E. sextant

9. The earth rotates 30 degrees in
   A. 1 hour   B. 2 hours   C. 3 hours   D. 4 hours   E. 5 hours

10. The earth is NEAREST the sun in the month of
    A. January   B. March   C. June   D. September   E. December

11. All parts of the earth have 12 hours of daylight on

    A. December 21st   B. June 21st   C. July 21st
    D. March 21st   E. November 21st

11.____

12. Eastern Double Daylight Saving Time corresponds to the standard time at the meridian of west longitude numbered

    A. 60   B. 75   C. 90   D. 105   E. 120

12.____

13. We see one-half of the lighted portion of the moon at the

    A. first quarter   B. full moon   C. new crescent
    D. new moon   E. old crescent

13.____

14. A planet whose orbit is between the sun and the orbit of the earth is

    A. Jupiter   B. Mars   C. Pluto   D. Saturn   E. Venus

14.____

15. The changing position of the stars during the night is MAINLY the result of the

    A. inclination of the earth's axis
    B. rotation of the earth
    C. rotation of the stars
    D. revolution of the earth
    E. revolution of the stars

15.____

16. The gravational force of the moon is exerted

    A. only upon the side of the earth nearest the moon
    B. only upon the point on the earth nearest the moon
    C. upon the center of the earth only
    D. upon the entire earth
    E. upon the water surfaces of the earth but not upon the land surfaces

16.____

17. The work done by tides is gradually slowing down the earth's period of rotation. It is, therefore, reasonable to predict that, millions of years from now,

    A. the earth will be farther away from the moon than now
    B. the frequency of tides will be greater than now
    C. days will be shorter than they are now
    D. phases of the moon will change more rapidly than now
    E. lunar months will be longer than they are now

17.____

18. The earth's gravitational attraction is GREATEST at

    A. the North Pole
    B. the equator
    C. a point on the earth's surface directly under the moon
    D. a point on the earth's surface exactly opposite the moon
    E. a point 10 miles above the earth's surface, whatever the position of the moon

18.____

19. The part of the seed that develops into the young plant is called the

    A. cotyledon   B. embryo   C. hilum
    D. micropyle   E. testa

19.____

20. The union of the sperm and the egg cells of flowers is called

    A. fertilization   B. maturation   C. parthenogenesis
    D. pollination   E. sporulation

21. An insect that eats no food during the adult stage is the

    A. grasshopper   B. bumblebee   C. cricket
    D. Japanese beetle E. Cecropia moth

22. The image of an object is formed in the eye on the

    A. cornea   B. pupil   C. iris   D. lens   E. retina

23. An organ located above the diaphragm is the

    A. stomach   B. liver   C. heart   D. pancreas   E. spleen

24. Of the following, an organ that is NOT connected with the alimentary canal is the

    A. pancreas   B. liver   C. kidney   D. salivary glands
    E. appendix

25. The ptyalin in saliva is a(n)

    A. auxin   B. chalone   C. enzyme   D. hormone   E. vitamin

26. Glucose is stored in the liver and muscles in the form of

    A. glycogen   B. levulose   C. glycocoll   D. fat   E. dextrose

27. A substance that is readily absorbed through the walls of the stomach is

    A. starch   B. sugar   C. alcohol   D. amino acids
    E. ascorbic acid

28. The poisonouc character of carbon monoxide is due to its tendency to unite chemically with

    A. water   B. synovial fluid   C. cerebrospinal fluid
    D. hemoglobin   E. gastric juice

29. A nutrient that contains nitrogen is

    A. fat   B. protein   C. starch   D. sugar   E. water

30. A substance that is a carbohydrate is

    A. glutenin   B. stearin   C. palmitin
    D. gliadin   E. dextrin

31. A food that contains no vitamins is

    A. white potato   B. cane sugar   C. dried beans
    D. lard   E. white bread

32. Of the following, the vegetable that contains the HIGHEST percentage of protein is the

    A. tomato   B. cabbage   C. carrot
    D. lima bean   E. head lettuce

33. When bread is toasted, much of the starch is changed to

    A. dextrose   B. maltose   C. maltase   D. dextrin   E. biotin

34. A preparation of dead or weakened bacilli used for developing immunity to a disease is called a(n)

    A. vaccine   B. virus   C. culture medium   D. antitoxin   E. immune serum

35. A disease caused by a virus is

    A. anthrax   B. dysentery   C. scurvy   D. smallpox   E. tuberculosis

36. Of the following diseases, the one that is NOT caused by a filtrable virus is

    A. syphilis   B. yellow fever   C. measles   D. mumps   E. infantile paralysis

37. A disease that may be prevented by the use of a vaccine is

    A. tuberculosis   B. poliomyelitis   C. rabies   D. gonorrhea   E. dementia praecox

38. Immunity to diphtheria may be detected by the use of

    A. the Dick test   B. the Schick test   C. arsphenamine   D. acetylsalicylate   E. the Wassermann test

39. A substance used to treat malaria is

    A. sodium perborate   B. atabrine   C. penicillin   D. salol   E. sulfathiazole

40. Silicosis may result from prolonged exposure to

    A. radium   B. poisonous gases   C. ragweed pollen   D. metallic dusts   E. rock dusts

41. Trichinosis is a disease contracted MOSTLY from

    A. chicken   B. beef   C. pork   D. lamb   E. fish

42. Delay in the removal of an inflamed appendix sometimes results in

    A. peritonitis   B. gingivitis   C. gastritis   D. phlebitis   E. meningitis

43. Blowing the nose hard during a cold is dangerous, PRIMARILY because the

    A. back pressure may force bacteria into the eustachian tubes
    B. lining of the nose may be damaged
    C. lungs may be overworked
    D. flow of mucus may be stopped
    E. nasal sinuses may burst

44. Mouth washes 44.____

    A. kill whatever germs are present in the mouth
    B. are effective in preventing diseases
    C. prevent germs from entering the mouth
    D. prevent the growth of germs in the mouth
    E. are of little or no health value

45. Dissolved impurities can be separated from water by 45.____

    A. aeration   B. chlorination   C. distillation
    D. filtration   E. settling

46. Lake or river water may be made safe to drink by letting the water stand one-half hour 46.____
    after adding

    A. two drops of tincture of iodine per quart
    B. one pint of ethyl alcohol per gallon
    C. one drop of sulfuric acid per quart
    D. 10 grams of table salt per gallon
    E. one aspirin tablet per pint

47. A dermatologist is a physician who specializes in the care of 47.____

    A. children   B. the hair   C. the skin   D. old people
    E. chronic diseases

48. Schizophrenia is a 48.____

    A. dangerous drug
    B. mental disorder
    C. dye used in staining tissue cells
    D. communicable disease
    E. hormone

49. An example of rationalization is 49.____

    A. building up an exaggerated tendency that is opposite to the unconscious wish
    B. justifying failure by means of arguments that excuse it
    C. complete forgetting of unfavorable experiences
    D. identifying oneself with a hero of some sort
    E. gratifying wishes by assuming an illness

50. The nutrient provided by milk and milk products that is MOST difficult to obtain from other 50.____
    common foods is

    A. vitamin A   B. calcium   C. complete protein
    D. niacin   E. vitamin C

KEY (CORRECT ANSWERS)

1. C	11. D	21. E	31. B	41. C
2. D	12. A	22. E	32. D	42. A
3. B	13. A	23. C	33. D	43. A
4. C	14. E	24. C	34. A	44. E
5. D	15. B	25. C	35. D	45. C
6. E	16. D	26. A	36. A	46. A
7. E	17. A	27. C	37. C	47. C
8. E	18. A	28. D	38. B	48. B
9. B	19. B	29. B	39. B	49. B
10. A	20. A	30. E	40. E	50. B

TEST 5

DIRECTIONS: Each question or incomplete statement is followed by several suggested answers or completions. Select the one that BEST answers the question or completes the statement. *PRINT THE LETTER OF THE CORRECT ANSWER IN THE SPACE AT THE RIGHT.*

Questions 1-7.

DIRECTIONS: Questions 1 through 7 refer to the passage that follows. Base your choice on the information in the passage *and on your own knowledge of science.*

    In the days of sailing ships, when voyages were long and uncertain, provisions for many months were stored without refrigeration in the holds of the ships. Naturally no fresh or perishable foods could be included. Toward the end of particularly long voyages the crews of such ships became ill and often many died from scurvy. Many men, both scientific and otherwise, tried to devise a cure for scurvy. Among the latter was John Hall, a son-in-law of William Shakespeare, who cured some cases of scurvy by administering a sour brew made from scurvy grass and watercress.
    The next step was the suggestion of William Harvey that scurvy could be prevented by giving the men lemon juice. He thought that the beneficial substance was the acid contained in the fruit.
    The third step was taken by Dr. James Lind, an English naval surgeon, who performed the following experiment with 12 sailors all of whom were sick with scurvy: Each was given the same diet, except that four of the men received small amounts of dilute sulfuric acid, four others were given vinegar and the remaining four were given lemons. Only those who received the fruit recovered.

1. Credit for solving the problem described above belongs to

   A. *HALL*, because he first devised a cure for scurvy
   B. *HARVEY*, because he first proposed a solution of the problem
   C. *LIND*, because he proved the solution by means of an experiment
   D. *both HARVEY and LIND*, because they found that lemons are more effective than scurvy grass or watercress
   E. *all three men*, because each made some contribution

2. A good substitute for lemons in the treatment of scurvy is

   A. fresh eggs   B. tomato juice   C. cod-liver oil
   D. liver   E. whole-wheat bread

3. The number of control groups that Dr. Lind used in his experiment was

   A. one   B. two   C. three   D. four   E. none

4. A substance that will turn blue litmus red is

   A. aniline   B. lye   C. ice   D. vinegar   E. table salt

5. The hypothesis tested by Lind was:

   A. Lemons contain some substance not present in vinegar.
   B. Citric acid is the most effective treatment for scurvy.
   C. Lemons contain some unknown acid that will cure scurvy.
   D. Some specific substance, rather than acids in general, is needed to cure scurvy.
   E. The substance needed to cure scurvy is found only in lemons.

6. A problem that Lind's experiment did NOT solve was:

   A. Will citric acid alone cure scurvy?
   B. Will lemons cure scurvy?
   C. Will either sulfuric acid or vinegar cure scurvy?
   D. Are all substances that contain acids equally effective as a treatment for scurvy?
   E. Are lemons more effective than either vinegar or sulfuric acid in the treatment of scurvy?

7. The PRIMARY purpose of a controlled scientific experiment is to

   A. get rid of superstitions
   B. prove a hypothesis is correct
   C. disprove a theory that is false
   D. determine whether a hypothesis is true or false
   E. discover new facts

Questions 8-15.

DIRECTIONS: Questions 8 through 15 refer to the passage that follows. Base your choice on the information in the passage and *on your own knowledge of science*.

Photosynthesis is a complex process with many intermediate steps. Ideas differ greatly as to the details of these steps, but the general nature of the process and its outcome are well established. Water, usually from the soil, is conducted through the xylem of root, stem and leaf to the chlorophyl-containing cells of a leaf. In consequence of the abundance of water within the latter cells, their walls are saturated with water. Carbon dioxide, diffusing from the air through the stomata and into the intercellular spaces of the leaf, comes into contact with the water in the walls of the cells, which adjoin the intercellular spaces. The carbon dioxide becomes dissolved in the water in these walls, and in solution diffuses through the walls and the plasma membranes into the cells. By the agency of chlorphyl in the chloroplasts of the cells, the energy of light is transformed into chemical energy. This chemical energy is used to decompose the carbon dioxide and water, and the products of their decomposition are recombined into a new compound. The compound first formed is successively built up into more and more complex substances until finally a sugar is produced.

8. The union of carbon dioxide and water to form starch results in an excess of

   A. hydrogen   B. carbon   C. oxygen
   D. carbon monoxide   E. hydrogen peroxide

9. Synthesis of carbohydrates takes place

   A. in the stomata
   B. in the intercellular spaces of leaves
   C. in the walls of plant cells
   D. within the plasma membranes of plant cells
   E. within plant cells that contain chloroplasts

10. In the process of photosynthesis, chlorophyl acts as a   10._____

    A. carbohydrate   B. source of carbon dioxide
    C. catalyst   D. source of chemical energy
    E. plasma membrane

11. In which of the following places are there the GREATEST number of hours in which photosynthesis can take place during the month of December?   11._____

    A. Buenos Aires, Argentina   B. Caracas, Venezuela
    C. Fairbanks, Alaska   D. Quito, Ecuador
    E. Calcutta, India

12. During photosynthesis, molecules of carbon dioxide enter the stomata of leaves because   12._____

    A. the molecules are already in motion
    B. they are forced through the stomata by the sun's rays
    C. chlorophyl attracts them
    D. a chemical change takes place in the stomata
    E. oxygen passes out through the stomata

13. Besides food manufacture, another useful result of photosynthesis is that it   13._____

    A. aids in removing poisonous gases from the air
    B. helps to maintain the existing proportion of gases in the air
    C. changes complex compounds into simpler compounds
    D. changes certain waste products into hydrocarbons
    E. changes chlorophyl into useful substances

14. A process that is ALMOST the exact reverse of photosynthesis is the   14._____

    A. rusting of iron   B. burning of wood
    C. digestion of starch   D. ripening of fruit
    E. storage of food in seeds

15. The leaf of the tomato plant will be unable to carry on photosynthesis if the   15._____

    A. upper surface of the leaf is coated with vaseline
    B. upper surface of the leaf is coated with lampblack
    C. lower surface of the leaf is coated with lard
    D. leaf is placed in an atmosphere of pure carbon dioxide
    E. entire leaf is coated with lime

Questions 16-24.

DIRECTIONS: Questions 16 through 24 refer to the passage that follows. Base your choice on the information in the passage and *on your own knowledge of science*.

The British pressure suit was made in two pieces and joined around the middle in contrast to the other suits, which were one-piece suits with a removable helmet. Oxygen was supplied through a tube, and a container of soda lime absorbed carbon dioxide and water vapor. The pressure was adjusted to a maximum of 2 1/2 pounds per square inch (130 millimeters) higher than the surrounding air. Since pure oxygen was used, this produced a partial pressure of 130 millimeters, which is sufficient to sustain the flier at any altitude.

Using this pressure suit, the British established a world's altitude record of 49,944 feet in 1936 and succeeded in raising it to 53,937 feet the following year. The pressure suit is a compromise solution to the altitude problem. Full sea-level pressure cannot be maintained, as the suit would be so rigid that the flier could not move arms or legs. Hence a pressure one-third to one-fifth that of sea level has been used. Because of these lower pressures, oxygen has been used to raise the partial pressure of alveolar oxygen to normal.

16. The MAIN constituent of air NOT admitted to the pressure suit described was

    A. oxygen   B. nitrogen   C. water vapor
    D. carbon dioxide   E. hydrogen

17. The pressure within the suit exceeded that of the surrounding air by an amount equal to 130 millimeters of

    A. mercury   B. water   C. air
    D. oxygen   E. carbon dioxide

18. The normal atmospheric pressure at sea level is

    A. 130 mm   B. 250 mm   C. 760 mm   D. 1000 mm   E. 1300 mm

19. The water vapor that was absorbed by the soda lime came from

    A. condensation
    B. the union of oxygen with carbon dioxide
    C. body metabolism
    D. the air within the pressure suit
    E. water particles in the upper air

20. The HIGHEST altitude that has been reached with the British pressure suit is about

    A. 130 miles   B. 2 1/2 miles   C. 6 miles   D. 10 miles
    E. 5 miles

21. If the pressure suit should develop a leak, the

    A. oxygen supply would be cut off
    B. suit would fill up with air instead of oxygen
    C. pressure within the suit would drop to zero
    D. pressure within the suit would drop to that of the surrounding air
    E. suit would become so rigid that the flier would be unable to move arms or legs

22. The reason why oxygen helmets are unsatisfactory for use in efforts to set higher altitude records is that

    A. it is impossible to maintain a tight enough fit at the neck
    B. oxygen helmets are too heavy
    C. they do not conserve the heat of the body as pressure suits do

D. if a parachute jump becomes necessary, it cannot be made while such a helmet is being worn
E. oxygen helmets are too rigid

23. The pressure suit is termed a compromise solution because

    A. it is not adequate for stratosphere flying
    B. aviators cannot stand sea-level pressure at high altitudes
    C. some suits are made in two pieces, others in one
    D. other factors than maintenance of pressure have to be accommodated
    E. full atmospheric pressure cannot be maintained at high altitudes

24. The passage implies that

    A. the air pressure at 49,944 feet is approximately the same as it is at 53,937 feet
    B. pressure cabin planes are not practical at extremely high altitudes
    C. a flier's oxygen requirement is approximately the same at high altitudes as it is at sea level
    D. one-piece pressure suits with removable helmets are unsafe
    E. a normal alveolar oxygen supply is maintained if the air pressure is between one-third and one-fifth that of sea level

25. If two 100-lb forces act concurrently so that their resultant is 50 lbs., the angle between them is which one of the following?

    A. Acute   B. Right   C. Obtuse   D. Straight   E. Oblique

26. The frequency of vibration of a string varies

    A. directly as the length
    B. directly as the square root of the tension
    C. inversely as the weight per unit length
    D. directly as the square root of the length
    E. directly as the length and inversely as the square foot of the tension

27. A 40 lb. force acting at an angle of 30° with a lever produces the same moment as a second force applied perpendicularly at the same point. The magnitude of this second force (in pounds) is

    A. 20   B. 35   C. 60   D. 80   E. 100

28. Assume that a simple pendulum has a period of one second. If the mass of the bob is doubled, and the length of the string is quadrupled, the new period (in seconds) is

    A. one   B. two   C. four   D. eight   E. sixteen

29. A given mass of an ideal gas is heated isothermally until it has a volume of 200 cm . If initially the gas had a volume of 100 cm^3 at a gauge pressure of 15 lb/in^2, the final guage pressure (in pounds per square inch) will be CLOSEST to which one of the following?

    A. zero   B. 7.5   C. 15   D. 30   E. 60

30. A pulley with a mechanical advantage of two is used to lift a 500 lb. weight 20 ft. The potential energy of the weight (in ft.lb) increased

   A. 500   B. 5,000   C. 10,000   D. 20,000   E. 40,000

31. Of the following, the natural process which might require an energy input of about 10^{24} ergs/hour is

   A. the glow of a firefly
   B. a hurricane
   C. a bird's flight
   D. insolation per square foot at the equator
   E. an earthquake

32. If the molecules in a cylinder of oxygen and those in a cylinder of hydrogen have the same average speed, then

   A. both gases have the same temperature
   B. both gases have the same pressure
   C. the hydrogen has the higher temperature
   D. the oxygen has the higher temperature
   E. the hydrogen has the higher temperature when the oxygen has the lower temperature

33. Of the following, which condition exists in a perfectly inelastic collision?

   A. Neither momentum nor kinetic energy are conserved
   B. Both momentum and kinetic energy are conserved
   C. Momentum is conserved, but not kinetic energy
   D. Kinetic energy is conserved, but not momentum
   E. There is no relationship between momentum and kinetic energy

34. A simple series circuit consists of a cell, an ammeter, and a rheostat of resistance R. The ammeter reads 5 amps. When the resistance of the rheostat is increased by 2 ohms, the ammeter reading drops to 4 amps. The original resistance (in ohms) of the rheostat R is

   A. 2.5   B. 4.0   C. 8.0   D. 10.0   E. 12.0

35. A simple steam engine receives steam from the boiler at 180° C and exhausts directly into the air at 100° C. The upper limit of its thermal efficiency (in percent) is CLOSEST to which one of the following?

   A. 17.6   B. 28.0   C. 35.5   D. 80.0   E. 92.6

36. Two lamps need 50V and 2 amp each in order to operate at a desired brilliancy. If they are to be connected in series across a 120V line, the resistance (in ohms) of the rheostat that must be placed in series with the lamps needs to be

   A. 4   B. 10   C. 20   D. 100   E. 200

37. As the photon is a quantum in electromagnetic field theory, which one of the following is considered to be the quantum in the nuclear field?

   A. Neutrino   B. Electron   C. Meson   D. Neutron
   E. None of them

38. A 5 diopter lens has a focal length (in cm) CLOSEST to which one of the following?   38._____

    A. 1/5   B. 5   C. 20   D. 50   E. 100

39. The infra-red spectrometer has a prism that is GENERALLY made of which one of the following?   39._____

    A. Quartz   B. Glass   C. Sodium chloride
    D. Carbon disulfide   E. Sodium disulfide

40. When an electron moves with a speed equal to 4/5 that of light, the ratio of its mass to its rest mass is which one of the following?   40._____

    A. 5/4   B. 5/3   C. 25/9   D. 25/16   E. 4/5

41. A pulley on an electric motor turns clockwise. A crossed belt turns a much larger pulley on a feed grinder. The pulley on the feed grinder turns   41._____

    A. clockwise and slower than the one on the motor
    B. counterclockwise and slower than the one on the motor
    C. clockwise and faster than the one on the motor
    D. counterclockwise and faster than the one on the motor
    E. clockwise and at the same speed as the one on the motor

42. The sprocket wheels and chain of a bicycle increase the   42._____

    A. power of the rider
    B. force applied to the rear wheel
    C. force applied to the road
    D. speed of the rear wheel
    E. energy output of the rider

43. Soda pop rises along a soda straw into one's mouth because   43._____

    A. nature abhors a vacuum
    B. there is capillary action in the straw
    C. the air pressure on the pop is greater than the pressure in one's mouth
    D. the vacuum in one's mouth pulls up the pop
    E. the carbon dioxide pressure in the pop forces it upwards

44. Which of the following principles BEST explains the propulsion of a jet plane?   44._____

    A. Every action has an equal and opposite reaction
    B. Energy can be neither created nor destroyed
    C. Every effect has a cause
    D. If pressure is applied to a confined gas, the volume of the gas will decrease
    E. Compression of a gas produces heat

45. To make an airplane bank on a left turn, the left   45._____

    A. elevator is raised and the right elevator is lowered
    B. pedal is pushed and the right pedal is pulled
    C. aileron is raised and the right aileron is lowered
    D. stabilizer is raised and the right stabilizer is lowered
    E. wing is tilted upward and the right wing is tilted downward

46. A ship entering a fresh-water river from the ocean will sink deeper because   46.____

   A. salt water has greater viscosity than fresh water
   B. salt holds objects up
   C. a cubic foot of salt water weighs more than a cubic foot of fresh water
   D. surface tension is greater in the river
   E. oceans are deeper

47. The fuel in the cylinder of a Diesel engine is ignited by   47.____

   A. an electric spark   B. a pilot light   C. the injector
   D. a supercharger   E. the heat of compression

48. A three-element vacuum tube in an electric circuit   48.____

   A. generates signals of increased voltage
   B. amplifies the grid bias
   C. controls the electron flow in the circuit
   D. rectifies the B-battery output
   E. increases the signal frequency

49. Some highways are lighted at night by lamps that produce a golden-yellow light. This color is due to the passage of electricity through the vapor of   49.____

   A. argon   B. helium   C. mercury   D. nitrogen   E. sodium

50. A fluorescent lamp produces light by the   50.____

   A. ionization of the Heaviside layer
   B. glowing of an incandescent filament
   C. production of X-rays
   D. action of infrared rays, which heat the glass
   E. action of ultraviolet rays on a mineral coating on the glass

---

KEY (CORRECT ANSWERS)

1. E	11. A	21. D	31. B	41. B
2. B	12. A	22. D	32. D	42. D
3. B	13. B	23. E	33. C	43. C
4. D	14. B	24. C	34. C	44. A
5. D	15. C	25. C	35. A	45. C
6. A	16. B	26. B	36. B	46. C
7. D	17. A	27. A	37. C	47. E
8. C	18. C	28. B	38. C	48. C
9. E	19. C	29. A	39. C	49. E
10. C	20. D	30. C	40. B	50. E

EXAMINATION SECTION
TEST 1

DIRECTIONS: Each question or incomplete statement is followed by several suggested answers or completions. Select the one that BEST answers the question or completes the statement. *PRINT THE LETTER OF THE CORRECT ANSWER IN THE SPACE AT THE RIGHT.*

1. An investigator uses Forms A, B, and C in filling out his investigation reports. He uses Form B five times as often as Form A, and he uses Form C three times as often as Form B.
   If the total number of all forms used by the investigator in a month equal 735, how many times was Form B used?
   A. 150   B. 175   C. 205   D. 235

   1.____

2. Of all the investigators in one agency, 25% work in a particular building. Of these, 12% have desks on the 14th floor.
   What percentage of the investigators work in this building but do NOT have desks on the 14th floor?
   A. 12%   B. 13%   C. 22%   D. 23%

   2.____

3. An investigator is given two reports to read. Report P is 160 pages long and takes the investigator 3 hours and 20 minutes to read.
   If Report S is 254 pages long and the investigator reads it at the same rate as he reads Report P, how long will it take him to read Report S? ____ hours ____ minutes.
   A. 4; 15   B. 4; 50   C. 5; 10   D. 5; 30

   3.____

4. A team of 6 investigators was assigned to interview 234 people.
   If half the investigators conduct twice as many interviews as the other half, and the slow group interviews 12 persons a day, how many days would it take to complete this assignment? ____ days.
   A. 4½   B. 5   C. 6   D. 6½

   4.____

5. The investigators in one agency conduct an average of 12 interviews an hour from 10 A.M. to 12 noon and from 1 P.M. to 5 P.M. daily. The director of his agency knows from past experience that 20% of those called in to be interviewed are unable to keep the appointments that were scheduled.
   If the director wants his staff to be kept occupied with interviews for the entire time period that has been set aside for this function, how many appointments should be scheduled for each day?
   A. 86   B. 90   C. 96   D. 101

   5.____

6. An investigator has a 430-page report to read. The first day, he is able to read 20 pages. The second day, he reads 10 pages more than the first day, and the third day, he reads 15 pages more than the second day.

   6.____

If, on the following days, he continues to read at the same rate as he was reading on the third day, he will complete the report on the _____ day.
A. 7th   B. 8th   C. 10th   D. 11th

7. The 36 investigators in an agency are each required to submit 25 investigation reports a week. These reports are filled out on a certain form, and only one copy of the form is needed per report.
Allowing 20% for waste, how many packages of 45 forms a piece should be ordered for each weekly period?
A. 15   B. 20   C. 25   D. 30

8. During the fiscal year, an investigative unit received $260 for stationery and telephone expenditures. It spent 43% for stationery and 1/3 of the balance for telephone service.
The amount of money that was left at the end of the fiscal year was MOST NEARLY
A. $49   B. $50   C. $99   D. $109

Questions 9-10.

DIRECTIONS: Questions 9 and 10 are to be answered SOLELY on the data given below.

Number of days absent per worker (sickness)	1	2	3	4	5	6	7	8 or Over
Number of Workers	96	45	16	3	1	0	1	0

Total Number of Workers: 500

9. The TOTAL number of man days lost due to illness in 2020 was
A. 137   B. 154   C. 162   D. 258

10. Of the 500 workers studied, the number who lost NO days due to sickness in 2020 was
A. 230   B. 298   C. 338   D. 372

Questions 11-13.

DIRECTIONS: Questions 11 through 13 are to be answered SOLELY on the basis of the following passage.

The rise of urban-industrial society has complicated the social arrangements needed to regulate contacts between people. As a consequence, there has been an unprecedented increase in the volume of laws and regulations designed to control individual conduct and to govern the relationship of the individual to others. In a century, there has been an eight-fold increase in the crimes for which one may be prosecuted.

For these offenses, the courts have the ultimate responsibility for redressing wrongs and convicting the guilty. The body of legal precepts gives the impression of an abstract and evenhanded dispensation of justice. Actually, the personnel of the agencies applying these precepts are faced with the difficulties of fitting abstract principles to highly variable situations emerging from the dynamics of everyday life. It is inevitable that discrepancies should exist between precept and practice.

The legal institutions serve as a framework for the social order by their slowness to respond to the caprices of transitory fad. This valuable contribution exacts a price in terms of the inflexibility of legal institutions in responding to new circumstances. This possibility is promoted by the changes in values and norms of the dynamic larger culture of which the legal precepts are a part.

11. According to the above passage, the increase in the number of laws and regulations during the twentieth century can be attributed to the
    A. complexity of modern industrial society
    B. increased seriousness of offenses committed
    C. growth of individualism
    D. anonymity of urban living

    11.____

12. According to the above passage, which of the following presents a problem to the staff of legal agencies? The
    A. need to eliminate the discrepancy between precept and practice
    B. necessity to apply abstract legal precepts to rapidly changing conditions
    C. responsibility for reducing the number of abstract legal principles
    D. responsibility for understanding offenses in terms of the real-life situations from which they emerge

    12.____

13. According to the above passage, it can be concluded that legal institutions affect social institutions by
    A. preventing change
    B. keeping pace with its norms and values
    C. changing its norms and values
    D. providing stability

    13.____

Questions 14-16.

DIRECTIONS: Questions 14 through 16 are to be answered SOLELY on the basis of information given in the following passage.

A personnel interviewer, selecting job applicants, may find that he reacts badly to some people even on first contact. This reaction cannot usually be explained by things that the interviewee has done or said. Most of us have had the experience of liking or disliking, of feeling comfortable and uncomfortable with people on first acquaintance, long before we have had a chance to make a conscious, rational decision about them. Often, too, our liking or disliking is transmitted to the other person by subtle processes such as gestures, posture, voice intonations, or choice of words. The point to be kept in mind is this: the relations between people are complex and occur at several levels, from the conscious to the unconscious. This is true whether the relationship is brief or long, formal or informal.

Some of the major dynamics of personality which operate on the unconscious level are projection, sublimation, rationalization, and repression. Encountering these for the first time, one is apt to think of them as representing pathological states. In the extreme, they undoubtedly are, but they exist so universally that we must consider them also to be parts of normal personality.

Without necessarily subscribing to any of the numerous theories of personality, it is possible to describe personality in terms of certain important aspects or elements. We are all aware of ourselves as thinking organisms.

This aspect of personality, the conscious part, is important for understanding human behavior, but it is not enough. Many find it hard to accept the notion that each person also has an unconscious. The existence of the unconscious is no longer a matter of debate. It is not possible to estimate at all precisely what proportion of our total psychological life is conscious, what proportion unconscious. Everyone who has studied the problem, however, agrees that consciousness is the smaller part of personality. Most of what we are and do is a result of unconscious processes. To ignore this is to risk mistakes.

14. The above passage suggests that an interviewer can be MOST effective if he
   A. learns how to determine other peoples' unconscious motivations
   B. learns how to repress his own unconsciously motivated mannerisms and behavior
   C. can keep others from feeling that he either likes or dislikes them
   D. gains an understanding of how the unconscious operates in himself and in others

15. It may be inferred from the above passage that the *subtle processes*, such as gestures, posture, voice intonation, or choice of words referred to in the first paragraph are USUALLY
   A. in the complete control of an expert investigator
   B. the determining factors in the friendships a person establishes
   C. controlled by a person's unconscious
   D. not capable of being consciously controlled

16. The above passage implies that various different personality theories are USUALLY
   A. so numerous and different as to be valueless to an investigator
   B. in basic agreement about the importance of the unconscious
   C. understood by the investigator who strives to be effective
   D. in agreement that personality factors such as projection and repression are pathological

Questions 17-19.

DIRECTIONS: Questions 17 through 19 are to be answered SOLELY on the basis of information contained in the following passage.

No matter how well the interrogator adjusts himself to the witness and how precisely he induces the witness to describe his observations, mistakes still can be made. The mistakes made by an experienced interrogator may be comparatively few, but as far as the witness is concerned, his path is full of pitfalls. Modern "witness psychology" has shown that even the most honest and trustworthy witnesses are apt to make grave mistakes in good faith. It is, therefore, necessary that the interrogator get an idea of the weak links in the testimony in order to check up on them in the event that something appears to be strange or not quite satisfactory.

Unfortunately, modern witness psychology does not yet offer any means of directly testing the credibility of testimony. It lacks precision and method, in spite of worthwhile attempts on the part of learned men. At the same time, witness psychology, through the gathering of many experience concerning the weaknesses of human testimony, has been of invaluable service. It shows clearly that only evidence of a technical nature has absolute value as proof.

Testimony may be separated into the following stages: (1) perception; (2) observation; (3) mind fixation of the observed occurrences, in which fantasy, association of ideas, and personal judgment participate; (4) expression in oral or written form, where the testimony is transferred from one witness to another or to the interrogator. Each of these stages offers innumerable possibilities for the distortion of testimony.

17. The above passage indicates that having witnesses talk to each other before testifying is a practice which is GENERALLY
    A. *desirable*, since the witnesses will be able to correct each other's errors in observation before testimony
    B. *undesirable*, since the witnesses will collaborate on one story to tell the investigator
    C. *undesirable*, since one witness may distort his testimony because of what another witness may erroneously say
    D. *desirable*, since witnesses will become aware of discrepancies in their own testimony and can point out the discrepancies to the investigator

18. According to the above passage, the one of the following which would be the MOST reliable for use as evidence would be the testimony of a
    A. handwriting expert about a signature on a forged check
    B. trained police officer about the identity of a criminal
    C. laboratory technician about an accident he has observed
    D. psychologist who has interviewed any witness who relate conflicting stories

19. Concerning the validity of evidence, it is clear from the above passage that
    A. only evidence of a technical nature is at all valuable
    B. the testimony of witnesses is so flawed that it is usually valueless
    C. an investigator, by knowing modern witness psychology, will usually be able to perceive mistaken testimony
    D. an investigator ought to expect mistakes in even the most reliable witness testimony

Questions 20-21.

DIRECTIONS: Questions 20 and 21 are to be answered SOLELY on the basis of information given in the following passage.

Since we generally assure informants that what they say is confidential, we are not free to tell one informant what the other has told us. Even if the informant says, "*I don't care who knows it; tell anybody you want to,*" we find it wise to treat the interview as confidential. An interviewer who relates to some informants what other informants have told him is likely to stir up anxiety and suspicion. Of course, the interviewer may be able to tell an informant what he has heard without revealing the source of his information. This may be perfectly appropriate where a story has wide currency so that an informant cannot infer the source of the information. But if an event is not widely known, the mere mention of it may reveal to one informant what another informant has said about the situation. How can the data be cross-checked in these circumstances.

20. The above passage IMPLIES that the anxiety and suspicion an interviewer may arouse by telling what has been learned in other interviews is due to the   20.____
    A. lack of trust the person interviewed may have in the interviewer's honesty
    B. troublesome nature of the material which the interviewer has learned in other interviews
    C. fact that the person interviewed may not believe that permission was given to repeat the information
    D. fear of the person interviewed that what he is telling the interviewer will be repeated

21. The above passage is MOST likely part of a longer passage dealing with   21.____
    A. ways to verify data gathered in interviews
    B. the various anxieties a person being interviewed may feel
    C. the notion that people sometimes say things they do not mean
    D. ways an interview can avoid seeming suspicious

Questions 22-23.

DIRECTIONS: Questions 22 and 23 are to be answered SOLELY on the basis of information given below.

The ability to interview rests not on any single trait, but on a vast complex of them. Habits, skills, techniques, and attitudes are all involved. Competence in interviewing is acquired only after careful and diligent study, prolonged practice (preferably under supervision), and a good bit of trial and error; for interviewing is not an exact science; it is an art. Like many other arts, however, it can and must draw on science in several of its aspects.

There is always a place for individual initiative, for imaginative innovations, and for new combinations of old approaches. The skilled interviewer cannot be bound by a set of rules. Likewise, there is not a set of rules which can guarantee to the novice that his interviewing will be successful. There are, however, some accepted, general guideposts which may help the beginner to avoid mistakes, learn how to conserve this efforts, and establish effective working relationships with interviewees; to accomplish, in short, what he sets out to do.

22. According to the above passage, rules and standard techniques for interviewing are   22.____
    A. helpful for the beginner, but useless for the experienced, innovative interviewer
    B. destructive of the innovation and initiative needed for a good interviewer
    C. useful for even the experienced interviewer who may, however, sometimes go beyond them
    D. the means by which nearly anybody can become an effective interviewer

23. According to the above passage, the one of the following which is a prerequisite to competent interviewing is   23.____
    A. avoid mistakes
    B. study and practice
    C. imaginative innovation
    D. natural aptitude

Questions 24-27.

DIRECTIONS: Questions 24 through 27 are to be answered SOLELY on the basis of information given in the following passage.

The question of what material is relevant is not as simple as it might seem. Frequently, material which seems irrelevant to the inexperienced has, because of the common tendency to disguise and distort and misplace one's feelings, considerable significance. It may be necessary to let the client "ramble on" for a while in order to clear the decks, as it were, so that he may get down to things that really are on his mind. On the other hand, with an already disturbed person, it may be important for the interviewer to know when to discourage further elaboration of upsetting material. This is especially the case where the worker would be unable to do anything about it. An inexperienced interviewer might, for instance, be intrigued with the bizarre elaboration of material that the psychotic produces, but further elaboration of this might encourage the client in his instability. A too random discussion may indicate that the interviewee is not certain in what areas the interviewer is prepared to help him, and he may be seeking some direction. Or again, satisfying though it may be for the interviewer to have the interviewee tell him intimate details, such revelations sometimes need to be checked or encouraged only in small doses. An interviewee who has "talked too much" often reveals subsequent anxiety. This is illustrated by the fact that frequently after a "confessional" interview, the interviewee surprises the interviewer by being withdrawn, inarticulate, or hostile, or by breaking the next appointment.

24. Sometimes a client may reveal certain personal information to an interviewer and subsequently may feel anxious about this revelation.   24.____
    If, during an interview, a client begins to discuss very personal matters, it would be BEST to
    A. tell the client, in no uncertain terms, that you're not interested in personal details
    B. ignore the client at this point
    C. encourage the client to elaborate further on the details
    D. inform the client that the information seems to be very personal

25. The author indicates that clients with severe psychological disturbances pose an especially difficult problem for the inexperienced interviewer.
The difficulty lies in the possibility of the client
    A. becoming physically violent and harming the interviewer
    B. rambling on for a while
    C. revealing irrelevant details which may be followed by cancelled appointments
    D. reverting to an unstable state as a result of interview material

26. An interviewer should be constantly alert to the possibility of obtaining clues from the client as to the problem areas.
According to the above passage, a client who discusses topics at random may be
    A. unsure of what problems the interviewer can provide help with
    B. reluctant to discuss intimate details
    C. trying to impress the interviewer with his knowledge
    D. deciding what relevant material to elaborate on

27. The evaluation of a client's responses may reveal substantial information that may aid the interviewer in assessing the problem areas that are of concern to the client. Responses that seemed irrelevant at the time of the interview may be of significance because
    A. considerable significance is attached to all relevant material
    B. emotional feelings are frequently masked
    C. an initial *rambling on* is often a prelude to what is actually bothering the client
    D. disturbed clients often reveal subsequent anxiety

Questions 28-30.

DIRECTIONS: Questions 28 through 30 are to be answered SOLELY on the basis of the following passage.

The physical setting of the interview may determine its entire potentiality. Some degree of privacy and a comfortable relaxed atmosphere are important. The interviewee is not encouraged to give much more than his name and address if the interviewer seems busy with other things, if people are rushing about, if there are distracting noises. He has a right to feel that, whether the interview lasts five minutes or an hour, he has, for that time, the undivided attention of the interviewer. Interruptions, telephone calls, and so on, should be reduced to a minimum. If the interviewee has waited in a crowded room for what seems to him an interminably long period, he is naturally in mood to sit down and discuss what is on his mind. Indeed, by that time, the primary thing on his mind may be his irritation at being kept waiting, and he frequently feels it would be impolite to express this. If a wait or interruptions have been unavoidable, it is always helpful to give the client some recognition that these are disturbing and that we can naturally understand that they make it more difficult for him to proceed. At the same time, if he protests that they have not troubled him, the interviewer can best accept his statements at their face value, as further insistence that they must have been disturbing may be interpreted by him as accusing, and he may conclude that the interviewer has been personally hurt by his irritation.

28. Distraction during an interview may tend to limit the client's responses. In a case where an interruption has occurred, it would be BEST for the investigator to
    A. terminate this interview and have it rescheduled for another time period
    B. ignore the interruption since it is not continuous
    C. express his understanding that the distraction can cause the client to feel disturbed
    D. accept the client's protests that he has been troubled by the interruption

29. To maximize the rapport that can be established with the client, an appropriate physical setting is necessary. At the very least, some privacy would be necessary.
    In addition, the interviewer should
    A. always appear to be busy in order to impress the client
    B. focus his attention only on the client
    C. accept all the client's statements as being valid
    D. stress the importance of the interview to the client

30. Clients who have been waiting quite some time for their interview may, justifiably, become upset.
    However, a client may initially attempt to mask these feelings because he may
    A. personally hurt the interviewer
    B. want to be civil
    C. feel that the wait was unavoidable
    D. fear the consequences of his statement

KEY (CORRECT ANSWERS)

1.	B	11.	A	21.	A
2.	C	12.	B	22.	C
3.	D	13.	D	23.	B
4.	D	14.	D	24.	D
5.	B	15.	C	25.	D
6.	D	16.	B	26.	A
7.	C	17.	C	27.	B
8.	C	18.	A	28.	C
9.	D	19.	D	29.	B
10.	C	20.	D	30.	B

TEST 2

DIRECTIONS: Each question or incomplete statement is followed by several suggested answers or completions. Select the one that BEST answers the question or completes the statement. *PRINT THE LETTER OF THE CORRECT ANSWER IN THE SPACE AT THE RIGHT.*

Questions 1-5.

DIRECTIONS: In Questions 1 through 5, choose the statement which is BEST from the point of view of English usage suitable for a business report.

1. A. The client's receiving of public assistance checks at two different addresses were disclosed by the investigation.
   B. The investigation disclosed that the client was receiving public assistance checks at two different addresses.
   C. The client was found out by the investigator to be receiving public assistance checks at two different addresses.
   D. The client has been receiving public assistance checks at two different addresses, disclosed the investigation

   1.____

2. A. The investigation of complaints are usually handled by this unit, which deals with internal security problems in the department.
   B. This unit deals with internal security problems in the department; usually investigating complaints.
   C. Investigating complaints is this unit's job, being that it handles internal security problems in the department
   D. This unit deals with internal security problems in the department and usually investigates complaints.

   2.____

3. A. The delay in completing this investigation was caused by difficulty in obtaining the required documents from the candidate.
   B. Because of difficulty in obtaining the required documents from the candidate is the reason that there was a delay in completing this investigation.
   C. Having had difficulty in obtaining the required documents from the candidate, there was a delay in completing this investigation.
   D. Difficulty in obtaining the required documents from the candidate had the affect of delaying the completion of this investigation.

   3.____

4. A. This report, together with documents supporting our recommendation, are being submitted for your approval.
   B. Documents supporting our recommendation is being submitted with the report for your approval.
   C. This report, together with documents supporting our documentation, is being submitted for your approval.
   D. The report and documents supporting our recommendation is being submitted for your approval.

   4.____

130

5.
A. Several people were interviewed and numerous letters were sent before this case was completed.
B. Completing this case, interviewing several people and sending numerous letters were necessary.
C. To complete this case needed interviewing several people and sending numerous letters.
D. Interviewing several people and sending numerous letters was necessary to complete the case.

5._____

Questions 6-20.

DIRECTIONS: For each of the sentences numbered 6 to 20, select from the options given below the MOST applicable choice, and mark your answer accordingly.
A. The sentence is correct.
B. The sentence contains a spelling error only.
C. The sentence contains an English grammar error only.
D. The sentence contains both a spelling error and an English grammar error.

6. He is a very dependible person whom we expect will be an asset to this division. 6._____

7. An investigator often finds it necessary to be very diplomatic when conducting an interview. 7._____

8. Accurate detail is especially important if court action results from an investigation. 8._____

9. The report was signed by him and I since we conducted the investigation jointly. 9._____

10. Upon receipt of the complaint, an inquiry was begun. 10._____

11. An employee has to organize his time so that he can handle his workload efficiantly. 11._____

12. It was not apparent that anyone was living at the address given by the client. 12._____

13. According to regulations, there is to be at least three attempts made to locate the client. 13._____

14. Neither the inmate nor the correction officer was willing to sign a formal statement. 14._____

15. It is our opinion that one of the persons interviewed were lying. 15._____

16. We interviewed both clients and departmental personel in the course of this investigation. 16._____

17. It is concievable that further research might produce additional evidence. 17._____

18. There are too many occurences of this nature to ignore. 18._____

19. We cannot accede to the candidate's request. 19.____

20. The submission of overdue reports is the reason that there was a delay in completion of this investigation. 20.____

Questions 21-2.

DIRECTIONS: Each of Questions 21 through 25 consists of three sentences lettered A, B, and C. In each of these questions, one of the sentences may contain an error in grammar, sentence structure, or punctuation, or all three sentences may be correct. If one of the sentences in a question contains an error in grammar, sentence structure, or punctuation, print in the space at the right the capital letter preceding the sentence which contains the error. If all three sentences are correct, print the letter D.

21. A. Mr. Smith appears to be less competent than I in performing these duties. 21.____
    B. The supervisor spoke to the employee, who had made the error, but did not reprimand him.
    C. When he found the book lying on the table, he immediately notified the owner.

22. A. Being locked in the desk, we were certain that the papers would not be taken. 22.____
    B. It wasn't I who dictated the telegram; I believe it was Eleanor.
    C. You should interview whoever comes to the office today.

23. A. The clerk was instructed to set the machine on the table before summoning the manager. 23.____
    B. He said that he was not familiar with those kind of activities.
    C. A box of pencils, in addition to erasers and blotters, was included in the shipment.

24. A. The supervisor remarked, "Assigning an employee to the proper type of work is not always easy." 24.____
    B. The employer found that each of the applicants were qualified to perform the duties of the position.
    C. Any competent student is permitted to take this course if he obtains the consent of the instructor.

25. A. The prize was awarded to the employee whom the judges believed to be most deserving. 25.____
    B. Since the instructor believes this book is the better of the two, he is recommending it for use in the school.
    C. It was obvious to the employees that the completion of the task by the scheduled date would require their working overtime.

KEY (CORRECT ANSWERS)

1.	B	11.	B
2.	D	12.	B
3.	A	13.	C
4.	C	14.	A
5.	A	15.	C
6.	D	16.	B
7.	A	17.	B
8.	A	18.	B
9.	C	19.	A
10.	A	20.	C

21. B
22. A
23. B
24. B
25. D

PREPARING WRITTEN MATERIAL
EXAMINATION SECTION
TEST 1

DIRECTIONS: Each of the sentences in this test may be classified under one of the following four categories:
  A. Faulty because of incorrect grammar or word usage
  B. Faulty because of incorrect punctuation
  C. Faulty because of incorrect capitalization or incorrect spelling
  D. Correct

Examine each sentence carefully to determine under which of the above four options it is best classified. Then, in the space to the right, print the capital letter preceding the option which is the BEST of the four suggested above. (Note that each faulty sentence contains but one type of error. Consider a sentence to be correct if it contains none of the types of errors mentioned, even though there may be other correct ways of expressing the same thought.)

1. He sent the notice to the clerk who you hired yesterday. 1.____

2. It must be admitted, however that you were not informed of this change. 2.____

3. Only the employee who have served in this grade for at least two years are eligible for promotion. 3.____

4. The work was divided equally between she and Mary. 4.____

5. He thought that you were not available at that time. 5.____

6. When the messenger returns; please give him this package. 6.____

7. The new secretary prepared, typed, addressed, and delivered, the notices. 7.____

8. Walking into the room, his desk can be seen at the rear. 8.____

9. Although John has worked here longer than She, he produces a smaller amount of work. 9.____

10. She said she could of typed this report yesterday. 10.____

11. Neither one of these procedures are adequate for the efficient performance of this task. 11.____

12. The typewriter is the tool of the typist; the cash register, the tool of the cashier. 12.____

135

13. "The assignment must be completed as soon as possible" said the supervisor. 13.____

14. As you know, office handbooks are issued to all new Employees. 14.____

15. Writing a speech is sometimes easier than to deliver it before an audience. 15.____

16. Mr. Brown our accountant, will audit the accounts next week. 16.____

17. Give the assignment to whomever is able to do it most efficiently. 17.____

18. The supervisor expected either your or I to file these reports. 18.____

KEY (CORRECT ANSWERS)

1.	A	11.	A
2.	B	12.	C
3.	D	13.	B
4.	A	14.	C
5.	D	15.	A
6.	B	16.	B
7.	B	17.	A
8.	A	18.	A
9.	C		
10.	A		

TEST 2

DIRECTIONS: Each of the sentences in this test may be classified under one of the following four categories:
    A. Faulty because of incorrect grammar or word usage
    B. Faulty because of incorrect punctuation
    C. Faulty because of incorrect capitalization or incorrect spelling
    D. Correct

Examine each sentence carefully to determine under which of the above four options it is best classified. Then, in the space to the right, print the capital letter preceding the option which is the BEST of the four suggested above. (Note that each faulty sentence contains but one type of error. Consider a sentence to be correct if it contains none of the types of errors mentioned, even though there may be other correct ways of expressing the same thought.)

1. The fire apparently started in the storeroom, which is usually locked.   1.____

2. On approaching the victim, two bruises were noticed by this officer.   2.____

3. The officer, who was there examined the report with great care.   3.____

4. Each employee in the office had a seperate desk.   4.____

5. All employees including members of the clerical staff, were invited to the lecture.   5.____

6. The suggested Procedure is similar to the one now in use.   6.____

7. No one was more pleased with the new procedure than the chauffeur.   7.____

8. He tried to persaude her to change the procedure.   8.____

9. The total of the expenses charged to petty cash were high.   9.____

10. An understanding between him and I was finally reached.   10.____

KEY (CORRECT ANSWERS)

1.	D		6.	C
2.	A		7.	D
3.	B		8.	C
4.	C		9.	A
5.	B		10.	A

TEST 3

DIRECTIONS: Each of the sentences in this test may be classified under one of the following four categories:
- A. Faulty because of incorrect grammar or word usage
- B. Faulty because of incorrect punctuation
- C. Faulty because of incorrect capitalization or incorrect spelling
- D. Correct

Examine each sentence carefully to determine under which of the above four options it is best classified. Then, in the space to the right, print the capital letter preceding the option which is the BEST of the four suggested above. (Note that each faulty sentence contains but one type of error. Consider a sentence to be correct if it contains none of the types of errors mentioned, even though there may be other correct ways of expressing the same thought.)

1. They told both he and I that the prisoner had escaped. 1.____

2. Any superior officer, who, disregards the just complaint of his subordinates, is remiss in the performance of his duty. 2.____

3. Only those members of the national organization who resided in the Middle West attended the conference in Chicago. 3.____

4. We told him to give the national organization assignment to whoever was available. 4.____

5. Please do not disappoint and embarass us by not appearing in court. 5.____

6. Although the office's speech proved to be entertaining, the topic was not relevent to the main theme of the conference. 6.____

7. In February all new officers attended a training course in which they were learned in their principal duties and the fundamental operating procedure of the department. 7.____

8. I personally seen inmate Jones threaten inmates Smith and Green with bodily harm if they refused to participate in the plot. 8.____

9. To the layman, who on a chance visit to the prison observes everything functioning smoothly, the maintenance of prison discipline may seem to be a relatively easily realizable objective. 9.____

10. The prisoners in cell block fourty were forbidden to sit on the cell cots during the recreation hour. 10.____

KEY (CORRECT ANSWERS)

1.	A	6.	C
2.	B	7.	A
3.	C	8.	A
4.	D	9.	D
5.	C	10.	C

TEST 4

DIRECTIONS: Each of the sentences in this test may be classified under one of the following four categories:
- A. Faulty because of incorrect grammar or word usage
- B. Faulty because of incorrect punctuation
- C. Faulty because of incorrect capitalization or incorrect spelling
- D. Correct

Examine each sentence carefully to determine under which of the above four options it is best classified. Then, in the space to the right, print the capital letter preceding the option which is the BEST of the four suggested above. (Note that each faulty sentence contains but one type of error. Consider a sentence to be correct if it contains none of the types of errors mentioned, even though there may be other correct ways of expressing the same thought.)

1. I cannot encourage you any. 1.____
2. You always look well in those sort of clothes. 2.____
3. Shall we go to the park? 3.____
4. The man whome he introduced was Mr. Carey. 4.____
5. She saw the letter laying here this morning. 5.____
6. It should rain before the Afternoon is over. 6.____
7. They have already went home. 7.____
8. That Jackson will be elected is evident. 8.____
9. He does not hardly approve of us. 9.____
10. It was he, who won the prize. 10.____

KEY (CORRECT ANSWERS)

1.	A	6.	C
2.	A	7.	A
3.	D	8.	D
4.	C	9.	A
5.	A	10.	B

TEST 5

DIRECTIONS: Each of the sentences in this test may be classified under one of the following four categories:
- A. Faulty because of incorrect grammar or word usage
- B. Faulty because of incorrect punctuation
- C. Faulty because of incorrect capitalization or incorrect spelling
- D. Correct

Examine each sentence carefully to determine under which of the above four options it is best classified. Then, in the space to the right, print the capital letter preceding the option which is the BEST of the four suggested above. (Note that each faulty sentence contains but one type of error. Consider a sentence to be correct if it contains none of the types of errors mentioned, even though there may be other correct ways of expressing the same thought.)

1. Shall we go to the park.   1.____
2. They are, alike, in this particular way.   2.____
3. They gave the poor man sume food when he knocked on the door.   3.____
4. I regret the loss caused by the error.   4.____
5. The students' will have a new teacher.   5.____
6. They sweared to bring out all the facts.   6.____
7. He decided to open a branch store on 33rd street.   7.____
8. His speed is equal and more than that of a racehorse.   8.____
9. He felt very warm on that Summer day.   9.____
10. He was assisted by his friend, who lives in the next house.   10.____

KEY (CORRECT ANSWERS)

1.	B	6.	A
2.	B	7.	C
3.	C	8.	A
4.	D	9.	C
5.	B	10.	D

TEST 6

DIRECTIONS: Each of the sentences in this test may be classified under one of the following four categories:
- A. Faulty because of incorrect grammar or word usage
- B. Faulty because of incorrect punctuation
- C. Faulty because of incorrect capitalization or incorrect spelling
- D. Correct

Examine each sentence carefully to determine under which of the above four options it is best classified. Then, in the space to the right, print the capital letter preceding the option which is the BEST of the four suggested above. (Note that each faulty sentence contains but one type of error. Consider a sentence to be correct if it contains none of the types of errors mentioned, even though there may be other correct ways of expressing the same thought.)

1. The climate of New York is colder than California. 1.____
2. I shall wait for you on the corner. 2.____
3. Did we see the boy who, we think, is the leader. 3.____
4. Being a modest person, John seldom talks about his invention. 4.____
5. The gang is called the smith street bos. 5.____
6. He seen the man break into the store. 6.____
7. We expected to lay still there for quite a while. 7.____
8. He is considered to be the Leader of his organization. 8.____
9. Although I recieved an invitation, I won't go. 9.____
10. The letter must be here some place. 10.____

KEY (CORRECT ANSWERS)

1.	A	6.	A
2.	D	7.	A
3.	B	8.	C
4.	D	9.	C
5.	C	10.	A

TEST 7

DIRECTIONS: Each of the sentences in this test may be classified under one of the following four categories:
- A. Faulty because of incorrect grammar or word usage
- B. Faulty because of incorrect punctuation
- C. Faulty because of incorrect capitalization or incorrect spelling
- D. Correct

Examine each sentence carefully to determine under which of the above four options it is best classified. Then, in the space to the right, print the capital letter preceding the option which is the BEST of the four suggested above. (Note that each faulty sentence contains but one type of error. Consider a sentence to be correct if it contains none of the types of errors mentioned, even though there may be other correct ways of expressing the same thought.)

1. I though it to be he. 1._____
2. We expect to remain here for a long time. 2._____
3. The committee was agreed. 3._____
4. Two-thirds of the building are finished. 4._____
5. The water was froze. 5._____
6. Everyone of the salesmen must supply their own car. 6._____
7. Who is the author of Gone With the Wind? 7._____
8. He marched on and declaring that he would never surrender. 8._____
9. Who shall I say called? 9._____
10. Everyone has left but they. 10._____

KEY (CORRECT ANSWERS)

1.	A	6.	A
2.	D	7.	B
3.	D	8.	A
4.	A	9.	D
5.	A	10.	D

TEST 8

DIRECTIONS: Each of the sentences in this test may be classified under one of the following four categories:
- A. Faulty because of incorrect grammar or word usage
- B. Faulty because of incorrect punctuation
- C. Faulty because of incorrect capitalization or incorrect spelling
- D. Correct

Examine each sentence carefully to determine under which of the above four options it is best classified. Then, in the space to the right, print the capital letter preceding the option which is the BEST of the four suggested above. (Note that each faulty sentence contains but one type of error. Consider a sentence to be correct if it contains none of the types of errors mentioned, even though there may be other correct ways of expressing the same thought.)

1. Who did we give the order to? 1._____
2. Send your order in immediately. 2._____
3. I believe I paid the Bill. 3._____
4. I have not met but one person. 4._____
5. Why aren't Tom, and Fred, going to the dance? 5._____
6. What reason is there for him not going? 6._____
7. The seige of Malta was a tremendous event. 7._____
8. I was there yesterday I assure you 8._____
9. Your ukulele is better than mine. 9._____
10. No one was there only Mary. 10._____

KEY (CORRECT ANSWERS)

1.	A	6.	A
2.	D	7.	C
3.	C	8.	B
4.	A	9.	C
5.	B	10.	A

TEST 9

DIRECTIONS: In each of the following groups of sentences, one of the four sentences is faulty in grammar, punctuation, or capitalization. Select the INCORRECT sentence in each case.

1. A. If you had stood at home and done your homework, you would not have failed in arithmetic.
   B. Her affected manner annoyed every member of the audience.
   C. How will the new law affect our income taxes?
   D. The plants were not affected by the long, cold winter, but they succumbed to the drought of summer.

   1.____

2. A. He is one of the most able men who have been in the Senate.
   B. It is he who is to blame for the lamentable mistake.
   C. Haven't you a helpful suggestion to make at this time?
   D. The money was robbed from the blind man's cup.

   2.____

3. A. The amount of children in this school is steadily increasing.
   B. After taking an apple from the table, she went out to play.
   C. He borrowed a dollar from me.
   D. I had hoped my brother would arrive before me.

   3.____

4. A. Whom do you think I hear from every week?
   B. Who do you think is the right man for the job?
   C. Who do you think I found in the room?
   D. He is the man whom we considered a good candidate for the presidency.

   4.____

5. A. Quietly the puppy laid down before the fireplace.
   B. You have made your bed; now lie in it.
   C. I was badly sunburned because I had lain too long in the sun.
   D. I laid the doll on the bed and left the room.

   5.____

KEY (CORRECT ANSWERS)

1. A
2. D
3. A
4. C
5. A

PREPARING WRITTEN MATERIAL

PARAGRAPH REARRANGEMENT
COMMENTARY

The sentences that follow are in scrambled order. You are to rearrange them in proper order and indicate the letter choice containing the correct answer at the space at the right.

Each group of sentences in this section is actually a paragraph presented in scrambled order. Each sentence in the group has a place in that paragraph; no sentence is to be left out. You are to read each group of sentences and decide upon the best order in which to put the sentences so as to form a well-organized paragraph.

The questions in this section measure the ability to solve a problem when all the facts relevant to its solution are not given.

More specifically, certain positions of responsibility and authority require the employee to discover connection between events sometimes, apparently, unrelated. In order to do this, the employee will find it necessary to correctly infer that unspecified events have probably occurred or are likely to occur. This ability becomes especially important when action must be taken on incomplete information.

Accordingly, these questions require competitors to choose among several suggested alternatives, each of which presents a different sequential arrangement of the events. Competitors must choose the MOST logical of the suggested sequences.

In order to do so, they may be required to draw on general knowledge to infer missing concepts or events that are essential to sequencing the given events. Competitors should be careful to infer only what is essential to the sequence. The plausibility of the wrong alternatives will always require the inclusion of unlikely events or of additional chains of events which are NOT essential to sequencing the given events.

It's very important to remember that you are looking for the best of the four possible choices, and that the best choice of all may not even be one of the answers you're given to choose from.

There is no one right way to solve these problems. Many people have found it helpful to first write out the order of the sentences, as they would have arranged them, on their scrap paper before looking at the possible answers. If their optimum answer is there, this can save them some time. If it isn't, this method can still give insight into solving the problem. Others find it most helpful to just go through each of the possible choices, contrasting each as they go along. You should use whatever method feels comfortable and works for you.

While most of these types of questions are not that difficult, we've added a higher percentage of the difficult type, just to give you more practice. Usually there are only one or two questions on this section that contain such subtle distinctions that you're unable to answer confidently. And you then may find yourself stuck deciding between two possible choices, neither of which you're sure about.

EXAMINATION SECTION

TEST 1

DIRECTIONS: The sentences that follow are in scrambled order. You are to rearrange them in proper order and indicate the letter choice containing the correct answer. *PRINT THE LETTER OF THE CORRECT ANSWER IN THE SPACE AT THE RIGHT.*

1. Below are four statements labeled W, X, Y and Z.   1.____
   W. He was a strict and fanatic drillmaster.
   X. The word is always used in a derogatory sense and generally shows resentment and anger on the part of the user.
   Y. It is from the name of this Frenchman that we derive our English word, martinet.
   Z. Jean Martinet was the Inspector-General of Infantry during the reign of King Louis XIV.
   The PROPER order in which these sentences should be placed in a paragraph is:
   A. X, Z, W, Y   B. X, Z, Y, W   C. Z, W, Y, X   D. Z, Y, W, X

2. In the following paragraph, the sentences, which are numbered, have been jumbled.   2.____
   I.   Since then it has undergone changes.
   II. It was incorporated in 1955 under the laws of the State of New York.
   III. Its primary purposes, a cleaner city, has, however, remained the same.
   IV. The Citizens Committee works in cooperation with the Mayor's Inter-departmental Committee for a Clean City.   3.____
   The order in which these sentences should be arranged to form a well-organized paragraph is:
   A. II, IV, I, III   B. III, IV, I, II   C. IV, II, I, III   D. IV, III, II, I

Questions 3-5.

DIRECTIONS: The sentences listed below are part of a meaningful paragraph but they are not given in their proper order. You are to decide what would be the BEST order in which to put the sentences so as to form a well-organized paragraph. Each sentence has a place in the paragraph; there are no extra sentences. You are then to answer Questions 3 through 5 inclusive on the basis of your rearrangements of these scrambled sentences into a properly organized paragraph.

In 1887 some insurance companies organized an Inspection Department to advise their clients on all phases of fire prevention and protection. Probably this has been due to the smaller annual fire losses in Great Britain than in the United States. It tests various fire prevention devices and appliances and determines manufacturing hazards and their safeguards. Fire research began earlier in the United States and is more advanced than in Great Britain. Later they established a laboratory specializing in electrical, mechanical, hydraulic, and chemical fields.

2 (#1)

3. When the five sentences are arranged in proper order, the paragraph starts with the sentence which begins
   A. "In 1887…"   B. "Probably this…"   C. "It tests…"
   D. "Fire research…"   E. "Later they…"

   3.____

4. In the last sentence listed above, "they" refers to
   A. the insurance companies   B. the United States and Great Britain
   C. the Inspection Department   D. clients
   E. technicians

   4.____

5. When the above paragraph is properly arranged, it ends with the words
   A. "…and protection."   B. "…the United States."
   C. "…their safeguards."   D. "…in Great Britain."
   E. "…chemical fields."

   5.____

KEY (CORRECT ANSWERS)

1. C
2. C
3. D
4. A
5. C

TEST 2

DIRECTIONS: In each of the questions numbered I through V, several sentences are given. For each question, choose as your answer the group of number that represents the MOST logical order of these sentences if they were arranged in paragraph form. *PRINT THE LETTER OF THE CORRECT ANSWER IN THE SPACE AT THE RIGHT.*

1. I. It is established when one shows that the landlord has prevented the tenant's enjoyment of his interest in the property leased.
    II. Constructive eviction is the result of a breach of the covenant of quiet enjoyment implied in all leases.
    III. In some parts of the United States, it is not complete until the tenant vacates within a reasonable time.
    IV. Generally, the acts must be of such serious and permanent character as to deny the tenant the enjoyment of his possessing rights.
    V. In this event, upon abandonment of the premises, the tenant's liability for that ceases.
    The CORRECT answer is:
    A. II, I, IV, III, V
    B. V, II, III, I, IV
    C. IV, III, I, II, V
    D. I, III, V, IV, II

    1.____

2. I. The powerlessness before private and public authorities that is the typical experience of the slum tenant is reminiscent of the situation of blue-collar workers all through the nineteenth century.
    II. Similarly, in recent years, this chapter of history has been reopened by anti-poverty groups which have attempted to organize slum tenants to enable them to bargain collectively with their landlords about the conditions of their tenancies.
    III. It is familiar history that many of the worker remedied their condition by joining together and presenting their demands collectively.
    IV. Like the workers, tenants are forced by the conditions of modern life into substantial dependence on these who possess great political aid and economic power.
    V. What's more, the very fact of dependence coupled with an absence of education and self-confidence makes them hesitant and unable to stand up for what they need from those in power.
    The CORRECT answer is:
    A. V, IV, I, II, III
    B. II, III, I, V, IV
    C. III, I, V, IV, II
    D. I, IV, V, III, II

    2.____

3. I. A railroad, for example, when not acting as a common carrier may contract away responsibility for its own negligence.
    II. As to a landlord, however, no decision has been found relating to the legal effect of a clause shifting the statutory duty of repair to the tenant.
    III. The courts have not passed on the validity of clauses relieving the landlord of this duty and liability.
    IV. They have, however, upheld the validity of exculpatory clauses in other types of contracts.

    3.____

V. Housing regulations impose a duty upon the landlord to maintain leased premises in safe condition.
VI. As another example, a bailee may limit his liability except for gross negligence, willful acts, or fraud.

The CORRECT answer is:
A. II, I, VI, IV, III, V
B. I, III, IV, V, VI, II
C. III, V, I, IV, II, VI
D. V, III, IV, I, VI, II

4.
I. Since there are only samples in the building, retail or consumer sales are generally eschewed by mart occupants, and in some instances, rigid controls are maintained to limit entrance to the mart only to those persons engaged in retailing.
II. Since World War I, in many larger cities, there has developed a new type of property, called the mart building.
III. It can, therefore, be used by wholesalers and jobbers for the display of sample merchandise.
IV. This type of building is most frequently a multi-storied, finished interior property which is a cross between a retail arcade and a loft building.
V. This limitation enables the mart occupants to ship the orders from another location after the retailer or dealer makes his selection from the samples.

The CORRECT answer is:
A. II, IV, III, I, V
B. IV, III, V, I, II
C. I, III, II, IV, V
D. I, IV, II, III, V

5.
I. In general, staff-line friction reduces the distinctive contribution of staff personnel.
II. The conflicts, however, introduce an uncontrolled element into the managerial system.
III. On the other hand, the natural resistance of the line to staff innovations probably usefully restrains over-eager efforts to apply untested procedures on a large scale.
IV. Under such conditions, it is difficult to know when valuable ideas are being sacrificed.
V. The relatively weak position of staff, requiring accommodation to the line, tends to restrict their ability to engage in free, experimental innovation.

The CORRECT answer is:
A. IV, II, III, I, V
B. I, V, III, II, IV
C. V, III, I, II, IV
D. II, I, IV, V, III

KEY (CORRECT ANSWERS)

1. A
2. D
3. D
4. A
5. B

TEST 3

DIRECTIONS: Questions 1 through 4 consist of six sentences which can be arranged in a logical sequence. For each question, select the choice which places the numbered sentences in the MOST logical sequent. *PRINT THE LETTER OF THE CORRECT ANSWER IN THE SPACE AT THE RIGHT.*

1.   I. The burden of proof as to each issue is determined before trial and remains upon the same party throughout the trial.
    II. The jury is at liberty to believe one witness' testimony as against a number of contradictory witnesses.
    III. In a civil case, the party bearing the burden of proof is required to prove his contention by a fair preponderance of the evidence.
    IV. However, it must be noted that a fair preponderance of evidence does not necessarily mean a greater number of witnesses.
    V. The burden of proof is the burden which rests upon one of the parties to an action to persuade the trier of the facts, generally the jury, that a proposition he asserts is true.
    VI. If the evidence is equally balanced, or if it leaves the jury in such doubt as to be unable to decide the controversy either way, judgment must be given against the party upon whom the burden of proof rests.
    The CORRECT answer is:
    A. III, II, V, IV, I, VI   B. I, II, VI, V, III, IV
    C. III, IV, V, I, II, VI   D. V, I, III, VI, IV, II

1.____

2.   I. If a parent is without assets and is unemployed, he cannot be convicted of the crime of non-support of a child.
    II. The term "sufficient ability" has been held to mean sufficient financial ability.
    III. It does not matter if his unemployment is by choice or unavoidable circumstances.
    IV. If he fails to take any steps at all, he may be liable to prosecution for endangering the welfare of a child.
    V. Under the penal law, a parent is responsible for the support of his minor child only if the parent is "of sufficient ability."
    VI. An indigent parent may meet his obligation by borrowing money or by seeking aid under the provisions of the Social Welfare Law.
    The CORRECT answer is:
    A. VI, I, V, III, II, IV   B. I, III, V, II, IV, VI
    C. V, II, I, III, VI, IV   D. I, VI, IV, V, II, III

2.____

3.   I. Consider, for example, the case of a rabble rouser who urges a group of twenty people to go out and break the windows of a nearby factory.
    II. Therefore, the law fills the indicated gap with the crime of inciting to riot.
    III. A person is considered guilty of inciting to riot when he urges ten or more persons to engage in tumultuous and violent conduct of a kind likely to create public alarm.
    IV. However, if he has not obtained the cooperation of at least four people, he cannot be charged with unlawful assembly.

3.____

153

V. The charge of inciting to riot was added to the law to cover types of conduct which cannot be classified as either the crime of "riot" or the crime of "unlawful assembly."
VI. If he acquires the acquiescence of at least four of them, he is guilty of unlawful assembly even if the project does not materialize.

The CORRECT answer is:
- A. III, V, I, VI, IV, II
- B. V, I, IV, VI, II, III
- C. III, IV, I, V, II, VI
- D. V, I, IV, VI, III, II

4.
I. If, however, the rebuttal evidence presents an issue of credibility, it is for the jury to determine whether the presumption has, in fact, been destroyed.
II. Once sufficient evidence to the contrary is introduced, the presumption disappears from the trial.
III. The effect of a presumption is to place the burden upon the adversary to come forward with evidence to rebut the presumption.
IV. When a presumption is overcome and ceases to exist in the case, the fact or facts which gave rise to the presumption still remain.
V. Whether a presumption has been overcome is ordinarily a question for the court.
VI. Such information may furnish a basis for a logical inference.

The CORRECT answer is:
- A. IV, VI, II, V, I, III
- B. III, II, V, I, IV, VI
- C. V, III, VI, IV, II, I
- D. V, IV, I, II, VI, III

KEY (CORRECT ANSWERS)

1. D
2. C
3. A
4. B

Food Sanitation Guide

INTRODUCTION

Restaurants, hotel and catering services in the country and the city serve millions of meals daily. This places tremendous responsibility upon them in safeguarding public health by preparing and serving only wholesome foods.

There are a number of cardinal principles which must be observed in preparing and serving wholesome foods. The bacterial contamination of these foods can be kept at a minimum if these principles are followed.

The food-handler must always be aware that he may contaminate the product by poor personal hygiene and work habits. He must always keep his person clean and work tools in a clean and sanitary condition.

Food must be stored in such a manner as to protect it from contamination. Unfortunately unless the food is sterilized, which is rarely practical, the presence of some bacteria is unavoidable. In order to keep their growth to a minimum, proper time and temperature control methods must be practiced.

Special care must be taken in the handling of foods which are to be served without further heat treatment. Ready-to-eat foods must not be subjected to contamination by coming into contact with unprocessed or partially processed foodstuffs or unsanitized work surfaces and implements.

Wholesome foods cannot be prepared in a dirty plant. The importance of good housekeeping cannot be minimized as a factor in the production of wholesome foods.

These general principles are more fully developed in the guide that follows.

I. Food Storage

The recommendations and prohibitions made below, if followed, will result in a wholesome and bacterialogically sound food product.

- A. Dry Storage Foods
    1. Dry stored foods are to be protected against contamination by insects, rodents, dust and other types of dirt.
    2. All food storage containers should be properly labeled.
- B. Cold Storage
    1. Frozen foods
        (a) During storage frozen foods are to be completely frozen until ready for use. ($0°$ F)
        (b) The freezer should be equipped with a thermometer so freezer temperatures can be determined without entering the holding box.
        (c) Foods are to be stored in an orderly manner to assure cold air circulation and are not to be stored directly on the floor.
- C. Chilled Foods
    1. Chilled foods should be kept at $45°F$ or less at all times. This may be done by the use of a walk-in refrigerator, reach-in refrigerator, refrigerated show cases, refrigerator counter and refrigerated tables, etc.
    2. Refrigerators should be supplied with appropriate thermometers.
    3. Containers holding foods should not be stored so that the bottom surface of the container rests on the surface of the food product in the container below it.
    4. Cooked foods should be stored so that they do not become contaminated by raw foods.
    5. All foodstuffs should be stored in such a manner as to protect them from contamination.
- D. Storage of Hot Foods

    Foods to be served hot soon after cooking should not at any time be allowed to drop below an internal temperature of $14°$ F. If food is not to be served immediately upon completion of the cooking, it may be kept at temperatures in excess of $14°$ F by the use of warming cabinets, steamtables, chafing dishes or any other devices suitable for these purposes. Hot perishable foods are not to be kept at room temperature when the internal and surface temperature of the food falls below $140°$ F. Rare roast beef can be an exception to this. (See handling of rare roast beef, Pages 7-9)

II. Cleaning and Sanitization of Equipment and Kitchen Utensils

Equipment, utensils and work surfaces which come in contact with food should be thoroughly cleaned and sanitized before and after food preparation.

- A. Methods of Cleaning and Sanitizing

    Prior to washing, manually remove all adhering food particles. Then wash, using a suitable soap or detergent, and hot water liberally applied by manual or mechanical means. After rinsing and removing all visible dirt and grease, sanitize using one of the following methods:
    1. Heat Sanitization
        (a) Clean hot water, $170°$ F or more, applied to all surfaces of the equipment or utensils for at least 30 seconds.

2. Chemical Sanitization

(a) Apply a commercial preparation (Sodium Hypochlorite type) being sure to follow label directions.

(b) If a commercial product is not available or desired, a suitable solution may be prepared by mixing 1/2 ounce of household bleach, (5.25% Sodium Hypochlorite) in one gallon of lukewarm water (do not use hot water). Flood the surfaces of the equipment and utensils with this solution for at least one minute. Do not rinse or wipe after this operation.

If necessary to dry, air dry. Do not use a solution which is more than two hours old. If more solution is required, prepare a fresh supply.

III. Principles of Food Preparation and Services

During food preparation, improper techniques may contaminate the product with disease-causing organisms. It is for this purpose that sanitary procedures must be observed. Listed below are some principles which should be followed.

A. Food that is to be served cold should be kept cold (45° F or less) through all stages of storage, processing, and serving. Thawing of frozen foods should be accomplished in such a manner so as to keep the surface and internal temperatures of the product 45° F or less at all times. If frozen food is to be thawed in water, running cold water is to be used.

B. Foods to be served hot are to be kept so that the internal and surface temperatures do not fall below 140° F. (See handling of rare roast beef - Pages 7-9). Care must be taken in the cooling of hot foods so they do not become contaminated by dust, contact with work clothes, human contact, etc. Cooling should be accomplished as quickly as possible by the use of fans, refrigeration, etc. To determine the temperature of foods, a food thermometer is to be used. (Hands are not to be used).

C. Partially processed and leftover foods are to be refrigerated at 45° F. or below. Just prior to service they are to be removed from the refrigerator and heated rapidly to serving temperatures so that the internal temperatures are not less than 140° F.

D. The holding of perishable foods between the temperatures of 140° and 45° F is to be kept at a minimum.

E. Contact of ready-to-eat foods with bare hands should be kept at an irreducible minimum and utensils should be used whenever possible.

F. Ready-to-eat foods should not be contaminated by coming in contact with work surfaces, equipment, utensils or hands previously in contact with raw foods until such surfaces, etc. have been cleaned and sanitized.

G. Do not place packing cases and cans on food work surfaces.

H. When necessary to taste foods during processing, a clean sanitized utensil should be used. When tasting again, either re-clean and re-sanitize utensil, or use another sanitized utensil.

I. Foods are to be cooked and processed as close to the time of service as possible.

J. Menu planning should be such as to prevent excessive leftovers, and leftovers are not to be pooled with fresh foods during storage.

IV. Transportation of Foods

In some food operations, it is necessary to transport food from a central kitchen (commissary) to an establishment where it is finally served. The food transported can be in a ready-to-eat state or a pre-cooked stage, which is finally processed at the place of service. The following practices should be observed to see that contamination is not introduced or possible previous bacterial contamination not afforded means for extensive multiplication during this period.

1. Transporting containers and vehicles should be clean and of sanitary design to facilitate cleaning.
2. Transporting containers and vehicles should have acceptable refrigerating and/or heating facilities for maintaining food at cold (45° F or below) or hot (above 140°) temperatures while in transit.
3. Food stored in transporting containers and vehicles should be protected from contamination.
4. A minimum amount of time is to be taken for the loading and unloading of foods from transporting vehicles so foods will not be exposed to adverse temperatures and conditions.

V. Food Processing Techniques Relative to Specific Types of Service

A. Displayed Food (Buffet, Smorgasbord, etc.)

1. Hot foods are to be kept at or above 140° F on the display table by use of chafing dishes, steam tables or other suitable methods.
2. Cold foods are to be at temperatures 45° F. or less before being displayed and not to be exposed at room temperature for more than one hour unless some means is employed, (ice, mechanical refrigeration, etc.) to keep cold foods at or less than 45° F.
3. All foods displayed and, therefore, subject to contamination must be discarded at the conclusion of the buffet service.

B. Protein Type Salads (Tuna, Ham, Shrimp, Egg, Chicken, Lobster, etc.)

These salads are always served cold and, therefore, all salad ingredients except the seasoning and spices are to be chilled to 45° F or less before use. Celery, which is almost always a component of these salads, should be treated so as to minimize its bacterial content by the immersing of the chopped celery in boiling water, using a hand strainer or colander for 30 seconds and then chilling immediately by holding under running cold tap water.

Before the mixing operation, the previously washed can opener, and tops of cans and jars holding salad ingredients should be wiped with a clean cloth containing sanitizing solution. The salad ingredients should be mixed with clean, sanitizing equipment, (sanitary type masher, sanitary mixing bowl, stainless steel long handled spon or fork, mechanical tumbler type mixer, etc.). There should be an absolute minimum of bare hand contact with the equipment and ingredients. The mixing operation is to be completed as quickly as possible and the finished salad immediately served or refrigerated.

C. Additional Instructions Relative to Specific Salads

1. Shrimp and Lobster Salad
   Immerse shrimp, or lobster meat in boiling water for 30 seconds and then chill to 45° F or less before adding to salad. Fast chilling can be accomplished by placing the meat in shallow pans in the freezer or refrigerator or on top of cracked ice.
2. Egg Salad
   After removing shell, use a hand strainer or colander to immerse hard-boiled eggs in boiling water for 30 seconds and then chill to 45° F or less before adding to salad. Chill the eggs by refrigerating or by placing strainer containing them under running cold tap water.
3. Chicken and/or Turkey Salad
   After removal from bones, immerse chicken or turkey meat in boiling water or boiling stock for 30 seconds and then chill to 45° F. before adding to salad. Fast chilling can be accomplished by placing the meat in shallow pans in the freezer, refrigerator or on cracked ice.
4. Ham Salad
   Immerse diced ham in boiling water or boiling stock for 30 seconds and then chill to 45° F. or less before adding to salad. Fast chilling can be accomplished by the same method used for chicken and shrimp.

D. Hot Meats and Poultry Served from Steamtables or Other Suitable Warming Devices
   1. Schedule the cooking of meats so they will be completed as close as possible to desired time of service.
   2. Upon removal from the oven or stove, cooked meats are to be kept at an internal temperature of 140° F or higher in a steamtable or other suitable device.
   3. Maintain the water in the steamtable at a temperature in excess of 180° F. The water must be brought to this temperature before any foods are placed therein. Water in the steamtable shall be kept at a steamtable depth so as to be in contact with the bottom and upper portions of the sides of the food container.
   4. Refrigerated ready-to-eat cooked meats, especially leftovers, gravies and stocks, are to be heated rapidly to an internal temperatures of 165° F or higher before being placed in the steamtable or warming device. Hot stock or meat gravies may be used to reheat meats. Steamtables or other warming devices should never be used to heat up cold meats.
   5. Cautions noted previously relative to hand contact, care of equipment storage, and menu planning should also be followed.

E. Roast Beef
   Because of consumer preference, roast beef is often served at an internal temperature of less than 140° F. Continuous warming and heating of this product, as for example on a steamtable, may not be practical as it causes the meat to become well done and thus less desirable to some consumers. It is, therefore, realized that instructions relative to maintenance of interior temperatures of meat cannot always be applied to this

product. It is essential, therefore, that Roast Beef be cooked as close to time of service as possible. Great care must be taken to prevent contamination. At large banquets this roast is sometimes stored or "rested" for excessive lengths of time, during which bacterial growth can occur.

1. Bone in Standing Rib Roast

    There are a number of methods to be used in the processing of this type of roast beef, which will help minimize bacterial contamination and growth.

    (a) Method No. 1

    The roast is boned and trimmed prior to cooking. Slicing is accomplished after cooking and immediately prior to serving. After removal from the oven, the surface temperature should be in excess of $140°$ F. This method minimizes the amount of handling after the cooking operations.

    (b) Method No. 2

    After cooking and storage the roast is boned, trimmed (all surfaces) and sliced immediately prior to service. This method removes almost all surface contamination.

    (c) Method No. 3

    The surface of the raw roast beef is coated with a concentration of coarse salt. The beef is cooked and stored with this coating intact and it is not removed until just prior to service, at which time, boning and trimming and slicing takes place. The salinity on the surface of the meat inhibits the bacterial growth. It has been found that after removal of the salt coating platibility of the meat is not impaired as there is practically no penetration of the salt into the edible portion of the meat.

2. Boneless Tied Roast Beef

    This type of roast beef is commonly machine sliced and used on sandwiches and platters. As stated above this type of roast beef is often desired rate where high internal temperatures cannot be applied.

    Menu planning should be such that the roast beef should be removed from the oven as close to the service time as possible.

    After removing a large roast beef from the oven, it should be cut into smaller pieces, each not to exceed 6 pounds. The surface temperature of the meat should not fall below $140°$., at which time the roast can be sliced for immediate service and placed in the refrigerator, warming oven or steamtable. The refrigerator temperature should be below $45°$ F and steamtable temperature in excess of $140°$ F.

    It is suggested that only one piece of roast be kept for immediate service and the other pieces be stored in the refrigerator or warming device. At the end of the day any piece of roast beef which has been partially used should be considered as a leftover. This piece of meat must be refrigerated overnight, and before being reused it is to be heated to an internal temperature in excess of $165°$ F. It is realized that after cooking at these temperatures, this product cannot be served again as rare roast beef.

The slicing machine used for this product should be dissassembled and cleaned at the end of the day's work, and left disassembled. Before beginning slicing operations the next day, it is to be sanitized and reassembled.

3. Steamship (Steamer) Beef Roasts

This type of roast consists of the whole beef round (top and bottom) usually served rare and stored at inadequate temperatures (less that 140°). This product is almost always hand carved. (The term hand carved is used to denote that it is not machine sliced). There is no need for hand contact inasmuch as this meat is sliced with the use of a chef's knife and fork and transferred to the sandwich or platter using these utensils. Since the normal means to prevent contamination cannot be excercised, it is mandatory that only properly sanitized equipment be used and the food-handler exert particular care not to contaminate the product. As stated above in paragraph 2, any unused portion of this roast should be refrigerated, and before being served again cooked to an internal temperature of 165° F. It is again realized that after recooking at this temperature this product cannot be served as rare roast beef.

F. Rare Steaks

If these are not cooked immediately prior to service, it is sometimes the practice to singe the outer surface of the meat, and then store it at room temperature until the time of service. It is cooked by broiling and served immediately.

For this type of meat service, it is important that the storage period is not over one hour, the meat does not come in contact with contaminated work surfaces or hands and the meat is subjected to sufficient surface terminal heat treatment just before serving.

G. Pre-cooked Hamburger Patties

It has become a practice in some restaurants to pre-cook hamburger patties, and store them in a warmer or above the stove or grill until needed for service. In most cases the temperatures and lengths of time the meat is kept can be such as to allow the growth of pathogenic organisms.

If this type of food preparation is practiced, extreme care should be taken to see that this product is not stored for more than one hour, the food is not contaminated by unclean hands or work surfaces, and it receives a thorough heat treatment (exceeding 16° F) just prior to its consumption.

H. Pre-cooked Chicken - (Barbecued Style)

This product, a whole eviscerated chicken of 2-3 pounds, is usually cooked in a rotisserie-type radiant heating device and stored for varying lengths of time and temperature. Again this type of food storage is advantageous for the growth of food poisoning organisms.

Precautions to be followed with this product are: all parts of the poultry are to be thoroughly and completely cooked (over 165° F); it is to be handled and stored so that it will not come in contact with contaminated hands or work surfaces; and it shall not be kept at temperatures between 45° F and 14° F for more than one hour anytime prior to consumption.

I. Poultry Stuffing

Often times adequate internal temperatures are not obtained in the cooking of stuffed poultry. The temperature of the stuffing is such as to incubate rather than destroy bacteria. It is therefore advisable to cook the stuffing separately from the poultry. When this is done adequate temperatures (165° F) are reached in both the stuffing and poultry. Thereafter the stuffing should be handled and/ or stored in a manner similar to that noted previously for perishable protein foods.

J. Custard-Filled Baked Goods

The problems with custard fillings arise after completion of the cooking operation during the cooling and handling period. The following recommendations are made:

1. Utensils and receptacles must be sanitized as previously noted.
2. The finished custard should be transferred to shallow stainless steel or aluminum trays to facilitate rapid cooling. It is important at this point not to contaminate the product with the foodhandler's hands or clothing.
3. A long-bladed flexible spatula of sanitary construction should be used to scrape the residue from the cooking receptacle.
4. The finished product should be refrigerated as quickly as possible and at no time should the product be exposed to room temperature for more than one hour.
5. The shallow pans of custard should be covered with wax or other clean paper while cooling and while being stored in the refrigerator.
6. Jelly-filling machines of sanitary design should be used. Multiple use pastry bags, after washing, are to be boiled or sanitized before use. A single service pastry bag can be fashioned out of wax or parchment paper. A desire method of filling eclair shells, cream puffs and similar type products is to cut the shell in half and apply the filling with a properly sanitized stainless steel spatula. This is the only method to be used in the production of napoleans.
7. Butter cream which is to be used as an ingredient of custard should be handled with the same precautions as actual custard.
8. The finished product, immediately after completion, must be kept under refrigeration (45° F or less) at all times until consumed. Commercial fillings, bavarian creams, etc., are often used instead of true custard. They are used, as per label directions, and are sometimes used with the addition of eggs, cream, butter cream, etc., depending on the recipe of the individual food processor. The same care, relative to the boiling and refrigeration of all ingredients, should be taken in the manufacture of these products as is observed with true custard.

K. Deviled Eggs

It has been the experience of the Food Processing Control Unit that this product is needlessly contaminated by poor handling techniques. The following is suggested to minimize contamination.

1. This product is to be prepared as close to service as possible.
2. After the shell is removed from the egg, the peeled egg is to be placed in a strainer or colander and then in boiling water for not less than 30 seconds and then immediately placed in running cold water and chilled to 45° F or less.
3. At this point, when it is unavoidable that the bare hands be used, it is mandatory that the food handler wash his hands thoroughly with a germicidal soap before proceeding with the process.
4. Whenever possible remove the yolk of the egg with a sanitized utensil, and when the yolk is mashed and mixed with seasonings, a sanitized utensil is also to be used.
5. In extruding the mashed yolk, a single service pastry bag is recommended. If a multiple use bag is desired it is to be sanitized by heat or chemical treatment prior to use.
6. If the finished product is not used immediately, it is to be refrigerated at 45° F or less until served.

L. Fresh Pork Products

Though it has been previously mentioned that meats are to be cooked to proper internal temperatures, it is felt that an additional warning be given concerning fresh pork products. Government inspection of fresh pork is not a guarantee against trichina contamination of this product. The trichina are not readily detectable except by microscopic examination and then only if an infested area is examined. It is therefore mandatory that fresh pork products be cooked to an internal temperature of at least 150° F.

M. Chopped Liver

This perishable, popular product is ordinarily literally manhandled in processing. Inasmuch as most of the handling takes place after cooking and the product is served without further heat treatment extra precautions must be taken to minimize hand contact.

Equipment must be cleaned and sanitized before use. It is best to clean, sanitize, and assemble equipment immediately prior to use. Ingredients should not be touched with bare hands after cooking. Cooked liver is to be handled with sanitized equipment only. Hard boiled eggs, after shells are removed, are to be placed in a colander or strainer and immersed in boiling water for 30 seconds and then placed in running cold water and chilled to 45°F or less. The peeled eggs are then to be handled by implements only. After mixing, the finished chopped liver is to be placed in stainless steel serving containers or molds without use of bare hands. If hand molding is required for a decorative display this is to be done immediately prior to service.

VI. Plant Sanitation and Maintenance

The unclean and defective condition of the physical plant, walls, floors, ceilings, doors, windows, etc., can adversely affect the final product from a bacterial standpoint. Care should be taken to see that they are clean and maintained in such a manner as to facilitate proper plant sanitation. It is known that bacterial organisms will establish themselves on encrusted foods such as is found on walls, light switches, room and refrigerator door handles, and other surfaces touched by food-handlers. Improper wall, window and door maintenance, ineffective cleaning and poor garbage disposal methods can also lead to insect and rodent infestations. These well known vectors of disease organisms can introduce food poisoning bacteria to foodstuffs in the establishment. (When necessary acceptable insecticides and rodenticides can be used to prevent or exterminate an infestation of these pests. Care should be observed to see they do not come in contact with foodstuffs.)

Adequate amounts of hot and cold running water should be supplied at properly maintained fixtures, strategically placed in parts of the plant, i.e., toilets, food processing areas, utensil cleaning areas, etc. Such fixtures should also be supplied with detergents, bactericides, and single service hand towels.

Equipment should be of sanitary design and maintained in a sanitary condition, cleaned after use and sanitized before use. Open seams and worn or defective surfaces which allow food particles to accumulate and prevent proper cleaning should be repaired forthwith.

Self-inspection and cleaning schedules should be devised for all areas of the plant and equipment. At routine periods all areas should be inspected to detail and findings noted on a form devised for this purpose. Follow-up on findings should be made as soon as feasible.

Cleaning and maintenance should follow every major production period. If production is continuous for a 12 or 18 hour period, "down" periods should be incorporated in the work schedule to allow for this sanitation program.

VII. Non-Commercial Food Operations

This guide is primarily for the use of the sanitarian and the operators of commercial food-processing establishments. In a city of this size, many large meals and buffets are prepared and served by private and volunteer organizations. These include church and synagogue socials, local charity and fund raising affairs, fraternal organizations, etc.

These types of affairs often lead to food-borne illnesses when proper precautions are not taken. It is therefore important that the recommendations contained herein also be practiced by these large non-commercial feeding operations.

VIII. Assistance to Food Processors

Commercial and non-commercial food operations are urged to use the expertise of this department by calling upon us to discuss and analyze problems occuring in their food handling programs.

SALAD PREPARATION GUIDE

1. Refrigerate all salad ingredients except seasoning and spices overnight or chill to 45° F or lower before use.
2. Purchase a sanitizing solution or prepare one by mixing one or two ounces of bleach to a gallon of cold water. This solution is effective for approximately two hours. Prepare a fresh solution if further sanitization is needed.
3. Clean work surfaces, equipment and utensils (pots, pans, spoons, spatulas, etc.) with soap and hot water, rinse with clean water, and then give a final rinse with sanitizing solution. Stainless steel utensils and equipment are preferred in preparation of these foods.
4. Clean hands, fingernails, and arms thoroughly with ger-micidal soap and hot water and dry with single use paper towels.
5. Individuals preparing salads are not to perform other tasks while engaged in salad preparation.
6. Clean and sanitize tops of cans and jars before openings. Do not use fingers to pry off can lids or drain off liquid contents.
7. Place diced celery, including pre-cut packaged celery in a strainer and immerse in boiling water for 30 seconds; then chill to 45° F or less.
8. Use clean sanitized utensils in mixing and handling of foods. Avoid hand contact with foods.
9. Refrigerate final salad product immediately in shallow pans.
10. Salads placed in bain-marie cold plates should have a minimum internal temperature of 45° F.
11. Do not fill trays above spill line.

Food Preparation-Handling and Storage

1. FOOD PREPARATION

    Begin with clean, fresh food. Handle food only when necessary.

    Don't dip fingers into food or use a stirring spoon to taste.

    Use oysters, clams and other frozen foods, fluid milk products and frozen milk desserts from approved sources.

    Never lean or sit on work surfaces.

    Foods should never be prepared in yards, alleys, stairs or hallways.

    Keep food that is on display covered so it can't be touched or coughed on by customers or contaminated by flies and other bugs.

    Always follow the recipe. Cook custards and cream sauces well. Chill them at once.

    Wash thoroughly with brush and clean water all vegetables and fruits which are to be served raw.

    As a food safeguard, boil leftover vegetables, gravies, soups, and other liquid foods before serving.

    Make sure that all mixing, grinding and chopping machines are thoroughly cleaned after each use. In order to properly clean one of these machines, one should know how to take it apart and assemble it.

    Work only in a well-lighted area that is well-ventilated.

2. FOOD STORAGE AND HANDLING

    Food should be stored well off the floor, away from walls or dripping pipes.

    Keep all food, bulk or otherwise, covered and safe from contamination.

    Check food daily and throw away any spoiled or dirty food.

    Store cleaning, disinfection, insect and rodent-killing powders and liquids away from foods, PLAINLY MARKED.

    Keep foods in refrigerator at temperature of 45° F or below.

    Check the temperature regularly with a good thermometer.

    Keep all cooling compartments closed except when you're using them.

    Store food in a refrigerator in such a way that inside air can circulate freely.

    Always refrigerate meats, creamed foods and custard desserts.

    Keep all refrigerated foods covered, and use up stored leftovers quickly.

    When dishes and utensils are sparkling clean, keep them that way by proper storage. Keep all cups and glasses inverted.

    Cakes, doughnuts and fruit pies may be kept inside a covered display area.

    The only goods that should be left on the counter uncovered are those which are wrapped and do not contain anything which could spoil at room temperature.

    Don't set dirty dishes, pots, cartons or boxes on food tables.

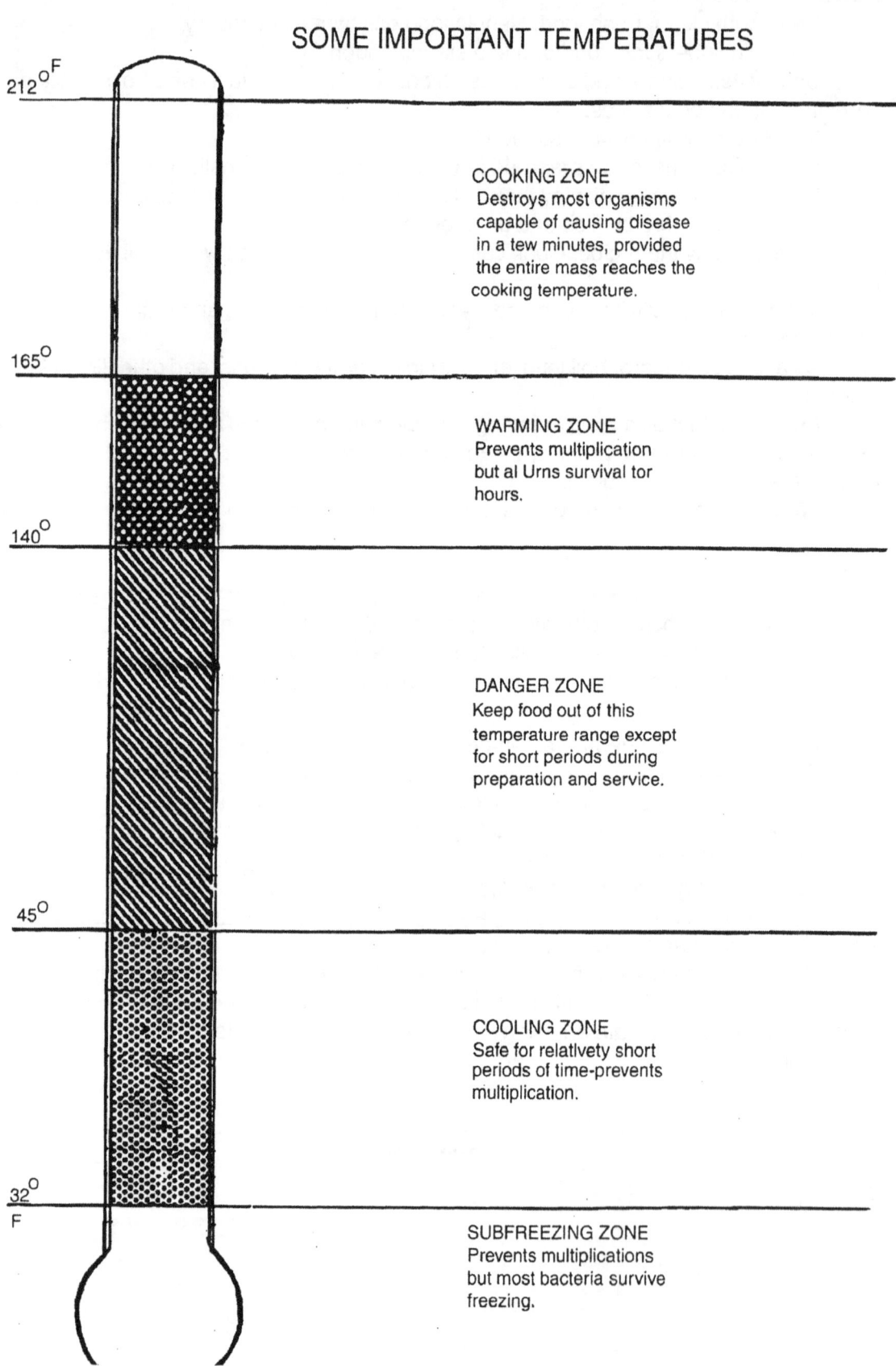

TEMPERATURE RANGE FOR SAFE STORAGE OF FOODS

Zone I   Sub-freezing temperatures 0° F to -15° F (-18° to -9.4° C)

   A. Frozen meat, fish, and vegetables
   B. Frozen fruits
   C. Ice Cream
   D. Homemade frozen deserts

Zone II   High Humidity (85%) and Moderate Air Circulation 34° to 37° F (1.1° to 2.7 °C)

   A. Fresh meat, chicken, and fish
   B. Sliced smoked ham and bacon
   C. Sliced cold cuts of meat
   D. Leftover canned and cooked meat

Zone III   38° to 40° F (3.3° to 4.4° C)

   A. Fresh milk, cream, and buttermilk
   B. Cottage cheese and butter (both covered)
   C. Fresh orange and tomato juice (covered)
   D. Bottled beverage (for chilling)

Zone IV   40° to 43° F (4.4° to 6.1° C) Moderate Humidity

   A. Berries, pears, and peaches
   B. Ripe grapefruit and oranges
   C. Ripe tomatoes (short time only)
   D. Fresh eggs
   E. Margarine
   F. Custards and puddings (day or two only)
   G. Prepared salads (for chilling)

Zone V   40° to 45° F (4.4° to 7.2° C) High Humidity

   A. Cherries and cranberries
   B. Lettuce and celery
   C. Spinach, kale, and other greens
   D. Beets, carrots, parsnips, and turnips
   E. Peas and lima beans
   F. Cucumbers and eggplant (short time only)

Zone VI   55° to 60° F (12.7° to 15.1° C) Fairly High Humidity and Moderate Circulation. (Good Fruit Cellar or Storage Cellar Well Ventilated).

   A. Apples, cabbage, potatoes, pumpkin, squash, unripened tomatoes, and maple syrup (in tight container)

Zone VII   Normal Room Temperature. Dry Storage
  A. Ready prepared cereals
  B. Crackers
  C. Bottled beverages

Zone VIII   Normal Room Temperature Storage

  A. Peanut Butter and honey
  B. Salad oils and vegetable shortenings
  C. Catsup and pickles
  D. Jelly and preserves
  E. Dried fruits and bananas (short time)
  F. Flour
  G. Dried peas and beans
  H. Sugar and salt

MICROBIOLOGY OF FOODS: BACTERIA

In order to understand the reasons behind food sanitation practices, it is necessary to know a few facts about the microorganisms which cause food spoilage and foodborne disease.

Bacteria, commonly called germs, are extremely small, plant-like organisms which must be viewed through a microscope in order to be seen. If 25,000,000 bacteria were placed in a line, that line would be only one inch long; one million could fit on the head of a pin. Like any living thing, bacteria require food, moisture, and the proper temperature for growth. Most of them need air, but some can thrive only in the absence of air (these are called anaerobic) and some can grow with or without air (facultative). Bacteria are found everywhere on the earth, in the air, and in the water. Soil abounds with bacteria which grow on dead organic matter.

SHAPES OF BACTERIA

One method of classifying bacteria is by their shape. All bacteria can be assigned to one of the following categories.

A. Cocci (plural of coccus) are round or spherical in shape. While they are able to live alone, they often exist in groups. Single chains are called streptococci. Those which form a grape-like cluster are called staphylococci, while those that form pairs are called diplococci. Some bacteria are named after the portion of the human anatomy they infect; for example, pneumococci infect the lungs, enterococci infect the intestines, and meningococci infect the meninges (protective sheath around the brain). Some of the common diseases caused by the cocci group are pneumonia, septic sore throat, scarlet fever, and meningitis.

B. Bacilli (plural of bacillus) are rod-shaped. Some of these also congregate in the single chain form, and are called streptobacilli. Some common diseases caused by bacilli are typhoid fever, tuberculosis, and anthrax.

C. Spirilla (plural of spirillum) are spiral or comma-shaped. Diseases caused by spirilla include cholera and syphilis.

SPORES

Some bacilli are able to protect themselves under adverse conditions by forming a protective shell or wall around themselves; in this form they are in the non-vegetative stage and are called spores. These bacterial spores can be likened to the seeds of a plant which are also resistant to adverse conditions. During the spore stage, bacteria do not reproduce or multiply. As soon as these spores find themselves under proper conditions of warmth, moisture, food and possibly air requirements. they resume their normal (vegetative) stage, and resume their growth. Since spores are designed to withstand rigorous conditions, they are difficult to destroy by the normal methods. Much higher killing temperatures and longer time periods are required. Fortunately, there are only a relatively few pathogenic or disease-causing bacilli which are spore formers. Tetanus, anthrax, and botulism are diseases caused by spore formers.

BACTERIAL REPRODUCTION

Bacteria reproduce by splitting in two, this is called binary fission. For this reason, their numbers are always doubling: one bacterium generates two; each of these generates two, resulting in a new total of four: etc. The time it takes for bacteria to double (generation time) is roughly fifteen to thirty minutes under good conditions.

TYPES OF BACTERIA ACCORDING TO THEIR EFFECT ON MAN

Types of bacteria, classified according to their effect on us, are:

- A. Harmful or disease-producing
- B. Undesirable
- C. Beneficial
- D. Benign

A. Harmful or disease-producing bacteria are known as pathogenic bacteria or pathogens. They cause various diseases of man, animals, and plants.

B. Undesirable bacteria, which cause decomposition of foods, are often referred to as putrefying bacteria. Bacteria that act on sugars in food, resulting in souring, are called saccharolytic bacteria.

C. Beneficial bacteria are used in the production of various foods, including cultured milk, yogurt, cheese, and sauerkraut.

The large intestine, or colon, contains millions of bacteria which are normal inhabitants of the intestinal tract, and we call this type *"coliform"* bacteria. It can be seen, therefore, that where coliform bacteria are found in food or water, they are an indication of fecal contamination. The coliforms themselves are not pathogenic, but where fecal contamination occurs, it is probable that other pathogenic organisms from the intestine may be present. The presence of coliform bacteria is often used as an index of good or bad sanitary practices.

Bacteria are essential in the operation of certain sewage disposal plants, known as *"activated sludge plants"*. In these plants the bacteria digest the organic sewage and either liquefy the solid matter which is in colloid form, or change it so that it settles out.

The greatest number of bacteria are found in the soil where they thrive on dead organic matter. They are constantly decomposing it, so that eventually it is changed into an inorganic form. This essential process of nature makes it possible for plants to absorb inorganic nutriment. Other types of bacteria *"fix"* nitrogen from the air, forming nitrates in the soil, generally on the roots of legumes.

D. Benign bacteria, as far as we know at the present time, are neither helpful nor harmful to man. Of the hundreds of thousands of strains of bacteria, most fall into this category.

It must be realized that may bacteria are essential in the balance of nature, and the destruction of all bacteria in the world would be catastrophic. Our main objective in public health protection, in which food handling plays a vital role, is the control and destruction of the pathogenic bacteria and those that cause food spoilage.

CONDITIONS FOR GROWTH

A. Food - Bacterial require food for growth. Food must be absorbed in liquid form through the cell wall of the organism. Generally bacteria prefer neutral foods (ph 6-8) but some can thrive on highly acid or alkaline media.

B. Moisture - Moisture (water) is an essential requirement. If moisture is not present, bacteria will not multiply and eventually may die. Processes which depend on removing available water, i.e., water in liquid form, from bacteria are used to preserve foods. Such methods include dehydration, freezing, and preserving in salt or sugar.

C. Temperature - In general, bacteria prefer a warm temperature and grow best between 90-100° F. (Optimum temperature) The temperature of the body, 98.6° F, is excellent for bacterial growth; when bacteria are cultured in the laboratory, they are kept at this temperature. However, different types of bacteria prefer different temperatures, and are as follows:

<u>Mesophilic</u>: Grow best at temperatures between 50-110° F. Most bacteria are in this group.

Thermophilic: Love heat. These grow best at temperatures between 110-150° F. or mo.re

Psychrophilic: Love cold. These grow best at temperatures below 50° F.

Where heat is employed to destroy pathogenic bacteria, the food processor often must contend with thermophilic or thermoduric bacteria, which may withstand the pasteurizing or sterilizing processes. These bacteria are not pathogenic, but may be putrefactive.

D. Air - With respect to air atmospheric oxygen, we find that some bacteria can grow only where air is present; these are called aerobes. Some bacteria can grow only in a medium where air is absent, and these are called anaerobes. They can thrive in a sealed can, jar, or bottle of food. Those bacteria which prefer to live where air is present but may grow without air are termed facultative aerobes, and those which prefer to grow in the absence of air but may grow where air is present are called facultative anaerobes.

LOCOMOTION

Bacteria cannot crawl, fly, or move about. A few types do have thread-like appendages called flagella, with which they can propel themselves to a very limited extent. Therefore, they must be carried from place to place by some vehicle or through some channel. The channels of transmission include: air, water, food, hands, coughing, sneezing, insects, rodents, dirty equipment, unsafe plumbing connections, and unclean utensils. Hands are one of the most dangerous vehicles. There is no doubt that better care of food handlers' hands would aid greatly in cutting down the transmission of disease.

DESTRUCTION BY HEAT

The most reliable and time-tested method of destroying bacteria is heat. This method is effective only when both time and temperature factors are applied. In other words, not only do we have to reach the desired temperature to kill bacteria, but we must allow sufficient time to permit the heat to kill the more sturdy members. The lower the temperature (to certain limits, of course) the longer the time required to kill bacteria. Conversely, the higher the temperature, the less time is necessary. An example of this principle involves the two accepted methods for pasteurizing milk. In the *"holding"* method, milk is held at a temperature of 145° F for thirty minutes. In the more recently developed *"flash"* or *"high temperature-short time"* method, milk is held at 161° F for fifteen seconds.

In sterilizing foods for canning, the type of food and size of the containers must be taken into consideration in determining the proper time and temperature. The smaller the container, the faster the heat will be conducted through the food.

It is important to note once more that in order to destroy spore-forming bacilli completely, very high temperatures, often higher than 212° F are required for long time periods.

DESTRUCTION BY CHEMICALS

Bacteria can be destroyed by chemical agents. Those which kill all bacteria are called germicides or bactericides. Examples are phenol (carbolic acid), formaldehyde, iodine, chlorine, and others, such as the group of chemicals known as quarternary compounds. The effectiveness of the chemical bactericide depends on the concentration and the method with which it is used. If it is used to kill pathogenic organisms only, it is called a disinfectant. If a mild concentration is used on wounds to inhibit the growth of disease organisms, it is called an antiseptic. Some chemicals have been used in foods to inhibit the growth of spoilage bacteria, and these are called preservatives. Examples of these are sulphur dioxide, benzoate of soda, salt, sugar, and vinegar.

OTHER METHODS OF DESTRUCTION

When exposed to air and sunlight, bacteria are destroyed due to the combined effects of lack of moisture and food and exposure to the natural ultraviolet rays of the sun. Ultraviolet lamps are used for bactericidal purposes but their field is limited. Aeration is not used commercially as the sole means of sterilizing a product.

REFRIGERATION

Refrigeration of foods in refrigerators (32-45° F) does not kill bacteria. However, these temperatures do inhibit the growth of bacteria, both putrefactive and pathogenic, so that foods under proper refrigeration remain wholesome and free from disease for some time.

MICROBIOLOGY OF FOODS: BACTERIA AND OTHER MICROORGANISMS

Extremely low freezing temperatures for prolonged periods may result in the death of some bacteria, while others may survive. However, refrigeration or freezing should never be considered as a means of destroying bacteria; these methods merely retard bacterial growth.

VIRUSES

Viruses are minute organic forms which seem to be intermediate between living cells and organic compounds. They are smaller than bacteria, and are sometimes called filterable viruses because they are so small that they can pass through the tiny pores of a porcelain filter which retain bacteria. They cannot be seen through a microscope (magnification of 1500 x) but can be seen through an electron microscope (magnification of 1,000,000 x). Viruses cause poliomyelitis, smallpox, measles, mumps, encephalitis, influenza, and the common cold. Viruses, like bacteria are presumed to exist everywhere.

YEASTS

Yeasts are one-celled organisms which are larger than bacteria. They, too, are found everywhere, and require food, moisture, warmth, and air for proper growth. Unlike some bacteria which live without air, yeasts must have air in order to grow. They need sugar, but have the ability to change starch into sugar. When yeasts act on sugar, the formation of alcohol and carbon dioxide results. In the baking industry, yeast is used to *"raise dough"* through the production of carbon dioxide. The alcohol is driven off by the heat of the oven. In wine production, the carbon dioxide gas bubbles off, leaving the alcohol. The amount of alcohol produced by yeasts is limited to 18%, because yeasts are killed at this concentration of alcohol.

Yeasts reproduce by budding, which is similar to binary fission. Generally, the methods described for the destruction of bacteria will kill yeasts as well.

Yeasts are not generally considered to be pathogenic or harmful although a few of them do cause skin infections. Wild yeasts or those that get into a food by accident rather than by design of the food processor cause food spoilage and decomposition of starch and sugar, and therefore are undesirable.

MOLDS

Molds are multicellular (many-celled) microscopic plants which become visible to the naked eye when growing in sufficient quantity. Mold colonies have definite colors (white, black, green, etc.) They are larger than bacteria or yeasts. Some molds are pathogenic, causing such diseases as athletes' foot, ringworm, and other skin diseases. However, moldy foods usually do not cause illness. In fact, molds are encouraged to grow in certain cheeses to produce a characteristic flavor.

The structure of the mold consists of a root-like structure called the mycelium, a stem (ariel filament) called the hypha, and the spore sac, called the sporangium. All molds reproduce by means of spores. Molds are the lowest form of life that have these specialized reproductive cells.

Molds require moisture and air for growth and can grow on almost any organic matter, which does not necessarily have to be food. Molds do not require warmth, and grow very well in refrigerators. Neither do molds require much moisture, although the more moisture present, the better they multiply.

Methods of destruction for molds are similar to those required for bacteria. Heat, chemicals, and ultraviolet rays destroy mold spores as well as the molds. Refrigeration does not necessarily retard their growth.

Certain chemicals act as mold inhibitors. Calcium propionate (Mycoban) is one used in making bread. This chemical when used in the dough, retards the germination of mold spores, and bread so treated will remain mold-free for about five days.

One of the most beneficial molds is the Penicillium mold from which penicillin, an antibiotic, is extracted. The discovery, by Dr. Alexander Fleming, of the mold's antibiotic properties open up a whold field of research, and other antibiotic products from molds have been discovered.

CLASSIFICATION OF FOODBORNE DISEASE

Several terms are used to describe illness in which the causative agent is obtained by ingestion of food; the expression *"food poisoning"* is commonly employed to describe any of these. However, such usage is inaccurate and confusing.

Foodborne diseases caused by bacteria are divided into two classes. The first is called food intoxication (this is the real food poisoning) and designates illnesses due to toxins (poisons) secreted by bacteria growing in large numbers on the food prior to ingestion. In the second type of bacterial disease, called food infection, the symptoms are caused by the activity of large numbers of bacterial cells, having grown to some extent in the contaminated food, within the gastrointestinal system of the victim.

Other microbial contaminants of food, such as viruses, rickettsiae, and protozoa, can cause disease, as can other parasites. Chemical poisonings are characterized by a relatively sudden onset of symptoms, often in minutes. In addition, certain plants and animals contain chemical poisons, some of which produce illness within a short period after ingestion.

I. Food Intoxications
    A. Botulism
1. Toxins are produced by growth of Clostridium botulinum in foods under anaerobic conditions. There are six major types of toxins: A, B, C, D, E and F. Types A, B, and E affect man. Antitoxins exist, although few hospitals routinely stock them.
2. Symptoms: Toxin affects the central nervous system, producing difficulty in swallowing, double vision, and difficulty in speech and respiration, followed by death from paralysis of muscles of respiration.
3. Onset of symtoms: 2 hours to 8 days, average 1 to 2 days.
4. Inactivation of toxins: 15 minutes at 212° F.
5. Foods usually involved: home-canned, low-acid vegetables. On rare occasions, commercially packed tuna, smoked fish, mushrooms, and vichysoisse.

    B. Staphylococcus Food Poisoning
1. Toxin produced by coagulase positive Staphylococcus aureus.
2. Symptoms: Nausea, vomiting, diarrhea, acute prostration, and abdominal cramps.
3. Onset of symptoms: 1 to 6 hours, average 2-3 hours.
4. Inactivation of toxin: Not inactivated by normal cooking times and temperatures.
5. Foods usually involved: Ham, poultry, cream-filled bakery goods, protein salads.

II. Bacterial Food Infections
    A. Salmonellosis
1. Salmonella typhimurium, Salmonella enteritidis, and others.
2. Symptoms: Abdominal pain, diarrhea, chills, fever, frequent vomiting, and prostration.
3. Onset of symptoms: 7 to 12 hours; average 12 to 24 hours.
4. Inactivation: 165° F for period of cooking or heating.
5. Foods usually involved: poultry, poultry products, inadequately cooked egg products, meats, and other foods.

B. Bacillary dysentery (Shigellosis)
  1. Various species of Shigella (Shigella dysenteriae, Shigella sonnei, and others.)
  2. Symptoms: Diarrhea, bloody stools, fever.
  3. Onset of symptoms: 1 to 7 days; average 2-3 days.
  4. Inactivation: 165° for period of cooking.
  5. Foods usually involved: Moist prepared foods and dairy products contaminated with excreta from carrier.

C. Streptococcal Infections (Scarlet fever or septic sore throat)
  1. Certain strains of beta-hemolytic streptococci
  2. Symptoms: Fever, sore throat.
  3. Onset of symptoms: 1 to 7 days; average 3 days.
  4. Inactivation: 165° F for period of cooking.
  5. Foods usually involved: Food contaminated with nasal or oral discharges from a case or carrier; raw milk from infected cows.

D. Enterococci (Fecal Streptococci)
  1. Various strains of Streptococcus fecalis.
  2. Symptoms: Nausea, sometimes vomiting and diarrhea.
  3. Onset of symptoms: 2 to 18 hours
  4. Inactivation: 165° F for period of cooking.
  5. Foods usually involved: Prepared food products contaminated with excreta.

E. Clostridium Perfringens
  1. Growth of Clostridium perfringens in food under anaerobic conditions.
  2. Symptoms: Acute abdominal pain and diarrhea, nausea, and rarely, vomiting.
  3. Onset of symptoms: 8 to 22 hours; average 8-12 hours.
  4. Inactivation: Variable, usually not inactivated by cooking temperatures.
  5. Foods usually involved: Poultry and meat products.

III. Viral Infections
  A. Infectious Hepatitis
    1. Virus of infectious hepatitis
    2. Symptoms: Fever, lack of appetite, malaise, fatigue, headache, nausea, chills, vomiting, jaundice may be present.
    3. Onset of symptoms: 14 to 35 days, average 25 days.
    4. Inactivation: not known.
    5. Foods usually involved: Shellfish (oyster, clams, mussels) taken from polluted waters and eaten raw; foods contaminated with excreta from an infected person.

IV. Parasitic Infections
  A. Trichinosis
    1. Trichinella spiralis.
    2. Symptoms: Nausea, vomiting, diarrhea (during digestion of trichinae); muscular pains, fever labored breathing, swelling of eyelids. Occassionally fatal.

3. Onset of symptoms: 2 to 28 days; average 9 days.
4. Inactivation: All parts of meat must reach 150° F to destroy cysts.
5. Foods usually involved: Raw or insufficiently cooked pork and pork products. Whale, seal, bear, and walrus meat have also been implicated.

B. Tapeworm (Taeniasis)
1. Taenia saginata (beef tapeworm); Taenia solium (pork tapeworm).
2. Symptoms: Beef tapeworm: abdominal pain, hungry feeling, vague discomfort. Pork tapeworm: varies from mild chronic digestive disorder to severe malaise.
3. Onset of symptoms: Several weeks.
4. Inactivation: All parts of the meat must reach 150° F.
5. Foods usually involved: Raw or insufficiently cooked beef or pork containing live larvae.

C. Fish Tapeworm Disease (Diphyllobothriasis)
1. Diphyllobothrium latum.
2. Symptoms: Anemia in heavy infections.
3. Onset of symptoms: 3 to 6 weeks.
4. Inactivation: All parts of fish meat must reach 150° F.
5. Foods usually involved: Raw or insufficiently cooked fish containing live larvae.

D. Amebic Dysentery
1. Entamoeba histolytica
2. Symptoms: Chronic diarrhea of varying severity or diarrhea alternating with constipation; occasionally fatal.
3. Onset of symptoms: 5 days to several months; average 3 to 4 weeks.
4. Inactivation: Cysts on vegetables destroyed by heating 30 minutes in water at 122° F.
5. Foods usually involved: Moist food contaminated with excreta from a carrier; contaminated water.

V. Poisonous Plants
A. Mushroom poisoning
1. Symptoms caused by phalloidine and other alkaloids of certain species of mushrooms.
2. Symptoms: Salivation: abdominal pain, intense thirst, nausea, vomiting, water stools, excessive perspiration, flow of tears; often fatal.
3. Onset of symptoms: 15 minutes to 15 hours.
4. Inactivation: Not inactivated by cooking.
5. Foods usually involved: Wild mushrooms, such as Amanita phalloides and Amanita muscaria, which are mistaken for edible mushrooms.

VI. Dangerous Chemicals
A. Antimony

1. Occurrence: Chipped grey enamelware in contact with acid foods and beverages.
2. Symptoms: Nausea, violent vomiting.
3. Onset of symptoms: 15 to 30 minutes.
4. Duration: Several hours.

B. Cadmium
1. Occurence: Cadmium used as plating, e.g., ice cube trays, dissolved in food or beverages.
2. Symptoms: Propulsive vomiting, nausea.
3. Onset of symptoms: 15 to 30 minutes.
4. Duration: Several hours.

C. Cyanide
1. Occurrence: Foods contaminated with silver polish containing cyanide.
2. Symptoms: Cyanosis (bluish discoloration of skin) mental confusion, glassy eyes, blue lips, often fatal.
3. Onset of symptoms: Almost instantaneous.

D. Lead
1. Occurrence: Food containers, solder containing more that 5% lead used on food equipment.
2. Symptoms: Blue line on gums, cramps in stomach, bowels, and legs, constipation, loss of appetite, headache, irritability.

E. Copper
1. Occurrence: Foods contaminated by copper salts (verdigris) on unclean copper utensils; beverages containing copper salts due to action of carbonation (carbon dioxide and water) on copper tubing.
2. Symptoms: Vomiting, abdominal pain, diarrhea.
3. Onset of symptoms: Usually immediate.

F. Zinc
1. Occurrence (rare): Acid foods cooked in galvanized (zinc-plated) utensils.
2. Symptoms: Dizziness, nausea, vomiting, tightness of throat.
3. Onset of symptoms: a few minutes to two hours.

G. Nitrites
1. Occurrence: Contamination of foods by nitrates, or nitrites used as a preservative in excess of 200 parts per million.
2. Symptoms: Cyanosis, shock, lowered blood pressure, methemoglobinemia (hemoglobin in blood combines with nitrites instead of oxygen producing internal asphyxiation.)
3. Onset of symptoms: 15 to 30 minutes.

H. Pesticides
1. Occurence: Foods accidentally contaminated with pesticides.

VII. Dangerous Animals
A. Shellfish
1. Occurrence: Shellfish grown in polluted waters, if eaten raw, can cause typhoid fever, cholera, and infectious hepatitis.

DISEASE PREVENTION IN RESTAURANTS

WHAT ARE THE MOST FAVORABLE CONDITIONS FOR THE GROWTH OF DISEASE GERMS?

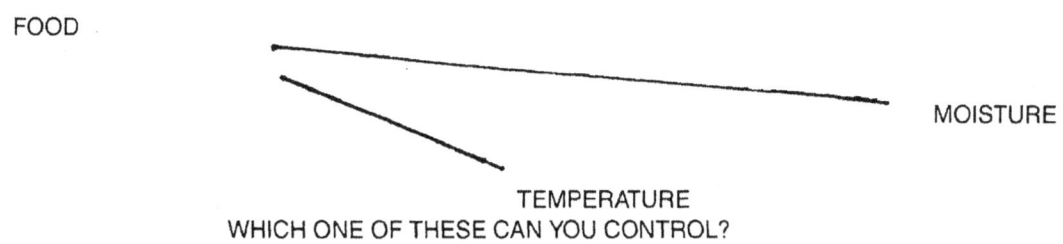

WHICH ONE OF THESE CAN YOU CONTROL?

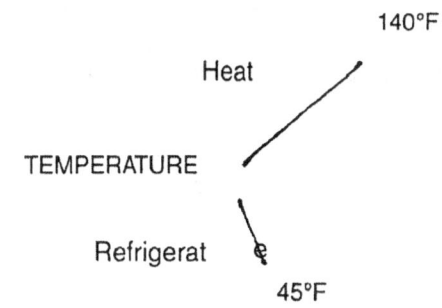

YOU CAN SPREAD DISEASE BY:

Carelessness
 Not washing hands before touching food, dishes, or utensils. Leaving food unprotected from dust, sneezes, rodents and insects. Using dirty equipment.
 Leaving food stand at room temperature.

Working when sick or with open sores
 Through food you infect.
 By direct contact with customers and fellow workers.
 By contaminating dishes and utensils.

YOU CAN GET DISEASE BY:
 Infection from a sick customer or fellow worker.
 Careless handling of soiled dishes.
 Eating infected food.
 Infection from rats, mice and insects.

FOOD PROTECTION

To Prevent Bacterial Food Poisoning and Infection
 Keep harmful bacteria out if possible.
 Keep them from growing if they do get in.
 How? By watching time and temperature, as well as cleanliness.

TIME
 Don't let food ready to serve stand longer than one hour at room temperature.

TEMPERATURE

Keep cold foods refrigerated at 45° F or lower until they are served.

Keep hot foods hot, above 140° F, until they are served.
WATCH THESE FOODS ESPECIALLY-BACTERIA LOVE THEM!
Cream filled or custard filled pastries, cakes and puddings.
Any dish made with cream sauce.
Meats, poultry and fish.
Dressing for poultry or meat.
Sandwiches, sandwich filling.

To Prevent Chemical Food Poisoning
- Be sure all poisons are clearly labeled.
- Never store poisons in food preparation areas.
- Don't use insect sprays over or near food.
- Don't keep any acid food or drink in a galvanized container.

SAFE STORAGE METHODS

Clean storage rooms, used for no other purpose.
All food stored at least six inches above floor.
Clean, neat refrigerator.
Food refrigerated in shallow containers, always covered.
Refrigerator shelves free of shelf-coverings.

SEVEN EASY RULES FOR SAFE FOOD

1. KEEP COLD FOODS COLD-HOT FOODS HOT. Don't let foods stand at room temperature.
2. KEEP HANDS CLEAN and touch food with hands as little as possible.
3. Don't let anyone with a skin infection or a cold handle food.
4. Keep kitchen, dining rooms and storage rooms free from rats, mice and insects.
5. Protect food from sneezes, customer handling, and dust.
6. Be sure poisons are well labeled and kept away from food preparation areas.
7. Wash dishes, glasses, silver and utensils by methods recommended by your health department.

Control of Rodents and Insects

CONTROL OF RODENT INFESTATION AND HORBORAGE

In combating rodent infestation the use of cats, traps and poisons are only temporary expendients and do not eliminate rodent life completely from your premises. The best method of permanently eliminating them is to *build the out*. Rodent life exists in buildings because of favorable conditions that permit them to hide, nest and breed. They will not remain where safe shelter or food is not available. To combat infestation in your premises, it is necessary to be able to recognize rodent harborages or hiding places, both actual and potential as they are the conditions favoring rodent life and propagation. There are three general types of rodent harborages:

      1- Temporary
      2- Incidental
      3- Structural

TEMPORARY RODENT HARBORAGES

These are conditions arising out of failure to maintain premises in a clean and sanitary condition, or faulty methods of operation, housekeeping, or storage of stock.

EXAMPLES

I. Mass storage of office supplies and old records, materials for repairs, food products or other store merchandise; boxes, crates, or cartons that are left undisturbed for periods of time and not rotated in use (using up older stock first).

II. Unused or obsolete fixtures or equipment, especially those having drawers, compartments or other hollow enclosures.

III. Miscellaneous junk, trash, odds and ends placed in closets, cellars, boiler rooms or out-of-the-way places, or portions of premises not in daily use having very little or no light.

IV. Garbage cans left uncovered overnight or having poorly fitting covers, or in a defective leaking condition.

V. Passageways used in transporting or storing garbage cans for removal, with spilled particles of food on floors, especially in corners.

VI. Accumulations of rubbish at bottom of airshafts, dumbwaiter or elevator shaft pits, under sidewalk or cellar window gratings, or other parts of premises not cleaned regularly.

PREVENTION

I. Unused materials should be stored neatly and away from walls, allowing enough space for a man to pass around in cleaning and should preferably be stored sufficiently high above the floor to permit cleaning underneath. The amount stored should be minimized as much as possible, and it should be disturbed or its position changed at least every three weeks to prevent nesting of rodents.

II. Avoid mass storage by arranging in rows with 2' wide aisles. If stock is placed on shelves, raise the lowest shelf about 6" to 8" above the floor. Remove all rubbish that usually accumulates about unused materials. Promptly clean up food scrapes that spill from garbage cans, or fall under, or behind slop sinks, equipment, and stock bins. (Rodents feed more readily on these than on bagged or packaged food supplies). Store all garbage in non-leaking metal receptacles with tightfitting covers.

III. Place soiled linen into suitable containers.

IV. Maintain clean and sanitary conditions at all times.

<u>INCIDENTAL RODENT HARBORAGES</u>

These are conditions arising from installing of fixtures or equipment incidental to their use on the premises, in such a manner that hollow spaces, enclosures, and inaccessible places are formed.

<u>EXAMPLES</u>

I. Fixtures, refrigerators, ovens, etc. not installed flush against walls but leaving a small space that is too narrow for proper inspection and cleaning.

II. Narrow spaces left between bottoms of counters, back bars, or other fixtures or equipment, and the floor.

III. Small spaces existing between ceilings and tops of fixtures, clothes lockers, refrigerators, closets and cabinets, large overhead pipes and ventilating ducts suspended a few inches from ceiling.

IV. Hollow partitions (double wall space).
Hollow furniture of fixtures with inaccessible enclosures. Boxed-in casings or sheathing around pillars, pipes, radiators, etc., forming hollow enclosures.

V. Bottom shelves, stock platforms or skids that are not set directly on the floor but allow a space of a few inches to exist underneath.

VI. Defective insulated sections of large refrigerators or pipe coverings (hollow enclosed spaces formed by damage to cork or asbestos).

VII. Loose foods stored in low, thin, wooden food bins, boxes, cartons, burlap bags, etc.

VIII. Partially enclosed spaces behind open metal grilles used on housing of motors or other mechanical equipment.

<u>PREVENTION</u>

I. Eliminate narrow, inaccessible spaces behind fixtures or equipment by placing flush against wall or leaving a space wide enough for inspection and cleaning. Solidly block out narrow spaces underneath, or install flush on floors or raise high enough for cleaning.

II. Avoid providing undisturbed rat runways in narrow space between ducts or long hoods, and the ceiling. Ducts should be placed flush against ceilings and preferably be found in shape, instead of square.

III. Remove decorative boxing-in around radiators, columns, etc., to avoid hollow enclosures, or protect gnawing margins with metal flashing extending at least 6" above the floors, if they must be sheathed for appearance, used sheet metal.

IV. Repair and securely close all breaks in insulation around pipes, refrigerators or cooling cabinets.

V. Line interiors of wooden bins with sheet metal, or store foods in rodent proof screening (mesh openings not greater than 1/4").

VI. Eliminate hollow spaces formed by false bottoms in counters, lockers, cabinets, back bars, etc.

VII. Alter hollow fixtures so that enclosures are exposed for easy cleaning.

STRUCTURAL RODENT HARBORAGES

These conditions are due to design or construction of a building that are defective from a rat-proof standpoint, or that developed during occupancy from failure to make proper repairs or to use rat-proof materials.

EXAMPLES

I. Openings made in outside building walls, around beams, or in interior walls, floors or ceiling for installation of pipes, cables, or conduits. They are made by plumbers, electricians, or other workmen. The openings are usually larger than necessary and the unused portions of holes are not closed up. Holes, large cracks, loose bricks, or other openings in floors, walls or ceilings are other examples.

II. Hollow spaces in double walls, between floor and ceiling of lower story, and in double ceilings of cellars.

III. Enclosed hollow spaces formed by sheathing the undersides of stairways, by installation of false floors in toilets, or by raised wooden floors over earthen floors of cellars.

IV. Entrance and cellar doors that are not tight-fitting or not provided with a proper door sill or saddle, permitting openings over 1/4" to exist and not protected around gnawing edges with metal flashing at least 6" above floor level.

V. Openings around ceiling or floor beams, or risers, where they pass through partitions.

VI. Openings of fans, ventilators, and louvers on the outside of buildings, or fancy metal grilles with openings over 1/4", not protected by rodent proof screening.

VII. Floor drain and sewer trap pits not kept clean and not provided with solid metal covers with preforations not exceeding 1/4". Cellar floors of earth, enabling rodents to burrow underneath.

PREVENTION

I. Promptly seal up all holes or openings around pipe lines or cables where they enter the building, with concrete mortar or cement mortar to which ground glass may be added for better results.

II. Place tight-fitting metal collars or flanges around pipes and risers. Provide escutcheon plates for all risers where they pass through floor slabs, unless same are waterproofed by pockets of mastic.

III. Seal up all openings around beams.

IV. Avoid using double-wall type construction with hollow interior spaces, or hollow tile block, hollow cement block, or similar material for partitions or walls of storage compartments or in cellars.

V. Inspect all parts of premises for holes and seal every opening in walls and ceilings with cement plastered smooth. Move away fixtures and stock that may hide holes in floors and use a flashlight so as not to miss any. Look for loose bricks, cracks or other openings in cellar foundation walls. Find all openings before rodents do. Inspect regularly and repair weak spots before actual breaks occur.

VI. Block out hollow spaces under raised wooden floors with concrete Refrigerators, ranges, ovens, etc., should be solidly based on concrete. Protect entrance, cellar doors, and windows with metal flashing around gnawing edges, and maintain in good repair.

VII. Replace earthen cellar floors with a floor of concrete at least 3" - 4" thick and tied securely into foundation walls.

VIII. Securely anchor window and door screens to the frames.

RODENT INFESTATION SURVEYS

In addition to trapping, surveys by operators will indicate presence and approximate extent of infestation, of which the following are some signs.

Excreta of Pellets

Physical state will indicate recent or old infestation. Soft, moist droppings indicate live rats or mice present, while hard and dry ones indicate old. Amount of droppings indicate heavy or light infestation. The size of pellets will show if the rodents are large or small; and if different sizes are present, it indicates litters of young are being reared.

Gnawings

If recent, will show fresh appearance of gnawings, shavings, debris or marks on food bags or containers, or damage to other merchandise, supplies or fixtures.

Rat Run

Difficult to tell by appearance if new or old. Use white chalk or paint on suspected rat run. The rat is a creature of habit and will continue to use the same pipe or beam. It will leave marks caused by dirt or grease on feet or fur.

FOR PERMANENT CONTROL MEASURES

I. Try to maintain permanent freedom rather than resort to temporary reduction of rat population by periodic drives employing trapping, poisoning or fumigation.

II. After carrying out all rat stoppage measures, a reliable employee should inspect entire premises weekly to insure cleaning and upkeep, and to repair any temporary breakages in windows and doors to the outside. Allow no accumulations of rubbish to form. Watch sky-lights, air shafts, dumbwaiter and elevator shafts, and all other means of ingress from outside, for breaks. Immediate repairs to be made to eliminate openings and harborages, with rat-proof material (impervious to gnawing). Relocate or alter fixtures with hollow enclosures. Prevent careless employees or workmen from leaving lower windows or cellar doors overnight or on weekends to rodent ingress from outside sources.

III. Include in the specifications for all new construction and repair contracts a specific provision that work is be done is to leave the building in a ratproof condition. Specifications may read as follows:

> *"This building is planned and detailed, and it is the intent of these specifications, to provide a structure that will prevent the penetration by rodent vermin of any vacant space where they might find a harborage. The contractor will he held responsible for securing this condition by the closing of all points of access to such spaces, including the passage of piping and conduits through all walls, partitions, ceilings and furred off spaces, the closing of access to void in hollow tile blocks, etc. There shall be a special inspection of the building with regard to this matter before final acceptance."*

IV. All permanent measures are aimed at eliminating the rodent's food supply and shelter. Architects need to be made more cognizant of conditions that prevent rodent harborage and infestation, so as to change design of new buildings to eliminate unnecessary enclosed spaces. Rat-proof construction should receive greater prominence in the future.

INSECT CONTROL

Proper restaurant or food plant sanitation must obviously include measures for the elimination of insects and vermin. Where insects infest food, such food cannot be used for human consumption and must be destroyed, entailing an economic loss. Even more important is the fact that insects carry millions of bacteria in and on their bodies and contaminate the food on which they crawl. Food establishments are particularly susceptible to insect infestation are attracted by the food.

GENERAL ENTOMOLOGY

Life Cycle: Insects have a life cycle that consists of: (a) the egg, (b) the larva (worm-like), (c) the pupa (web, cocoon) and (d) the adult. Some insects have only three stages: (a) egg, (b) nymph, and (c) adult.

Structure: The general external structure of insects consists of three parts:

1. Head

    (a) Compound eyes - often more efficient than human eyes; enables them to see in all directions.
    (b) Antennae - hair-like structures that act as feelers.
    (c) Mouth - may be constructed for use as a hypodermic needle (mosquito), for chewing (beetle) or sucking (fly).

2. Thorax

    (a) Wings
    (b) Spiracles (breathing vents)
    (c) Feet

3. Abdomen - used for digestion, reproduction, and excretion. Insect "specks" may be from excreta or vomit.

Flies are vicious public health enemies. They breed in filth and carry diarrheal diseases to the food we eat. Flies have a life span of about four weeks. One female may lay 150 eggs at one time and usually prefers manure, garbage, or some other filthy waste matter for this purpose. In four weeks, the eggs hatch in eight hours into the larva stage (maggots) which become fully developed in four to five days. Each larva then becomes a pupa and five days later the adult fly emerges. Hence there are ten days from the egg to adult stage but this elapsed time varies according to the temperature. The female may start laying eggs four days after reaching the adult stage.

Flies generally die in the early autumn, partly due to a fungus disease that attacks them, and partly due to the cold temperature. They do not hibernate, but larvae may survive in manure piles or beneath the soil over the winter months and start the new generations of flies the following summer.

The fly cannot eat solid food. It alights on food and vomits a liquid through its proboscis-like mouth. The dissolved food is then sucked back, but, of course, all or a portion of this "vomit" may remain on the food. The excreta also remains on the food.

Examination of flies has disclosed as many as 28,000,000 bacteria on the inside and 5,000,000 on the outside of the body of the fly. Flies infest manure piles, privies, toilets, and other waste materials and then may alight on food. It is obvious that they may easily pick up millions of harmful bacteria and infect our food. They constitute a dangerous channel of disease transmission that must be eliminated.

A very large outbreak of bacillary dysentery in an army encampment was definitely traced to flies as the vectors of this disease. Thousands of cases of illnesses are undoubtedly due to flies, even though it may be difficult to prove.

Prevention: Remove all breeding places that may be found in or adjacent to the establishment, e.g., piles of manure, garbage, filth in general. Keep garbage cans tightly covered, and thoroughly clean them when emptied. Screen all openings to the outer air.

Destruction: Swat the fly, use fly paper, or use fly sprays.

Fly Sprays: These generally contain a contact poison, such as pyrethrum, as the active ingredient, dissolved in a nonodorous organic solvent, usually kerosene which has been deodorized or to which some perfume has been added. Such sprays act on the nervous system of the fly and are very effective, provided the spray contacts the insect.

Pyrethrum: Is a powder that is obtained from the chrysanthemum flower. The active ingredients are known as pyrethrins and a good insect spray should contain 100-120 milligrams of pyrethrins per 100 cubic centimeters of liquid.

Pyrethrum is not toxic to man but kills the fly by contact. When a dose of this insecticide is absorbed, it stupefies the insect by acting on the nervous system and causes the insect to drop to the floor. It may remain alive for several hours (even twenty-four hours) before death occurs, depending on the lethal dose of insecticide that is has absorbed. Pyrethrum is relatively unstable and loses strength on exposure to air or heat.

Pyrethrum Synergists: An insecticidal synergist is a chemical which, when combined with an insecticide, increases the killing power of the combination beyond what might be expected by the simple addition of each. Common pyrethrum synergists and piperonyl butoxide, sulfoxide, and MFK-264.

Golden Malrin: This effective fly-killer is a sugar bait.

Residual Fly Sprays:
Diazinon: 5-1%
Malathion: 2%
Rotenone Baygon: 1%

Note: Chlordane, DDT, and Lindane are banned in New York State. Parathion is a dangerous organic phosphate and under no conditions may it be used in home or food establishments.

INSECT CONTROL: ROACHES

The elimination of roaches in food establishments is a greater problem than flies. Roaches also carry disease bacteria on their bodies and deposit them on the food through their excreta, vomit, and bodily contact.

The most common household roach is the German roach. It is one-half to one inch in size, light brown in color with two dark stripes on the back, very agile, and very prolific. The female lays twenty-five to thirty eggs at one time, enclosed in a leathery pouch one-quarter inch long. The life span of a roach is one to one and a half years, and the female will lay five batches of eggs in one year. The egg hatches into a nymph and the nymph grows by molting its shell-like skin. After five molts, the roach reaches adult size. The length of time required for hatching eggs depends on the temperature, and ranges from one to five months.

Roaches are cunning and quick to sense danger. They can survive for long periods under unfavorable conditions and their flat oval shapes facilitate hiding in cracks and crevices into which they can glide with lightning rapidity. They generally travel and feed at night. While they prefer starchy foods, they can feed on leather, felt, or wood. All loose foods should be kept in covered containers.

CONTROL

I. It is difficult to prevent the invasion of a food establishment with insects, especially roaches, thay may come from an adjoining building or in packages delivered to the plant. The emphasis must be placed on eliminating of harborages and breeding places within the establishment as well as extermination.

II. All cracks and holes in the floor, walls, and ceilings should be eliminated as far as possible by filling with cement, plaster, putty, or plastic wood. Seams in fixtures and equipment should receive the same treatment. III. Equipment and fixtures should be placed flush against the wall and floor; if not, then a sufficient distance away from the wall and above the floor to facilitate cleaning around it. Wherever possible, wooden fixtures should be replaced with metal.

IV. All potential insect breeding places, such as rubbish, debris and stagnant water, should be eliminated. Garbage should be kept in tightly covered metal cans, and the cans should be thoroughly cleaned after being emptied. The room in which garbage is kept, prior to removal, should be constructed of impervious washable material, preferably cement, and should have can washing facilities. If this room can be refrigerated, the cold temperature will prevent insects from breeding, and odors from decomposing garbage will be inhibited.

V. Good housekeeping is a very important factor in insect control. The food establishment and equipment therein should be completely cleaned each night before closing, not only for good sanitation, but to remove all grease, food encrustation, and food particles on which the insects can feed.

VI. In addition, roaches can be destroyed with effective insecticides.

DESTRUCTION BY POISON (EXTERMINATION)

I. Space sprays are not very effective against roaches. The spray or powder used must actually contact the body and so aerosol types of sprays are not used for roaches. Where powder is used, it is generally spread with a mechanical device or "gun".

II. Insecticides may be classified as contact poisons or stomach poisons. A contact poison is one that only requires contact with the preparation to injure or destroy the insect. This occurs when the insecticide enters the external breathing apparatus or is deposited upon other vulnerable portions of the body. A stomach poison is one which is required to enter the insect's digestive apparatus in order to kill the pest. This may occur when poison is mixed with the food bait so that it is eaten by the insect, or when the insect walks through an insecticide (which may be a contact or stomach poison) and grooms itself, (licks its feet and antennae,) inadvertently ingesting the poison.

III. In extermination by insecticides, it is important to remember that the Health Code prohibits the use of any poisonous insecticides in a food establishment. Artificially colored blue fluoride powder is the only exception to this rule. When new insecticides are offered on the market for use in food establishments, they must be accepted by the Fumigant Board of the Health Department as to their non-poisonous character.

Insecticides commonly used for roach destruction are:

I. <u>Pyrethrum:</u> Non-poisonous to man but effective against roaches. It is non-stable and loses its strength rapidly when exposed to air, moisture, and sun. It is used in several forms, usually as a powder or spray. It is also used in the form of a pyrethrum vapor that penetrates every crack and crevice in the room. Various devices exist in which steam is generated that passes through a narrow horizontal nozzle to which is attached a bottle of pyrethrum dissolved in kerosene. The stream of steam causes this solution of pyrethrum to vaporize throughout the room in which the device is used, and the roaches leave their hiding places to get air and generally die on the floor where they can be swept up.

II. <u>Rotenone:</u> Is non-poisonous to man. It is a product extracted from plants known as Derris Root, Cube, and Timbo. It is an effective roach killer and is generally spread as a powder, although it may also be used in sprays.

SUSPECTED ROACH INFESTATION SUGGESTIONS FOR INSPECTION

1. Locations where commonly found Kitchen, vegetable preparation area, serving counter, garbage area, walls and shelving adjacent thereto; behind hanging pictures and signs, beneath paper shelf lining, at electric and steam meters. All warm, slightly moist, seldom disturbed dark spots.

2. Structural Defects Harborages as cracks, crevices, seams, fissures in walls, fixtures, furniture, pipes, and wire passageways.

3. Storage Conditions

   A. Accumulations of seldom disturbed paper goods as menus, newspapers, paper stock, bags, cups, cartons, containers, straws.
   B. Accumulations of empty unrinsed food containers as milk, beer and soda bottles, ice cream containers, milk cans, meat, fish and bakery boxes.

4. Insanitary Conditions

   A. Unclean garbage can exterior surface and adjacent floor area.
   B. Dried food scraps on surfaces of floor, walls, shelving; beneath and adherent to fixtures and equipment such as mixers, slicers, dicers, peeler impact about can opener and within seams of cutting boards, chopping blocks and work tables.

PESTICIDE USE IN FOOD SERVICE OPERATIONS

ARE YOU HARMING.....

.....yourself?
.....your employees?
.....your customers?

You may be - without realizing it - if you are using pestices improperly.

You may also be breaking the law.

THE LAW

State law requires that anyone using pesticides, except farmers or homeowners on their own property, be certified as a "commercial applicator" with the State Department of Environmental Conservation (DEC). This applies even to arerosol cans of pesticides, available at most grocery stores.

Persons applying pesticides in restaurants, institutional kitchens or other food service operations need special certification from DEC's Bureau of Pesticides Management. Under the State Sanitary Code, a food service operation can be closed down by the State Health Department if pesticides are applied by a person not certified to do so, or if pesticides or other toxic substances are improperly used, stored or labeled.

WHY?

All pesticides are toxic. After all, their purpose is to kill roaches, rats and other pest. Proper use of pesticides is essential to everyone's safety.

If pesticides are used improperly, food, utensils or other food-preparation equipment can become contaminated. Improper handling of pesticides can also lead to direct exposure through the nose, mouth or skin. The result may be future health problems for those exposed.

State or local health department sanitarians check for proper labeling, storage and use of pesticides during their routine inspections of food service establishments. Sanitarians also make sure that only registered businesses or certified persons are applying pesticides. Violations found during these inspections can result in fines, closure or both.

DO'S AND DON'TS

Help insure the safest control of pests in your food service operation by following these do's and don'ts:

DO be concerned about your health and safety, and that of your employees and customers.

DO ask your pest controller for proof of certification by DEC'S Bureau of Pesticides Management.

DO report uncertified pest controllers to a DEC pesticide inspector at the DEC pesticide inspector at the DEC Regional Office.

DO make a pest's life difficult by maintaining extra-clean conditions and by eliminating possible pest entry routes.

DO know what pest species you are dealing with, and what pesticides are being used. Ask your pest controller or health department sanitarian about options for pest control, including chemical and non-chemical methods. (A combination of both is often most effective.)

DO get instructions from both the pest controller and a sanitarian on what you should do following treatment.

DO read and follow the label instructions carefully when using any pesticide product.

DON'T hire an uncertified pest controller.

DON'T apply any pesticide in a food service operation yourself unless you are certified.

DON'T permit the application of pesticides while food is being prepared or served, or in an area where utensils, unprotected food or containers are stored.

FOR MORE INFORMATION .....

To learn more about pest control, or for details on how to become certified to apply pesticides, contact your local health department or DEC regional pesticide office.

RODENT AND INSECT CONTROL

HOW CAN WE CONTROL RATS AND MICE?

I. GET RID OF THEIR NESTING PLACES
Clean up all piles of rubbish, inside and outside the premises.

II. BUILD THEM OUT
Block all possible rat entrances. Rat-proof foundations.

III. STARVE THEM OUT
Protect food at night. Keep garbage containers closed. Do a thorough clean-up job.

IV. KILL THEM
Use traps for temporary control.

HOW CAN WE CONTROL FLIES?

I. GET RID OF THEIR BREEDING PLACES
Control the sources.

II. KEEP THEM OUT
Screen doors and windows properly. See that all doors open out and are self-closing. Install overhead fly fans or air curtains.

III. DO A GOOD JOB OF HOUSEKEEPING
Keep foods covered. Keep garbage containers sealed. Remove food accumulations promptly.

IV. KILL THEM
Use a pyrethrin insect spray inside the buildings. CAUTION: Don't use sprays with any food or food surfaces exposed in the room.

HOW CAN WE CONTROL COCKROACHES AND OTHER INSECTS?

I. BE ALERT TO FIRST SIGNS OF INFESTATION
Destroy infested foods.

II. DO A GOOD JOB OF HOUSEKEEPING AND STORAGE

III. USE PROPER INSECTICIDES (CAREFULLY)

THEN IF RATS, MICE, FLIES, COCKROACHES OR OTHER INSECTS STILL INFEST YOUR ESTABLISHMENT, CONTACT YOUR LOCAL HEALTH DEPARTMENT!